'This book of psychoanalytic essays on identity is timely, as this is such a general preoccupation in our society. The analytic sense of what one might call "core identity", based on current and ancestrally derived relationships, is often lost in the demands for the acknowledgement of a multiplicity of self-selected "identities". The different chapters arose out of a Workshop run by John Steiner, which meets regularly to discuss clinical practice and theoretical psychoanalytic issues in a way that is unique and greatly admired. It provides an opportunity for thinking and original ideas under the branches of the tree of psychoanalytic knowledge and experience led by John and shared by all the writers. The fruits of that are evident in this book and cover various aspects of the interplay of social and internal relationships that inform self-identification throughout life. It is stimulating, thought-provoking and should be read by all those interested professionally in human relations – as well as by many others keen to know more about themselves and others.'

Ronald Britton *FRCPsych, is a distinguished fellow at the British Psychoanalytical Society*

'This book leads us right to the germinal centre of psychoanalytic thinking. It gives a vivid account of John Steiner's postgraduate workshop where experienced colleagues work together for many years to share and discuss their clinical experiences and create new models for their understanding. The contributions by renowned analysts invite the reader to share the unique atmosphere of the seminars and to witness nascent new theory about the basic concept of identity.'

Prof. Dr. Heinz Weiss *is head of the department of Psychosomatic Medicine, Robert-Bosch-Krankenhaus, Stuttgart, managing director of the Medical Section, Sigmund-Freud-Institut, Frankfurt a.M., teaches at the University of Tübingen (Germany) and is chair of the Education Section of* The International Journal of Psychoanalysis

'This book is a collection of papers by members of John Steiner's Workshop, a group of experienced psychoanalysts who have been meeting for over 10 years, discussing psychoanalytic theory as well as their own clinical cases. It contains an extensive theoretical preface by Steiner, and is expertly edited and introduced by Sharon Numa, who has also written a scholarly overview of the development of this complex subject in Kleinian theory. The clinical chapters study identity as it can be seen over a landscape of cases and pathologies by clinicians all substantially informed by Klein's and Steiner's contributions, but also open to different influences and, most importantly, each with their particular sensitivity and a mind of their own. Each explores the deepest layers of identity formation, addressing the continuous conflict between development and integration and the obstacles created by primitive defences. I strongly recommend this rich and satisfying collection, a fit homage to Steiner's influence and originality.'

Ignes Sodre *is a training and supervising psychoanalyst of the British Psychoanalytic Society*

ON BEING ONE'S SELF

On Being One's Self emerges from discussions in John Steiner's Workshop and investigates the meanings of self and identity, including the many ways in which the development of personal identity can be subverted, interrogating what can facilitate the development of a reasonably stable identity.

The variety of problems that can arise in relation to the development of a unique identity is reflected in rich clinical material that vividly illustrates 'identities' felt to be weak, unformed, fluid or brittle, in many cases demonstrating how the sense of self is held together by pathological defences and organisations. The book examines several long-term adult analytic cases, suggesting that a mature personal identity involves not only 'knowing who one is' but also the capacity for empathic identification with the experience of others as separate human beings.

The question of 'having' an identity, or the fear of losing it, is a central concern of individuals, and this volume, which will be of interest to psychoanalysts and psychotherapists alike, considers these issues by looking at the deepest conflicts around self and identity as they emerge and are relived in the transference relationship.

Sharon Numa is a Fellow of the Institute of Psychoanalysis who has been working as an analyst in private practice for thirty years. Originally working as a Clinical Psychologist in the NHS she subsequently trained at the Tavistock Clinic. She is a training supervisor and therapist for psychotherapy associations and teaches clinical and theory seminars both in London and, in the last few years, in Beijing.

THE NEW LIBRARY OF PSYCHOANALYSIS
General Editor: Anne Patterson

The *New Library of Psychoanalysis* was launched in 1987 in association with the Institute of Psychoanalysis, London. It took over from the International Psychoanalytical Library which published many of the early translations of the works of Freud and the writings of most of the leading British and Continental psychoanalysts.

The purpose of the *New Library of Psychoanalysis* is to facilitate a greater and more widespread appreciation of psychoanalysis and to provide a forum for increasing mutual understanding between psychoanalysts and those working in other disciplines such as the social sciences, medicine, philosophy, history, linguistics, literature and the arts. It aims to represent different trends both in British psychoanalysis and in psychoanalysis generally. The *New Library of Psychoanalysis* is well placed to make available to the English-speaking world psychoanalytic writings from other European countries and to increase the interchange of ideas between British and American psychoanalysts. Through the *Teaching Series*, the *New Library of Psychoanalysis* now also publishes books that provide comprehensive, yet accessible, overviews of selected subject areas aimed at those studying psychoanalysis and related fields such as the social sciences, philosophy, literature and the arts.

The Institute, together with the British Psychoanalytical Society, runs a low-fee psychoanalytic clinic, organizes lectures and scientific events concerned with psychoanalysis and publishes the *International Journal of Psychoanalysis*. It runs a training course in psychoanalysis which leads to membership of the International Psychoanalytical Association – the body which preserves internationally agreed standards of training, of professional entry, and of professional ethics and practice for psychoanalysis as initiated and developed by Sigmund Freud. Distinguished members of the Institute have included Michael Balint, Wilfred Bion, Ronald Fairbairn, Anna Freud, Ernest Jones, Melanie Klein, John Rickman and Donald Winnicott.

Previous general editors have included David Tuckett, who played a very active role in the establishment of the New Library. He was followed as general editor by Elizabeth Bott Spillius, who was, in turn, followed by Susan Budd, Dana Birksted-Breen and most recently by Alessandra Lemma. Current members of the Advisory Board include Giovanna Di Ceglie, Liz Allison, Anne Patterson, Josh Cohen and Daniel Pick.

Previous members of the Advisory Board include Christopher Bollas, Ronald Britton, Catalina Bronstein, Donald Campbell, Rosemary Davies, Sara Flanders, Stephen Grosz, John Keene, Eglé Laufer, Alessandra Lemma, Juliet Mitchell, Michael Parsons, Rosine Jozef Perelberg, Richard Rusbridger, Mary Target and David Taylor.

A full list of all the titles in the *New Library of Psychoanalysis* main series is available at https://www.routledge.com/The-New-Library-of-Psychoanalysis/book-series/SE0239.

For titles in the *New Library of Psychoanalysis* 'Teaching' and 'Beyond the Couch' subseries, please visit the Routledge website.

ON BEING ONE'S SELF

Clinical Explorations in Identity from John Steiner's Workshop

Edited by Sharon Numa

LONDON AND NEW YORK

Cover image: chiawut, Shutterstock.com
First published 2023
by Routledge
4 Park Square, Milton Park, Abingdon, Oxon OX14 4RN
and by Routledge
605 Third Avenue, New York, NY 10158

Routledge is an imprint of the Taylor & Francis Group, an informa business

© 2023 selection and editorial matter, Sharon Numa; individual chapters, the contributors

The right of Sharon Numa to be identified as the author of the editorial material, and of the authors for their individual chapters, has been asserted in accordance with sections 77 and 78 of the Copyright, Designs and Patents Act 1988.

All rights reserved. No part of this book may be reprinted or reproduced or utilised in any form or by any electronic, mechanical, or other means, now known or hereafter invented, including photocopying and recording, or in any information storage or retrieval system, without permission in writing from the publishers.

Trademark notice: Product or corporate names may be trademarks or registered trademarks, and are used only for identification and explanation without intent to infringe.

British Library Cataloguing-in-Publication Data
A catalogue record for this book is available from the British Library

Library of Congress Cataloging-in-Publication Data
Names: Numa, Sharon, 1952– editor.
Title: On being one's self: clinical explorations in identity from john steiner's workshop / edited by Sharon Numa.
Description: 1 Edition. | New York, NY: Routledge, 2022. |
Includes bibliographical references and index. |
Identifiers: LCCN 2022005697 (print) | LCCN 2022005698 (ebook) |
ISBN 9781032210742 (hardback) | ISBN 9781032210759 (paperback) |
ISBN 9781003266624 (ebook)
Subjects: LCSH: Identity (Psychology) | Self.
Classification: LCC BF697 .O424 2022 (print) | LCC BF697 (ebook) |
DDC 155.2—dc23/eng/20220613
LC record available at https://lccn.loc.gov/2022005697
LC ebook record available at https://lccn.loc.gov/2022005698

ISBN: 9781032210742 (hbk)
ISBN: 9781032210759 (pbk)
ISBN: 9781003266624 (ebk)

DOI: 10.4324/9781003266624

Typeset in Bembo
by codeMantra

CONTENTS

List of contributors   *xi*
Acknowledgements   *xiii*
Foreword by Dr John Steiner   *xiv*

Introduction   1
SHARON NUMA

1 An outline of the Kleinian model of the mind and its implications for the understanding of personal identity   25
SHARON NUMA

2 Identification and pathological identification: implications for identity   58
ANNE AMOS

3 The cerebral mind versus the body mind: containing and recovering unknown parts of the self   77
SUSAN LAWRENCE

4 Orientation, disorientation and identity development: an illustration from Dante's *Divine Comedy*   99
GIOVANNA RITA DI CEGLIE

5 A mind of one's own: the growth of identity in an adult patient   123
CAROLINE GARLAND

CONTENTS

6 Failure to mourn: idealisation, illusion and identity 145
SHARON NUMA

7 Identity and the struggle to "be" in the face of distorting projections from an ill object 171
PHILIP CROCKATT

8 A lost child: the failure to develop an identity 192
JUDITH JACKSON

9 Forming an identity: from somatisation and hypochondriasis to hysteria and beyond 215
ANNE AMOS

10 'If you are not my mum, who are you?': a woman's analytic journey from a melancholic identification to an identity of her own 230
ORNA HADARY

11 Liquid fear: a dissolving identity 245
SHARON NUMA

12 Identity as the threads of meaning through a person's life 269
DENIS FLYNN

Index *293*

CONTRIBUTORS

Anne Amos is a training and supervising analyst of The British Psychoanalytical Society. For over twenty years she practised in London and now practises in Edinburgh. She teaches in the UK and abroad, is part of the long-standing Kleinian Seminar in Ukraine and also helped establish a similar seminar in Belarus.

Philip Crockatt trained at the Tavistock Clinic and the Institute of Psychoanalysis. He worked in private practice for forty years, and is a past Director of the Camden Psychotherapy Unit and the London Clinic of Psychoanalysis. A training analyst and supervisor for psychotherapy trainings he currently organises an online clinical training for Chinese psychotherapists.

Giovanna Rita Di Ceglie is a training analyst of the BPAS. She qualified in medicine and specialised in psychiatry at the University of Perugia, Italy. She worked in adult psychiatry and then in child and adolescent psychiatry at the Tavistock Centre. She has written several papers on symbolic thinking and more recently on orientation/disorientation in early development and clinical work. She lectures in the UK and abroad.

Denis Flynn is a training and supervising analyst and child and adolescent analyst of the British Psychoanalytical Society/IPA working in private practice. He formerly ran an NHS Inpatient Adolescent Unit, is Chair of Education at the Institute of Psychoanalysis, teaches widely and has published both papers and books on child analysis and psychoanalysis more generally.

CONTRIBUTORS

Caroline Garland is a practising psychoanalyst and clinical psychologist. She worked for thirty years in the National Health Service at the Tavistock Clinic. She has a particular interest in trauma and in group psychotherapy, having produced books on both. She lectures and teaches both nationally and internationally.

Orna Hadary is a training analyst of the British Psychoanalytical Society, in full-time private practice. She previously worked as a clinical psychologist. She teaches at the Institute of Psychoanalysis and taught at the Tavistock Clinic and other psychotherapy organisations.

Judith Jackson is a child and adult psychoanalyst and a fellow of the Institute of Psychoanalysis. She teaches and supervises at the Tavistock Clinic, Institute of Psychoanalysis and in many other countries. She has presented at several IPA congresses and published papers in English and French journals, as well as books.

Susan Lawrence is a training and supervising analyst of the British Psychoanalytical Society, in full-time private practice in London. She is interested in the communication of psychoanalysis and has been Chair of Outreach for the British Society.

Sharon Numa is a fellow of the British Psychoanalytical Society in private practice. She first qualified as a clinical psychologist and worked in the NHS before training at the Tavistock Clinic. She is a training supervisor and analyst for the BpF interested in teaching and supervising both in London and in Beijing.

ACKNOWLEDGEMENTS

Thanks to Alessandra Lemma, former Editor of the New Library Series, for her help and guidance; and to Anne Patterson her successor, for her patience and encouragement through this long process which extended through the time of Covid. Thanks to the anonymous reviewers for the New Library who gave up their valuable time to carefully read and comment on the manuscript. Our gratitude to Grainne Lucey who offered us much-needed editorial help in the earlier stages of this work.

We would also like to thank the Melanie Klein Trust for their financial contribution to editorial costs.

With gratitude to John Steiner whose clinical acumen, teaching and intellectual generosity have been a source of inspiration for so many years, to our colleagues in the seminar for many enriching discussions and to our patients, without whom none of these explorations would be possible.

FOREWORD

Perhaps the most important contribution psychoanalysis can make to the understanding of identity is to explore its dependence on our relationship to internal objects. To a significant degree, we gain an identity through identifications with the primary objects of infancy and gradually with other significant parental figures as we grow up. Later these are extended to prominent figures in society and in literature and myth. In this way we gain an identity from a family, a school, a nation, a religion, a profession, a gender or a race. The ability to announce, "I am an Englishman, a Christian, or a Socialist", can create a sense of belonging and communicate a set of values that help answer the question, "Who am I?"

However, a wish to discover a personal identity separate from that of the parents is part of a drive towards separation and individuation in development. When successful this leads to a personal identity based on an internal self, separate from but in a relationship with internal parents. However, the situation is complicated because the wish to be separate is in conflict with the wish to cling on and the process of separation is obstructed through the operation of defence mechanisms that prevent change. In particular, introjective and projective identifications lead to self and object becoming entangled with each other so that neither of them is able to relinquish possession of the other and both are distorted and misrepresented.

Nevertheless, a degree of separateness between self and object normally emerges because the identifications are normally flexible and reversible. This enables the individual to both accept an identity as an individual and retain his membership of the family group.

Sometimes however, separateness is firmly resisted and self-object conglomerates become difficult to unpack. It is then not possible to sort out what belongs to self and what belongs to the object and a personal identity separate from that of the group fails to emerge. In these cases, the object is possessed and distorted by introjective and projective identifications and exists in the internal world as a concrete body not properly differentiated from the self.

Generational Change

The evolution of personal identity begins early in development and continues throughout life. Separateness is linked with sleeping alone, going to school, and forming peer groups and a critical moment that epitomises the process takes place when, as young adults we leave home to establish a new family of our own. Here the conflict between individuation and possession becomes stark and unavoidable because a break away from dependent ties on the parents is required for a new family to be established. Other steps in adult life, which involve the capacity to think independently whilst simultaneously being rooted in developments in the past, make true independence possible. Creative developments in various fields of endeavour and new discoveries in science, literature and art require both a dependence on the old and a willingness to overthrow previous dogmas.

An important indicator of an independent personal identity lies in the individual's creative capacity which comes to represent the successful espousal of the new over the old. This aspect of identity is nicely stated in the biblical phrase, "Ye shall know them by their fruits" (Matthew 7:16), which implies that our identity is reflected in our actions. Creativity above all requires a move from our primary objects to those in our own generation and a break from the family is necessary even if it is painful and frightening. Indeed, in unconscious phantasy, such a break is experienced as an oedipal murder and when the murder is taken seriously the consequences have to be faced. The overthrow of the parents leads to feelings of anxiety and loss but also to feelings of regret, remorse and guilt which can release loving feelings and a wish to make reparation. After a successful rebellion, the working through of the mourning for the lost parents restores the relationship with them but now as objects separate from the self. Creativity depends on the capacity to symbolise and that capacity depends on the capacity to mourn: to move from the concrete possession of the actual object to a relationship with a symbolic representation of it.

The Emancipation of the Ego from the Dominance of the Super-Ego

An important quality that is commonly assigned to parental figures is the function of judgement itself. The super-ego can be seen as the agency that sets standards of excellence by which we are judged but it acquires a severity when it also acts as a judge of how these standards have been met. Britton (2003) pointed out that making judgements is an ego function through which we evaluate the state of things as they are. When usurped by the super-ego, the capacity to judge acquires a moralistic connotation which is concerned with what "should be" rather than "what is". If the patient can "emancipate" his ego from dominance by the super-ego, he can begin to weigh up his own decisions and even pass judgement on his super-ego figures. Good and bad elements in ourselves and our parents become discernible so that we can identify with aspects we value and oppose those we disagree with. It is this differentiation that is so difficult when unconscious projective and introjective identifications distort what belongs to self and object. Following Strachey (1964), we can recognise that an important goal of analysis is to modify the severity of the super-ego, but Britton's approach helps us to see that it is sometimes just as important for the patient to be able to stand up to a tyrannical super-ego.

FOREWORD

True and False Identities

All such developments involve the risk of conflict with powerful internal and external objects and at times may create a gap between a private view of ourselves and a mask or public persona behind which we need to hide. Winnicott (1960), for example, has described a true self that more directly expresses wishes and desires which is hidden beneath a false-self, presented in deference to external opinion. These conflicts may weaken confidence in a personal identity that depends on the integrity of the ego especially when the gap between the two identities is not recognised. Multiple identities such as those seen in "as-if" personalities or even in impostors may result (Deutsch, 1955). On the other hand, we all have hidden secret parts of the self that we know about but may not wish to show to the world. If we recognise that secret identities are universal, it is easier to respect our patient's and our own wish to exercise a right to privacy. The poet Elisabeth Bishop refused to speak about her sexuality in public asserting that she relied on "closets, closets and more closets" (Tóibín, 2015).

The Critical Role of Mourning in the Establishment of Separateness

We have seen that the drive to individuation is thwarted unless, at least in phantasy, a violent break from the dominance of internal super-ego figures is undertaken. Sometimes this requires heroic actions in which omnipotence plays a part and the cost is often high. When the violence subsides and a return to reality is established, we become aware that the figures we hated and had to escape from are also the figures we loved and valued. The damage done becomes apparent and gives rise to regret, remorse and guilt. It is these feelings that make us aware of our love and together can lead to a move towards reparation.

It is in the process of working through such losses, accepting responsibility for them and mourning them that enables projections previously attributed to objects to be returned to the self (Steiner,

1996). Freud described how, in the work of mourning (1917), each memory of the lost object is taken out and the verdict of reality applied to it. This verdict separates what is alive from what is dead, what can be retained and what is lost, and it enables elements of the self previously projected into the object to be returned to the ego. In this way, the ego is strengthened and the object becomes less distorted. These changes help establish a personal identity based on a stronger ego while establishing internal relationships with less distorted super-ego figures.

The Conflict between Holding-On and Letting-Go of Primary Objects

The anxiety created by the move towards independence can be so threatening that powerful defences are deployed that retain a possessive hold to prevent loss and to control and limit the freedom of the object. Projective and introjective identifications are again deployed to re-create an amalgam of self and object that is resistant to change. These types of object relationship have been studied under a variety of headings such as Narcissistic Organisations (Rosenfeld, 1971) and Self-Objects (Kohut, 1971), and they involve mechanisms involving power such as those described by Freud as a drive for *Mastery* (Freud, 1905). This theme has been studied by French analysts (Laplanche and Pontalis, 1973; Denis, 1997), and amongst these Dorey (1986) has made a detailed examination of power relations which he found were particularly prominent in perverse and obsessional patients. In the perverse type, sexual excitement plays a critical role and sado-masochistic phantasies cruelly imprison the object. In the obsessional type, phantasies of anal control set up an alternation between possession and release, leading to cruelty which repeatedly needs to be undone and checked. Introjective and projective identifications with bad objects can lead to an idealisation of power which is felt to be stronger than love and can become ego-syntonic and be established as a character trait.

FOREWORD

The issue of mastery is also relevant to the object relations seen in melancholia in which a damaged or dying object is identified with and possessed. Freud described how the object then casts its shadow on the ego and separateness is prevented unless it can be relinquished and mourned.

To end this short foreword I will briefly mention the importance of irony in the appraisal of identity. The ability to entertain doubts, to avoid grandiosity and to laugh at one's pretensions requires a capacity to stand back and view oneself dispassionately. Taking an ironic view means that we can entertain more than one view of ourselves and smile at the contradictions that emerge. This makes us less rigid and also more tolerant of others. Identity itself has long-term implications and does not change from moment to moment, but our view of ourselves may sometimes change dramatically so that we can feel successful sometimes and then plunge into a depression following a disappointment. It is irony that helps support both views as we admit that we cannot always sustain the image of ourselves that we would like to have. Similarly, the dependence on both tradition and innovation means that we sometimes adopt the identity of family, nation or religion and then realise that we actually have independent views that shape our identity. An ironic stance is difficult to sustain if object relations are concrete and self and object are confused as in the pathological organisations discussed above. When the object is more separate symbolic function is facilitated and with it irony becomes possible.

These thoughts linking object relations with a sense of identity arise from the clinical experience of patients such as those described in the various chapters of this book. The bi-monthly seminars where the cases were discussed included a clinical hour followed by one in which theory was read and studied. This meant that the theory was always clinically based and that the clinical material was thought about in terms of theory. Perhaps the members of the seminar established a kind of group identity through working together over a considerable period of time but also retained the individual identity that can be discerned in the separate chapters.

FOREWORD

REFERENCES

Britton, R. S. (2003) Emancipation from the Super-Ego, (Job). In *Sex, Death and the Super-Ego* (Chapter 7, pp. 103–116). London: Karnac.

Denis, P. (1997) *Emprise et Satisfaction. Les deux formants de la pulsion*. Paris: Presses Universitaires de France.

Dorey, R. (1986) The Relationship of Mastery. *Int. J. Psychoanal.*, 13: 323–332.

Deutsch, H. (1955) The Impostor—Contribution to Ego Psychology of a Type of Psychopath. *Psychoanal. Q.*, 24: 483–505.

Freud, S. (1905) Three Essays on the Theory of Sexuality. *SE* 7: 123–243.

Freud, S. (1917) 'Mourning and Melancholia', *SE* 14: 237–258.

Kohut, H. (1971) *The Analysis of the Self*. New York: International Universities Press.

Laplanche, J. & Pontalis, J.B. (1973) *The Language of Psychoanalysis*. London: Hogarth Press. Originally published as *Vocabulaire de la Psychoanalyse*. Paris: Presses Universitaires de France, 1967.

Steiner, J. (1996) The Aim of Psychoanalysis in Theory and in Practice. *Int. J. Psycho-anal.*, 77: 1073–1083.

Tóibín, C. (2015) *On Elizabeth Bishop*. Princeton, NJ and Oxford: Princeton University Press.

Winnicott, D. W. (1960) Ego Distortions in Terms of True and False Self. In *The Maturational Process and the Facilitating Environment* (pp. 140–157). London: Hogarth Press, 1965.

INTRODUCTION

Sharon Numa

The idea of writing a book on the question of identity arose during an ongoing workshop led by Dr John Steiner which, over time, has been a fertile space for exploring a number of different topics. The membership of the group has changed over the last fifteen years, but a core of members has been involved for at least a decade. John Steiner has emphasised the value of appreciating the total transference situation (Joseph, 1985), taking note of the mood or atmosphere of the session and of any emerging configurations that might orient our thinking about our cases. Ideas emerge from the clinical material rather than being imposed upon it; indeed, it is a feature of John Steiner's approach that an attitude of openness better serves the patient than a rush to premature 'understanding'. The movement between putting oneself in the patient's shoes (identifying sympathetically) and stepping back to think and observe the analytic couple, perhaps from the position of the 'third' object, has often been an integral part of our reflections. This type of fluidity is referred to in the more general context of separation and identification in the Foreword. Theoretical papers form the second part of the Workshop and this tends to lead to a dialectical relationship between theory and clinical cases.

A few years ago, the group began to discuss and deepen our understanding of the problems and disturbances associated with developing a sense of self and identity, problems that were reflected in the clinical cases presented. The results of this exploration, including some of the clinical cases which helped us to understand the obstacles to developing or maintaining a relatively stable sense of identity, are brought together in this collection by a small group of analysts within the Workshop. Our investigation however went beyond the cases included here, as a wide range of cases were discussed from the perspective of identity. Many that could not be included here (some for reasons described in the following section) nevertheless contributed to the work and understanding represented in the ensuing chapters.[1]

As we embarked on this project, we encountered a difficult and paradoxical issue in relation to confidentiality. A concern for patients' privacy means that we were mindful of the privileged access we have to the internal and external lives of patients, which, as is always the case, led us to disguise or remove the identifying features which relate to their external circumstances and social identities as much as possible. In studying 'identity', this became 'paradoxical' since concerns for confidentiality often precluded the use of important aspects of patient's 'identities' – which can for example include gender, ethnicity, colour, country of birth, religion, class and so on – depending on the patient and their circumstances. In addition, what we consider to be one of the main aims of this book (the use of in depth analytic cases to demonstrate the impact of the analytic work on the patient's conflicts around developing a separate identity) is a form of presentation that is in its nature revealing since it unfolds over time, spanning a variety of patients' external situations. While maintaining privacy, we strove to be true to the important elements of the analysis itself and to those aspects of their external lives that would not specifically identify them. Our focus is on the inner world (the relationship between external and internal reality), but we are aware that the social aspect of identity is implicated in this and recognise the inherent limitations of writing a book about the self or identity while restricting ourselves in terms of the more social aspects of identity, particularly at a time when 'identity politics' has been the subject of intense general interest. Nevertheless, we feel that from a psychoanalytic point of view, there is value in looking in detail at what certain adult patients might teach us about identity formation

INTRODUCTION

and stability as phantasies and object relationships are relived in the analytic situation and in the transference.

It seemed to us that the question of 'identity' as a topic in itself had been neglected in the Kleinian *oeuvre* – and we hope that this book will contribute in some measure to the process of filling that gap. The mechanisms and attendant phantasies associated with splitting, projective identification, introjection and pathological identification have a central place in the development of British object relations theory; yet they have not generally been used to focus on and further our understanding of what it means to have a sense of self or identity, despite the fact that it is often problems associated with disturbances in the sense of identity that bring patients to analysis.

In discussing our analytic cases, we found that certain recurring themes emerged and these have been taken up throughout the book. Each chapter approaches these central themes with its own particular emphasis, led by the clinical material, though there is considerable convergence around those themes. An analysis is however never just about 'one thing' and even in regard to the specific theme of identity there is also a particularity in each patient's struggle towards, and away from, integration. Our cases attempt to follow a thread in the analysis relating to the obstacles to the patient's identity development or stability, obstacles which have resulted in defensive positions or pathological organisations upon which they had come to depend. Such restricting dependence, in turn, prevents emancipation in favour of the development of a separate sense of self. There are a number of 'solutions' to the problems of identity that appear in the case studies here, in the form of compromise positions; for example, false identities or borrowed identities – some more rigid and organised than others. There are also, however, 'unformed' or markedly unintegrated personality structures where the sense of identity is weak or absent.

This collection relies on adult cases (with a considerable age range) from the Workshop, and a fuller account might certainly wish to include children and adolescent cases as well as patients in later stages of life. While we see the 'achievement' of a sense of identity as an ongoing, life-long process marked by challenges and revisions at each important phase, what we hope to do here is to tease out what might lie at the deepest layers of identity formation (on which family and society will undoubtedly make their mark). In that endeavour, it seemed to us that certain basic Kleinian concepts could be fruitfully brought to bear on our understanding of the developing sense of self and identity, and particularly on its disturbance, in a more coherent way than has hitherto generally been the case. In that sense, we are not offering 'new' theory but rather seeing which aspects of our theory of object relationships are most helpful in elucidating the problems of identity. As Margaret Mahler (1982) has pointed out, the development of the sense of self 'reveals itself by its failure much more readily than by its normal variations' (p. 827). We would agree with her that observation and inference drawn from pathology are often the route by which psychoanalysis in general has progressed, and the same can be said for the investigation of identity.

While I have indicated that we are not putting forward any new theory, this collection of detailed long-term clinical studies we believe does throw fresh light on the processes involved in achieving a sense of identity. The chapter on Dante takes a literary perspective on this process. Each paper describes a unique individual striving to achieve as well as defend against the process of separation and mourning that we regard as integral to stabilising a sense of personal identity. While all the contributing psychoanalysts share a common Kleinian theoretical paradigm, the papers and clinical experiences that have emerged from our work and make up this book are nevertheless varied. It is one of the difficulties in thinking about identity that it extends into wide areas of psychoanalytic thought. It was therefore helpful to restrict our investigation to the clinical manifestations of 'identity problems' in a small group of patients in order to formulate ideas that we hope will advance our understanding of what might constitute 'necessary' conditions for developing a stable sense of identity, and what internal impediments might interfere with or foreclose that process.

INTRODUCTION

The rest of this Introduction will look at definitions and the use of terms and will also give brief descriptions of other approaches to identity from within the psychoanalytic field as well as a note on the social aspects of identity, ending with an outline of the basic Kleinian ideas that inform our own view. Chapter 1 (An Outline of the Kleinian model of the mind and its implications for the understanding of personal identity) will detail our account of identity, focusing on the recurrent themes that emerged from our clinical cases and make reference to the Workshop reading against which contributors' chapters are described.

Definitions of Identity

The Oxford English dictionary defines identity as follows:

> The sameness of a person or thing at all times or in all circumstances; the condition of being a single individual; the fact that a person or thing is itself and not something else; individuality, personality.
>
> (2nd ed., 1989)

'Identity' does not figure in either Jean Laplanche's dictionary *The Language of Psychoanalysis* (Laplanche and Pontalis, 1988) or in Robert Hinshelwood's *A Dictionary of Kleinian Thought* (Hinshelwood, 1991). It does however figure within *ego psychology*, a strand of psychoanalysis which began to develop in America shortly after Freud's death and which I will be referring to later.

While identity has not been directly explored in the classical psychoanalytic literature, it is a topic, however, that Leon Grinberg (1990) from the Argentinian psychoanalytic school has written about; he considers identity in its three dimensions – spatial, temporal and social – and much of what he writes in fact resonates with our own approach to identity. Identities are said to develop, and yet to remain the same. The very word identity is derived from the Latin *idem* meaning 'same'; Grinberg captures the two aspects in his definition of identity as the capacity 'to continue feeling oneself to be the same person over a succession of changes' (1990, p. 45). This forms the basis of what he calls the *emotional experience of identity*. He suggests that identity is developed from the *successive assimilation of introjective identifications and the sorting out of projective processes*. He argues that certain identifications gradually become integrated and contribute to the enrichment of the ego, especially in the early periods of life. The idea of a 'succession of changes while remaining the same' introduces the aspect of time and continuity, and in our view, this sense of internal coherence and continuity – something that can be said to be 'identical' within a person in a profound way – is vitally important. This core sense of self goes beyond notions of social role or self-image. The 'self over time' is also reflected in the philosopher Richard Wollheim's idea of 'the thread of life'. Wollheim (1984) speaks of the continuity of experience, and of both conscious and unconscious phantasy as important constituents of the sense of identity.

The above definitions, which we find useful, nevertheless, illustrate the complexity of the concept: we are immediately confronted with issues of time and continuity, identifications, the notion of 'being oneself', introjective and projective processes, the idea of a 'person', the notion of a self and so on. Identity cannot be conveniently reduced to a single psychological force with a single developmental line. This undoubtedly makes it an unwieldly concept, and further confusion has arisen over time with respect to the use of terms.

The term 'identity' has frequently been used interchangeably with 'sense of self', which, like 'identity', is also sometimes referred to as 'ego' or 'personality'. There are also terms such as 'character' vying with 'personality'. To some degree, Freud was responsible for the early confusion by his interchangeable use of 'self' and 'ego'. In his *On Narcissism* paper of 1914, he also introduces the ego preservative instincts, whose fate is ultimately to be transformed into the ego ideal. This, in turn, becomes the route to the recovery of the narcissistic perfection of childhood, the self-love enjoyed in childhood by the actual ego (Freud's primary narcissism).

INTRODUCTION

However, the gap between ego and ego ideal is watched and measured by a conscience essentially in identification with the critical admonishing parents as well as with social demands and mores. A thorough discussion of Freud's thinking can be found in Sandler et al. (1963) but we can see here that Freud comes very close to his later structural model. The idea of self-assessment, self-regard and self-observation (all of which we might now think of as being connected to identity) are, thus, brought into play.

Hanly (1984) suggests that the term 'ego ideal' marks a 'relative distinction within the superego between its prohibitive and its goal-setting functions' (p. 259) but regards these functions as two sides of the same coin. He argues that the term 'ideal ego', on the other hand, could be reserved for the more 'secret, private, purely subjective representation of the self as being perfect, as being lovable and loved' (ibid., p. 254). The essential point seems to be that the ego ideal refers to an ideal unrealised potential, a goal or standard as yet to be achieved while the ideal self represents the self as already being in that state of perfection (that is, a self which is distorted by idealisation). The ego ideal is subject to scrutiny and revision in the light of reality in a way that an ideal ego is not since the latter (which may, as Hanly suggests, be consolatory) is the hallmark of a self-idealising grandiose narcissism. We see in some of the clinical chapters here the patient's struggle with shame and potential humiliation as the encounter with reality forces them to revise their sense of self in the light of failures to live up to their ego ideal as their omnipotent phantasies of an ideal self collapse.

The capacity to move between the subjective experience of self into a more 'objective', observing role is well described by Britton (1998). He draws a distinction between 'being oneself' and 'knowing oneself'. He suggests that the ability to view the self from the outside, from a 'third position', is based on a developmental achievement whereby the child can tolerate a position in triangular space as *witness* to the couple, a link from which the subject (child) is excluded; this, he argues, is essential for developing an authentic and realistic sense of self. This has implications for our clinical work where oedipal conflicts may not have been confronted and worked through. The 'third position' also seems relevant to the point made by John Steiner in the Foreword on the nature of irony, which involves an ability to observe ourselves, our self-deceptions and inconsistencies, with humour. As he writes: 'Taking an ironic view means that we can entertain more than one view of ourselves and smile at the contradictions that emerge'.

The Ego and Identity

Originally based on Freud's structural model, ego psychology was refined and advanced by Heinz Hartmann (e.g. 1950, 1964) and his colleagues Kris and Loewenstein (1946). With their emphasis on conflict-free ego functions and the 'average expectable environment', these studies aimed to rectify what they believed was an imbalance in the classical psychoanalytic approach to the ego. While Freud attributed to the ego the function of reality testing and orientation as well as an inhibitory role in relation to instinctual discharge, ego psychologists sought to expand our view of the role of the ego, shifting the balance towards its 'synthetic', 'integrating' and 'organizing' functions (Nunberg, 1931). This was seen as a move away from the focus on pathology to the positive environmental and maturational influences on personality development harnessed by the coherent, organised functioning of the ego.

For an authoritative reading of ego psychology and Hartmann's 'autonomous ego', the reader may refer to the references already quoted above.

Ego psychology has had many contributors from a variety of perspectives (see Schafer's 1970 overview) including Erik Erikson from the psychosocial perspective. A German born psychoanalyst, Erik Erikson was impressed by the work of Freud and became one of the most influential thinkers of the twentieth century, proposing a psychosocial theory of identity development. In this way, he developed away from Freud's more 'psycho-sexual' theory. His extensive studies (1950, 1966a,b, 1968, for example) move between classical psychoanalysis, ego psychology and social theory and encompass a

INTRODUCTION

broader spectrum than our own psychoanalytic one, but his view on development has remained of interest to anyone investigating this area. He also regarded identity development as a process extending through the entire life span. Erikson saw adolescence as *the* critical period for differentiation (the identity crisis) necessary for establishing a mature identity, and the earliest, most vulnerable period of a child's life as the most crucial for providing a basis for identity (the phase of 'Trust vs Mistrust'). Processes of identification and dis-identification have since been firmly placed on the map in the consideration of identity development and stability. He believed that a sense of identity was a deep subjective feeling, a sense of 'an invigorating sameness and continuity', the recognition of something identical within the core of the individual that says 'This is me', often though not always at moments of opposition to a 'compact majority' (which resonates with Steiner's point in the Foreword concerning breaking away from the group, the family or tradition). Erikson argued for a two-fold development resulting in an inner synthesis comprising both personal growth and integration into the 'group'. To quote Charles Rycroft's *Critical Dictionary of Psychoanalysis* (1968) on Erikson's definition of identity:

> Many of the problems of identity centre around the part played by identifications in enhancing or diminishing identity. Failure to identify with parents, particularly the parent of one's own sex, during childhood, is held to diminish the sense of identity, but failure to dis-identify with them in adolescence has a similar effect.
>
> (pp. 76–77)

In her book *Inside Lives* (2002), the psychoanalyst Waddell also explores the fate of identifications in puberty, early and mid-adolescence, pointing to the disruption of certainty, however fragile, as confusions arise over good and bad, adult and infantile, male and female.

Erikson recognised both 'negative' and 'positive' identities (negative aspects of identity being particularly marked in stigmatised or marginalised individuals whose circumstances rob them of choice). Historical trauma, associated with threats to 'self-continuity', is seen as disrupting identity integration; he references native Americans, the holocaust and the centuries of slavery in America.

Erikson sees conflict at each developmental stage serving as a turning point with the potential for growth, or for failure. He also addresses the importance of becoming 'competent', developing a sense of mastery. He argues that the feeling of mastery adds to 'ego strength', but its failure can lead to shame and a sense of inadequacy. This is a point also made by the psychoanalyst Grinberg; he writes that 'confidence in the ego capacity is one of the most important supports of identity' guaranteeing permanence, stability and the integrity of the ego over time (p. 111). Many of the cases within these pages confirm the importance of feelings of inadequacy, incompetence and related shame as a deeply inhibiting factor in identity development, which impacts on the individual's self-esteem. Identification with a primary object (frequently the paternal object) felt to be weak and inadequate often plays a significant role.

Authors such as Otto Kernberg and Margaret Mahler also form a bridge between ego psychology and object relations. Kernberg (1975) writing of borderline personality disorders – (referred to in Chapter 11) – holds pathological levels of splitting responsible for 'identity diffusion' ('emptiness' resulting from the lack of an integrated self-concept and unstable object relationships), while Mahler's work with disturbed young children has contributed much to the analytic understanding of separation and individuation.

Self-Psychology

Heinz Kohut, a very influential American psychoanalyst in the 1960s and 1970s, was Hartmann's natural heir but, in fact, took a different direction. Somewhat disappointed with classical psychoanalysis, and with ego psychology's inability to address problems that lie more deeply below the surface, he developed what became

INTRODUCTION

known as Self-Psychology. In his paper, *Introspection, Empathy and Psychoanalysis*, Kohut (1959) redefined the observational position of the analyst, arguing that the exploration of the internal world requires an empathic, introspective stance. He ultimately moved away from the structural model of id ego and superego entirely and posited a 'nuclear self' – part of a 'self-selfobject matrix'. His view of the 'bipolar self' described a tension between the poles of self-assertion and self-esteem on the one hand (said to require a 'mirroring selfobject') and the pole of values and ideals on the other hand (which requires an idealisable selfobject). For Kohut, pathology arises in states of imbalance between these poles and it is the task of therapy to correct them through empathy and corrective re-enactments within the therapeutic field.

What has become known as 'Relational psychoanalysis' (Greenberg and Mitchell, 1983; Aron, 1991; Orange, Atwood and Stolorow, 1997, 1998) to name only a few among a very large number of writers and adherents of this approach has become increasingly popular in the US. It is in part a development from Kohutian Self-Psychology but is also influenced by the Hegelian philosophical tradition, by post-modernism and by the British object relations school. Despite the latter legacy, the relational approach has largely promoted a shift away from the centrality of unconscious phenomena to a 'psychology of consciousness' (Mills, 2005), with a number of different views around the idea of 'intersubjectivity'. In placing the relation to the object as central to development and to the sense of self, there is an area of shared ground with our own approach, but the differences are marked, both at a theoretical and clinical level. As I understand it, little weight is given by most relational analysts to unconscious phantasy which demarcates it rather sharply from the Kleinian (and, indeed, generally British) view of how the inner world is built up and shaped through the interaction of the external world with unconscious phantasies (particularly those relating to projection and introjection). While *some* relational analysts might agree with our view that there is a 'kernel' of something we recognise as 'ourselves' which is continuous across time, despite developmental changes, this would not, I believe, go so far as to include continuity of fantasy and unconscious phantasy.

A number of relational authors are decisive in their rejection of Freud's drive theory and the central place he gave to instinctual forces (relating, therefore, mainly to his earlier theoretical formulations) which they feel ignores the role of the object. However, it is also true that Freud in his later work (most notably in 'Mourning and Melancholia' (1917)) introduces the idea of an internal object relationship, which was expanded by Melanie Klein. Moreover, though using a libidinal model for understanding mental life in his earlier writings, he also recognised the importance of the relation of the individual to others, particularly his or her primary objects (this is also evident in his case studies). In 'Group Psychology and the Analysis of the Ego' (1921), he writes:

> …It is true that individual psychology is concerned with the individual man and explores the paths by which he seeks to find satisfaction for his instinctual impulses; but only rarely and under certain exceptional conditions is individual psychology in a position to disregard the relations of this individual to others. In the individual's mental life someone else is invariably involved, as a model, as an object, as a helper, as an opponent; and so from the very first individual psychology, in this extended but entirely justifiable sense of the words, is at the same time social psychology as well.

"The relations of an individual to his parents and to his brothers and sisters, to the object of his love, and to his physician – in fact, all the relations which have hitherto been the chief subject of psycho-analytic research – may claim to be considered as social phenomena" (p. 69).

There are considerable differences in clinical technique and practice, for example in what is considered or valued as the 'analytic attitude' (well described in one of Klein's early lectures, in Steiner ed., 2017). Relational analysis leads to a different clinical

INTRODUCTION

stance which favours mutual revelations between analyst and patient including what the analyst feels, thinks and experiences, and possibly even dreams, with respect to the patient, on the grounds that we are inevitably part of the 'intersubjective field' which, I think, is believed to create an autonomous system arising from the contact. In contrast, while we see countertransference experiences as an integral part of 'what is going on', these are largely viewed as unconsciously driven so that feelings that may have disturbed the usual 'flow' need to be reflected upon in order to be made fully conscious and understood rather than necessarily being revealed, with all the increased dangers of enactment. While, unlike in Freud's early view of countertransference, we now consider that countertransference experiences can be and are helpfully (though necessarily imperfectly) used, they are not explicitly revealed.

While we are exploring identity in terms of separation mourning and loss, the focus of relational analysis is on the view of analyst and patient as 'co-constructing a relationship in which neither of them can be seen as *distinct* from the other' (Seligman, 2003, p. 484). In the clinical chapters of this book, unconscious processes of projection and identification are given primacy, and identity is seen as relating to the mourning of cherished and defensive unconscious phantasies which become clear through the patient's resistance to as well as struggle towards accepting the separateness of self and object while taking back projections, that is, owning disavowed aspects of the self, whether good or bad.

While the approaches described above share certain points of contact with the British object relations school, they would also seem to diverge in significant ways in terms of theory and technique. However, we have no pretensions to a comparative study here, for which a proper investigation into relational psychoanalysis and self-psychology would be indicated. As will become apparent, our thoughts on identity, however, also show the influence of both Erik Erikson and Margaret Mahler. The reader can use any of the above references as a starting point for pursuing the wealth of publications on the relational trend.

SHARON NUMA

A Note on the Social and Cultural Aspects of Identity

To integrate the social, cultural and personal aspects of identity would be an enormous task, and not one that we can tackle in this book. It is, nevertheless, important to acknowledge the significance of its scope and implications, no more so than at the current time when these wider issues of national and individual identity are so intensely felt and debated. To cite one example, a number of important issues are outlined in the recent book by the political scientist Francis Fukuyama, *Contemporary Identity Politics and the Struggle for Recognition* (2018). The works of Hannah Arendt on nationalism, identity and difference in fact remain relevant today. There have been a large number of publications over the last twenty years covering identity, sexuality and gender: to name a few, the influential work of Judith Butler (1993, 2006) on 'performative acts' that she regards as constituting gender, Jessica Benjamin who over several publications discusses psychoanalysis, intersubjectivity and gender issues (1988, 2004, 2013) and Avtar Brah's work on 'contesting identities' (1996). The intersection of race and sex in relation to identity also features in a number of works by sociologists such as Brah (ibid.), Wekker (2006), Ruth Frankenberg (1993) and Sara Ahmed (2012, 2017). There are many more contemporary writings on these subjects which represent a substantial body of work.

The idea of race (itself a contested notion) together with culture and class in relation to identity are concepts widely explored by a number of writers, the most distinguished and impressive being the public intellectual and sociologist Stuart Hall whose works spanned his lifetime. Many of his best-known essays are brought together in the collections *Cultural Identity* (with Paul Du Gay, first published 1996) and two volumes of *Essential Essays* in a 2019 collection. Paul Gilroy's interesting exploration of 'black diasporic identity' is laid out in *Black Atlantic: Modernity and Double Consciousness* (1993). Franz Fanon's seminal book *Black Skins White Masks* (1952) brought a psychoanalytic perspective on race, and a number of writers such as Curry (1964–1965) in an early paper, Altman

INTRODUCTION

(2006), Msebele and Brown (2011), Fletchman Smith (2000), Evans Holmes (2016) and White (2002) address racial identity and the psychotherapeutic process. A contemporary psychoanalytic view of race and difference can be found in Fahkry David's book *Internal Racism* (2011).

There is no doubt that the societal role in identity disruption or enhancement, the strengthening of identity through group membership and the challenges posed by group exclusion are significant in determining our overall self-perception and even our actions (this has been well documented, for example by Erving Goffman (1956, 1963, 1967) and Émile Durkheim (1895)). Notions of 'belonging' and the importance of 'home' – that world that lies between the internal and external – is a preoccupation reflected not only in psychoanalytic writings (e.g. Salman Akhtar's work on migration and mourning (1999) or that of Grinberg and Grinberg (1989) on migration and exile) but also in literature.

However, how we experience socially ascribed qualities, particularly in relation to attributes that are stigmatised, will in some part depend on how solid an internal structure we have to support our identity. Given the central role of the object in the model we use here (see p. 12), it seems clear that the *state of the object* will have a significant impact on the child's developing sense of self. A parent who feels socially diminished, stigmatised, or who is denied supportive resources out of poverty, racial hatred or class inequality, or who has had to endure refugee status in an inhospitable land, may struggle with damaged self-esteem, shame, anger, a sense of unfairness, injustice or grievance. Where it has been feasible, some of our cases in this book refer to situations where, derailed by trauma – such as the holocaust – the object's capacity for containment appears to have been profoundly damaged. We know that the internal state of the object is critical to the projective and introjective processes between infant and mother so that in this often unintentional but powerful unconscious way the infant also 'ingests' the emotional impact of a social context and experience which has found a place in the inner world of the object.

SHARON NUMA

A Kleinian View of the Self

If we take Klein's description of the paranoid schizoid and depressive positions as a useful and fundamental starting point, we would suggest that a coherent and realistic sense of self is an achievement of the depressive position. Klein herself, and most Kleinians and post-Kleinians, have emphasised that the primary achievement of the depressive position is the move from a fragmented sense of self and object based on unconscious phantasies of splitting and projective identification, to a more integrated state based on greater accommodation to reality. Most writers have focused on the emotional consequences for the child of the child's new awareness of the whole object, which is characteristic of the depressive position. This emphasis follows naturally from Klein's important discovery that in the depressive position the child's central anxiety shifts from fear of annihilation of the endangered self to fear of the loss and death of the object, occurring alongside the development from the narcissism of the paranoid-schizoid position towards fuller object relations which encompass genuine concern for the object. Less studied are the implications of Klein's simultaneous discovery that in the depressive position the ego, or self, becomes more integrated as the child discovers that the good and bad self are one and the same (the discovery of the whole self), which we believe provides the basis for a sense of identity. It is this area we have explored and extended in these pages.

The 'Self' in the Paranoid-Schizoid Position

In the paranoid-schizoid position, the self is split into a 'good self' containing pleasure, satisfaction, love, gratitude (positive experiences) and a 'bad self' made up of fear, frustration, pain, hatred, envy – (negative experiences). At this early stage, the infant projects the bad self and bad experiences into the object, through omnipotent phantasies of splitting and projective identification, losing parts of the self and becoming vulnerable to paranoid anxieties. At the same time, the infant also splits off and introjects the good

INTRODUCTION

self (linked to good experiences), experiencing manic beliefs in his power and total goodness. Identity, at this stage, oscillates between experiences of an idealised, 'good' self, fused and confused with idealised elements of the object, and an amplified experience of the 'bad' self, also confused with elements of the 'bad' object.

Identifications, at this stage, both projective and introjective, tend to be primitive, omnipotent, total and narcissistic. They result in the infant having the delusion of 'becoming' the good or bad self, the split between these two selves being intensified by confusion with the good and bad object, which is filled with the infant's projections. Although Klein emphasises that there is an early ego operating from the start, responsible both for these primitive defences, and, perhaps in phases of calm for moments of relative integration, it is primitive, split mental states and confusion with the object that predominate in the paranoid-schizoid position. At this stage, the self is fragmented and incoherent. Klein further suggests that if splitting and projective identification is extreme, too intense or frequent, such that it cannot be managed by the ego, what would otherwise be a normal feature of the developing infant mind could instead lead to disintegration, schizophrenia, developmental failure and depersonalisation.

The 'Self' in the Depressive Position

In our clinical examples, we focus on the shift from these relatively fragmented experiences of the self to the more integrated experience of the self that becomes possible in the depressive position. We emphasise, as did Klein, that like the 'achievement' of the depressive position the 'achievement' of a coherent sense of self and of personal identity is never fixed once and for all. We all move constantly backward and forward between more fragmented and integrated states, particularly at times of stress or trauma. In this book, the authors suggest that the achievement of identity involves a series of painful developments, involving the modification of the sense of self (and self-image) ushered in by the recognition of hatred, destructiveness and envy.

Klein has also described the anxiety that arises when the infant realises that his attacks aimed at the 'bad' object also injure, or in phantasy may be felt to destroy, the object of his love. This is the nature of depressive anxiety which sets in motion the wish to make reparation. The infant can no longer bask in an idealised and wholly benevolent view of the self (gained through projective identification with an ideal object); relinquishing that view is painful and involves mourning, disillusion and an anxiety that the loving parts of the self may have been damaged or lost. This can trigger the terror of falling to pieces. If internal stability is fragile, disillusionment can set in train a narcissistic collapse, a disastrous encounter with failed ego ideals.

The impact of acknowledging and owning unwelcome split off parts of the self often triggers a sense of great vulnerability which involves potential shame as well as the mental pain of mourning (Steiner, 1989). We link this to Steiner's description of the problems encountered as the individual emerges from a pathological defensive system, often a 'psychic retreat' (1993). This adds to what is generally associated with identity development.

I think that much of the clinical work in this book focuses on the difficulties our patients have at this delicate stage which prompts us to reflect not only on the material of the session but on technical issues concerning tact and avoidance of humiliation in how we communicate and interpret to our patient. In the 'Lectures on Technique' edited by Steiner (2017), Klein discusses 'the psychoanalytic attitude'. While stressing the search for truth and 'good co-operation between several different parts of our mind', she singles out a serious obstacle to the progress of an analysis: the development of 'feelings of power and superiority' in the analyst (p. 6). A sense of reality and humility will, she notes, keep this in check. One might say that the analyst has to have a reality-based view of his or her own 'identity', to know about his/her own weaknesses and limitations in order to maintain the proper 'analytic attitude'.

What became clear in the course of our studies and is reflected in the chapters that follow is that a central struggle in identity, as

INTRODUCTION

stated so clearly in the Foreword, is our dependence on the relationship to internal objects and the conflicts this engenders. For many patients, the prospect of separateness and loss is experienced as a catastrophe that threatens to fragment the ego and the self.

The infant's ability to face these difficulties of separation is partly based on innate levels of aggression, tolerance of frustration, the level of ego strength and the degree of mental pain involved. However, it also requires the presence of a containing object able to transform the infant's anxieties, an object that can respond to the terrors the infant faces, allowing access and understanding rather than, for example, immediately projecting back that which is projected. This will be discussed more fully but it is a feature not often thought about in a specific way with respect to identity development.

Interestingly, some of our cases alerted us to the possibility that when issues of identity are uppermost in the analysis the analyst will, through the processes of projective identification and enactment, inevitably, at moments, feel their own analytic identity under threat. The patient communicates the experience of their primitive, fused and confused states, often their defence against the pain of separation. (There may be repeated failures in the cycle of development towards separateness, and retreats often signal a return to the imagined safety of a pathological organisation.) The analyst may first need to work through difficult countertransference feelings and to find a way of recovering or holding onto his or her own analytic identity. This countertransference experience can often illuminate the particular nature of the patient's problems of identity (as for example in Chapters 3, 5, 6, 7, 8 and 9); this may be a hypothesis that can be further developed.

While there is a certain elusive quality both to the term 'self' and even to that inner experience we think of as a 'sense of self', perhaps accepting the complexity and the many different levels of functioning involved in the concept of a personal identity does some justice to the question which patients (often silently) bring (who am I?). To summarise what has been discussed up to this point, we could think of the 'self' as an overarching concept describing the conscious and unconscious interactions between the id, ego and superego in the confrontation with the internal and external world. As Klein has shown, at an object relations level, there are dynamic relations in phantasy not only between internal and external objects but between our internal objects; aspects of the ego or superego can also be split off and located in objects. The ego as agency with its functional, organising and reality-oriented activities is critical for the experience of mastery and efficacy, important in the struggle towards an individual identity. A sense of inadequacy in the face of the demands of life (poor ego functioning being one possible causal factor) may also prompt a feeling of inferiority and even condemnation or contempt from the superego, further weakening the ego. Freud understood that 'self-regard' could be diminished in a number of ways – through melancholic identifications, by experiencing loss of love (whether from the external or internal object in the form of the superego), or by the inability to love, leading to feelings of inferiority and impoverishment of the ego. A benign superego *sustains* and strengthens the ego, reducing the need for denial and splitting as Melanie Klein would later propose. Klein concurs with Freud's view that if mourning can be worked through, the ego is enriched due to the gradual introjection of the loved object.

Note

1 *Michael Mercer, Renata Li Causi, Erika Bard, Martin Kinston, Katya Golynkina, Philip Lucas.*

References

Ahmed, S. (2012) *On Being Included: Racism and Diversity in Institutional Life*. Durham NC and London: Duke University Press Books.

Ahmed, S. (2017) *Living a Feminist Life*. Durham, NC and London: Duke University Press Books.

Akhtar, S. (1999) 'The Immigrant, the Exile, and the Experience of Nostalgia'. *J. Appl. Psychoanal. Stud.*, 1(2): 123–130.

INTRODUCTION

Altman, N. (2006) 'Whiteness'. *Psychoanal. Quarterly*, 75(1): 45–72.

Aron, L. (1991) 'The Patient's Experience of the Analyst's Subjectivity'. *Psychoanal. Dial.*, 1(1): 29–51.

Benjamin, J. (1988) *The Bonds of Love: Psychoanalysis, Feminism and the Problems of Domination*. New York: Pantheon Books Inc.

Benjamin, J. (2004) 'Beyond Doer and Done to': An Intersubjective View of Thirdness'. *Psychoanal. Quarterly*, 73(1): 5–46.

Benjamin, J. (2013) 'The Bonds of Love: Looking Backward'. *Studies in Gender and Sexuality*, 16(4): 271–277.

Brah, A. (1996) *Cartographies of Diaspora: Contesting Identities*. London: Psychology Press.

Britton, R. (1989) 'The Missing Link: Parental Sexuality in the Oedipus Complex'. In J. Steiner (Ed.), *The Oedipus Complex Today* (pp. 83–101) London: Karnac

Britton, R. (1998) 'Subjectivity, Objectivity and Triangular Space'. In E. Bott Spillius (Ed.), *Belief and Imagination* (pp. 41–58) London and New York: New Library of Psychoanalysis/Routledge.

Butler, J. (1993) *Bodies That Matter: On the Discursive Limits of Sex*. New York and London: Routledge.

Butler, J. (2006) *Gender Trouble: Feminism and the Subversion of Identity*. London: Routledge.

Curry, A.E. (1964–1965) 'Myth, Transference and the Black Psychotherapist'. *Psychoanal. Rev. D*, 51(4): 7–14.

Davids, F. (2011) *Internal Racism: A Psychoanalytic Approach to Race and Difference*. London: Palgrave MacMillan.

Erikson, E.H. (1950) *Childhood and Society*. New York: WW Norton and Company. Also (1977) Triad/Paladin: St Albans, Herts.

Erikson, E.H (1966a) *The Concept of Identity in Race Relations: Notes and Queries Daedalus* (Vol. 95, No. 1, pp. 145–171). Cambridge MA: MIT Press.

Erikson, E.H. (1966b) 'The Problem of Ego Identity'. *J. Am. Psychoanal. Assn.*, 4: 56–121.

Erikson, E.H. (1968) *Identity, Youth and Crisis*. London: Faber and Faber.

Evans Holmes, D. (2016) 'Culturally Imposed Trauma: The Sleeping Dog Has Awakened. Will Psychoanalysis Take Heed?' *Psychoanal. Dial.*, 26(6): 641–654.

Fanon, F. (1952) *Black Skin, White Masks.* (C.L. Markmann, Trans.) London: Pluto Press, 1986.

Fletchman Smith, B. (2000) *Mental Slavery: Psychoanalytic Studies of Caribbean People.* London: Routledge.

Frankenberg, R. (1993) *White Women, Race Matters: The Social Construction of Whiteness.* MN: University of Minnesota Press.

Freud, S. (1917) 'Mourning and Melancholia'. In *The Standard Edition of the Complete Psychological Works of Sigmund Freud. S.E.* Ed. J. Strachey (Vol. 14, pp. 237–258). London: The Hogarth Press.

Freud, S. (1921) *Group Psychology and the Analysis of the Ego. S.E.* Ed. J. Strachey (Vol. 18, pp. 67–142).

Fukuyama, F. (2018) *Identity: Contemporary Identity Politics and the Struggle for Recognition.* London: Profile Books Ltd.

Gilroy, P. (1993) *The Black Atlantic.* London and New York: Verso.

Goffman, E. (1959) *The Presentation of Self in Everyday Life.* New York: Doubleday.

Goffman, E. (1963) *Stigma: Notes on the Management of Spoiled Identity.* New York: Touchstone.

Goffman, E. (1967) *Interaction Ritual: Essays on Face-to-Face Behaviour.* New York: Pantheon Books.

Greenberg, J. and Mitchell, S. (1983) *Object Relations in Psychoanalytic Theory.* Cambridge, MA: Harvard University Press.

Grinberg, L. (1990) *The Goals of Psychoanalysis.* London: Karnac Books.

Grinberg L. and Grinberg, R. (1989) *Psychoanalytic Perspectives on Migration and Exile.* New Haven and London: Yale University Press.

Hall, S. (1996) *Questions of Cultural Identity.* Eds. S. Hall and P. Gay. London: Sage Publications.

Hall, S. (2019) *Essential Essays* (Vol. 1 and 2). Durham and London: Duke University Press.

Hanly, C. (1984) 'Ego Ideal and Ideal Ego'. *Int. J. Psychoanal.*, 65: 253–261.

Hartmann, H., Kris, E. and Loewenstein, R.M. (1946) 'Comments on the Formation of Psychic Structure'. *Psychoanal. St. Child*, 2: 11–38.

Hartmann, H. (1950) 'Psychoanalysis and Developmental Psychology'. *Psychoanal. St. Child*, 5: 7–17.

Hartmann, H. (1964) *Essays on Ego Psychology.* New York: International Universities Press.

Hinshelwood, R.D. (1991) *A Dictionary of Kleinian Thought*. London: Free Association Books.

Joseph, B. (1985) 'Transference: The Total Situation'. *Int. J. Psychoanal.*, 66: 447–454. Reprinted in Psychic Equilibrium and Psychic Change, Selected Papers of Betty Joseph. London: Routledge, 1989.

Mahler, M.S. and McDevitt, J.B. (1982) 'Thoughts on the Emergence of the Sense of Self, with Particular Emphasis on the Body Self'. *J. Am. Psychoanal. Assn.*, 30: 827–848.

Kernberg, O.F. (1975) *Borderline Conditions and Pathological Narcissism*. New York: Jason Aronson.

Kohut, H. (1959) 'Introspection, Empathy and Psychoanalysis: An Examination of the Relationship between Mode of Observation and Theory'. *J. Am. Psychoanal. Assn.*, 7: 459–483.

Laplanche, J. and Pontalis, J.B. (1988) *The Language of Psychoanalysis*. London: Karnac Books.

Mills, J. (2005) 'A Critique of Relational Psychoanalysis'. *Psychoanaly. Psych.*, 22(2): 155–188.

Msebele, N. and Brown, H. (2011) 'Racism in the Consulting Room: Myth or Reality?' *Psychoanal. Rev.*, 98(4): 451–492.

Nunberg, H. (1931) 'The Synthetic Function of the Ego'. *Int. J. Psychoanal.*, 12: 123–140.

Orange, D.M., Atwood, G. and Stolorow, R.D. (1997) *Working Intersubjectively: Contextualism in Psychoanalytic Practice*. Hillsdale, NJ: Analytic Press.

Orange, D.M., Stolorow, R.D. and Atwood, G.E. (1998) 'Hermeneutics, Intersubjectivity Theory and Psychoanalysis'. *J. Am. Psychoanal. Assn.*, 45: 779–806.

Rycroft, C. (1968) *A Critical Dictionary of Psychoanalysis*. New York: Basic Books.

Sandler, J., Holder, A. and Meers, D. (1963) 'The Ego Ideal and the Ideal Self'. *Psychoanal. Study Child*, 18: 139–158.

Schafer, R. (1970) 'An overview of Heinz Hartmann's Contributions to Psycho-analysis'. *Int. J. Psychoanal.*, 5: 425–446.

Seligman, S. (2003) 'The Developmental Perspective in Relational Analysis'. *Contemp. Psychoanal.*, 39(3): 77–507.

Steiner, J. (1989) 'The Aim of Psychoanalysis'. *Psychoanal. Psychotherapy*, 4(2): 109–120.

Steiner, J. (1993) *Psychic Retreats: Pathological Organizations of the Personality in Psychotic Neurotic and Borderline Patients.* London: Routledge.

Steiner, J. (ed.) (2017) *Lectures on Technique by Melanie Klein.* London and New York: Routledge.

Waddell, M. (2002) *Inside Lives: Psychoanalysis and the Growth of the Personality.* London: Karnac.

Wekker, G. (2006) *The Politics of Passion: Women's Sexual Culture in the Afro-Surinamese Diaspora.* New York: Columbia University Press.

White, K.P. (2002) 'Surviving Hating and Being Hated: Some Personal Thoughts about Racism from a Psychoanalytic Perspective'. *Contemporary Psychoanal.*, 38(3): 401–422.

Wollheim, R. (1984) *The Thread of Life.* Cambridge University Press, and (1999) New Haven and London: Yale University Press.

1

AN OUTLINE OF THE KLEINIAN MODEL OF THE MIND AND ITS IMPLICATIONS FOR THE UNDERSTANDING OF PERSONAL IDENTITY

Sharon Numa

This chapter is intended to place our study of identity in relation to Bion's concept of 'container-contained' as a model of experience against which the emergence of a sense of self can be understood. It will also describe the recurrent themes that emerged during the Workshop discussions in relation to our clinical cases, set in the context of the seminar reading that influenced and helped us formulate our thoughts on identity.

A model for the 'achievement' of identity

In line with a Kleinian approach to the development of the internal world, it is fundamental to our view of identity that *the early determinants of the sense of self and identity are located in our early object relationships*. The model of identity we use therefore considers the development of identity, as *part* of the infant's overall normal mental and emotional development, to be governed by the nature of the object relationship and the ongoing mechanisms of introjection and projection – the introjection into the ego of both good and bad objects, for which the mother's breast is the prototype (Klein, 1935). *The authors here are persuaded that the internalisation of a good object is crucial to a relatively stable sense of identity.* This is facilitated by an experience of continuity as well as by the infant's innate resilience. (While trauma for instance can severely disrupt continuity, there is also the more everyday matter of whether the child feels held in the object's mind, over time.) It also has implications for the role of the object in that process and for the defences that are likely to be recruited when pressures on integration and stability arise. An insecurely established internal object leaves the individual prone to greater persecutory anxieties – and defences against such anxieties – in periods of vulnerability.

The unconscious phantasies that accompany affect and perception all influence, and are influenced by, the early to and fro of emotional experience between infant and mother. Within this context, the mother contains and transforms the infant's anxieties, digesting and de-toxifying experiences of anxiety and fragmentation. Through this 'alpha function' (Bion, 1962) and maternal reverie *meaning* is formed; anxiety is given a meaningful context. Bion has emphasised the function of the breast in this regard. While the breast both satisfies and frustrates, it confers meaning and creates context. There can be little emotional development or psychic growth without meaning, and moreover, it is crucial for the capacity to learn. Bion's notion of 'container/contained' therefore provides a useful model for both normal and pathological emotional and cognitive development, providing a link between the growth of a sense of self (through the projection of infantile fears of fragmentation and disintegration, containment of these anxieties by the object and then re-introjection by the infant), on the one hand, and the capacity for thought and learning on the other hand. Both lie at the nucleus of identity formation.

This model, however, does involve a dependence on the strength and capacity of the object so that, to a great degree, the infant's first identifications will be based on this link with the mother. However, *a further step* is required to find and use a personal identity. We have not only to acquire an identity but to make it our own (Steiner, 1989). This will in part involve a process of 'dis-identification'. To progress towards true personal identity necessitates mourning, relinquishing the phantasy of 'possessing' the object and its desired qualities, hitherto felt to be under the omnipotent control of the self. Painful though this can be, filling the child with feelings of loss and anxiety (and potentially marking a deep narcissistic wound), the differentiation between what belongs to the self and what to the object makes possible a real and separate identity. There is a sense of loss as phantasies of omnipotence and fusion with the object are relinquished, but there is also a strengthening of the sense of identity as aspects of the self (whether good or bad) that had been projected into the object are taken back. This process is repeated over and over again until a more or less stable individual identity is achieved.

If this process goes well, it can lead to the emotional experience of 'having a unique identity'; if it does not and there is a sense of emptiness, meaninglessness or other emotional deficit, then we can expect defensive systems to become established with further consequences for the coherence of identity and personality.

Our understanding of identity *disturbance and pathology* is in line with our view of normal identity development described above. That is, it is understood in terms of the early failure of containment, disturbances relating to the process of identification, the excessive use of splitting and projective identification, the resulting inability to internalise the good object securely and the failure of mourning. Problems may arise at any or all of these points since they are so closely connected, and they may also manifest in various ways – including concretely in the body, a reflection perhaps of early sensory-somatic disturbances relating to a failure of containment.

Recurrent themes emerging from the clinical cases

From our readings, we established a number of headings or themes under which to organise our understanding of the development of self and personal identity vis-à-vis psychoanalytic thought.

The various clinical chapters of the book inevitably address more than one of these recurrent themes (listed below) while emphasising different aspects.

- Splitting, identification, projective identification
- Containment: The role of the body, the maternal object and alpha function
- The inauthentic self: Defensive formations
- Mourning, psychic reality and separateness
- Structure: Ego and superego

Summary of clinical chapters

As mentioned above, Freud's move between models was significant for our own thinking about identity. At the time of writing 'On Narcissism', Freud was largely guided by an energic libidinal model, but by the time he published 'Mourning and Melancholia' (1917) and later the 'Wolf Man' (1918), the importance of projection, identification with the object (already present in his Leonardo paper of 1910) and its link to narcissism allowed for a shift away from instinct theory. It further became the basis of Melanie Klein's extensive mapping of object relations and the internal world. This shift enables us to look at identity less in terms of gaining and losing quantities of narcissistic supplies (self-love in balance with object love), but rather through the lens of identifications with primary objects, separation and dis-identification, and the crucial process of internalisation of the object. We frequently observed narcissistic identifications to be a major obstacle to identity development and stabilisation.

A review of the fundamental notion of identification is the subject of Chapter 2 by Anne Amos where she summarises the main psychoanalytic ideas on unconscious identifications from Freud's Leonardo paper of 1910 onwards. Understanding identification has always been, as she notes, the 'bread and butter' of much analytic work. She discusses the formation of primary identifications through the processes of projection and introjection, discussing some of the ways in which these processes can go wrong. The self and object may become merged, or alternatively an 'identificate' may be formed – a concrete construction – instead of a true internal object, depleting the ego by persistent projection. Two cases illustrate the fixed and unyielding nature of identifications with bad internal objects and the impact on identity in the respective patients.

Phyllis Greenacre (1958) in her paper 'The early physical determinants in the development of the sense of identity' suggests that there is a development from an incipient self to an image of the self, first involving an experience of the body-self. She believes that the sense of identity, or awareness of identity, involves comparison and contrast, with special attention called to obvious unlikeness (face, eyes and genitals). Even for the individual, his inner sense of himself is not enough to produce a sense of identity. The individual's self-image, she suggests, is a fusion of implicit, but generally not clearly focused awareness of his own form and functioning, together with his wishes as to how he would like to appear or to function (forerunners and derivatives of identifications and ideals). These form the core on which his sense of his own identity is built. Greenacre feels that in the first weeks of life, the relationship to the other is mediated largely through the touch of the skin and the mouth (sucking), with hearing and vision playing important but secondary roles. Other parts of the body attain greater significance as directed movement becomes possible for the infant, allowing exploration of the world and ushering in the child's 'love affair with the world'. She focuses on the 'build-up' of the body image suggesting that we can often trace the development of disturbances in sexual identity to this period of self/other body differentiation.

In her seminal paper 'The Experience of the Skin in Early Object Relationships' (1968), Esther Bick argues that in its most primitive form, the parts of the personality are felt to have no binding force holding them together and this must be experienced externally – the skin functions as a boundary. She writes:

> But this internal function of containing the parts of the self is dependent initially on the introjection of an external object, experienced as capable of fulfilling this function. Later,

identification with this function of the object supersedes the unintegrated state and gives rise to the fantasy of internal and external spaces.

(p. 484)

In the absence of this, she states, confusions of identity will become manifest. The need for a containing object in her view produces a frantic search for an object – 'a light, a voice, a smell, or other sensual object' – which can hold the attention and thereby be experienced, momentarily at least, as holding the parts of the personality together. *The optimal object is the nipple in the mouth, together with the holding and talking and familiar smelling mother.* Bick describes disturbances in this important skin-boundary function leading, in many cases, to the formation of a 'second skin', a pseudo-independence not unlike Mahler's 'muscular defence' referring to a bodily defence which attempts to hold the self tightly together (see Chapter 8 for an example of this defensive use of the body). Both Freud and later writers have affirmed the importance of the unity of body and mind; bodily sensations, mental and physical pain or pleasure are clearly interwoven and linked in unconscious phantasy to an object.

In Chapter 3, Susan Lawrence describes a patient who presents a number of somatic symptoms and in whom early splitting between the body and mind resulted in the patient surviving on a thin, unintegrated sense of self. She argues that this early splitting has a serious impact on identity development, illustrated by this patient whose entire survival was based on the extreme separation of his 'cerebral mind' from his body and much of his ordinary lived experience. It was in the body that he located a state of extreme collapse and catastrophic anxieties so that the analyst's containment was crucial in the patient recovering split off parts of himself. In addition to the work of Klein, Bion and Britton, Lawrence draws on Harfung and Steinbrecher's work on the somatic countertransference, as she describes the somatic resonance of the patient's bodily states in the analyst which raises interesting questions about projective processes.

Giovanna Rita Di Ceglie outlines in Chapter 4 Bick's central ideas on the infant's perceptual and somatic connection with the mother and explores the struggle towards what the author notes is a *mutual orientation* between mother and baby, which she links to Antonio Damasio's idea of an 'autobiographical self'. This chapter uses Dante's *Divine Comedy* as a literary example of Bick's paradigm describing the infant's 'reaching towards the mother', as a basis for depicting Dante's psychic journey from disorientation to re-orientation to the primary object, in the process of which he rediscovers his sense of identity, a process shared with us in *The Divine Comedy*.

Margaret Mahler's work (1972) draws our attention to a number of issues relevant to identity. She writes of the psychological achievement in moving from a 'good symbiotic union' towards individuation and object constancy but also notes that we oscillate between being fully in the world yet also apart from it; this evolving intra-psychic process reverberates throughout the life cycle and is never finished. She considers the shift towards aspiration and individuation to be the principal psychological achievement of development involving the body, its function and the relation to the primary love object. From visual and tactile forms of differentiation, we move to locomotor skills and experimentation with distance and separateness from the object. The sense of autonomy and mastery in the relation to the world signals an important moment for the child's narcissistic investment in both his own functioning and his own body and locomotor skills. She refers to the child's pleasure and excitement at his or her new capacities (akin to Greenacre's 'love affair with the world'). In the cycle of separation-individuation, the child begins to separate from the mother unaware for the time being of the reality of his smallness, which will soon have to be faced. At this moment, there is not only likely to be a physical 'fall' but also a psychic one; shame and humiliation become a real potential with consequences for confidence and security of the self. Recovery from this 'fall' will be discussed later in relation to the work of Ignes Sodre and John Steiner.

In this regard, the response of the object is central: pride and support for the child's striving as opposed to the damaging effects of indifference, or shaming and humiliation. The child oscillates between the elation of escape with attendant phantasies of omnipotence and the pull back towards the object. The mother is required to be sensitive to both the child's vulnerability and helplessness and its striving towards individuation. The outcome will depend on both the internal resources of the child and the mother's capacity to respond appropriately. A well-supported child can confront and tolerate the degree of object loss that this process entails. Failures in this stage, Mahler argues, can impact negatively on the later adult's self-esteem and sense of identity.

Donald Winnicott follows Klein, attending more closely, however, to the role of the maternal object and environment, and the early infant's absolute dependency on the mother (which resonates with Erikson's emphasis on the early stage of absolute vulnerability and dependency). He states that 'the inherited potential of an infant cannot become an infant unless linked to maternal care' (1960, p. 588). He draws our attention to the role of the mother's eyes, arms and holding capacity which he argues are critical in the infant's first sense of 'self'; he states that what is reflected in the mother's eye is the baby-self, and this influences how the infant defines itself: a 'good' or 'bad' baby, loved or unloved. If there is both holding and environmental provision in space and time ('living with'), with good enough maternal care and a build-up of memories of maternal care on which the infant can draw, then the infant can, in his view, emerge from the merged state with mother to a 'not-me' position towards differentiation of a separate personal self. Such a mother provides *continuity of being* for the infant which promotes the infant's capacity to develop towards separateness, without excessive impingements to which he or she must 'react', in the grip of primitive fears of annihilation. It is interesting that to different degrees dissociative identity disorders and experiences of depersonalisation are associated with loss of memory, or 'dissociative amnesia' as well as disturbances in the individual's relation to time, that is, trauma resulting in breaches in the sense of time and in the ongoing sense of self. Such states, where there is a blurring of the sense of identity, point to continuity and memory as essential components in the subjective experience of identity. Winnicott also explores the question of reality and illusion. He describes how there is no possibility for an infant to proceed from the pleasure to the reality principle, beyond primary identification, unless there is a 'good enough mother' (1953, p. 94).

The 'good enough mother' makes an active adaptation to the child's needs, an adaptation that gradually lessens, according to the infant's growing capacity to tolerate frustration. In this process, the child gains from the experience of frustration since there is inevitably an incomplete adaptation to need, which makes the object real, that is to say hated as well as loved. Winnicott also stresses the child's narcissistic illusion that he is the breast or the breast is part of him and emphasises the positive value of, in fact the necessity of, illusion. For a time, a good enough mother allows the child the opportunity to believe the breast is part of the infant as if under the infant's omnipotent magical control, 'created' by the infant (ibid.). The transitional phase that follows leaves silent the question of who created the breast; eventually, the painful reality that the breast belongs to the object is reached. A good enough mother can help the child negotiate through these phases, through a 'gradual disillusionment'. Like the maternal object, the analyst needs to have a capacity to survive the patient's hatred and to tolerate with understanding the experience of being the 'bad object'. For Winnicott, the 'real' self cannot be born without this inevitable mix of loving and hating feelings towards the mother and cannot develop without the mother being able to hold onto her awareness of the child's love while being hated.

As noted earlier, the question of identity brings even more clearly into focus the fact that with the splitting of the object *there is a complementary splitting of the self* into a 'good' and 'bad' *self*. Splitting and projective processes are mental mechanisms that underwrite a large number of other defences (for example denial, idealisation or intellectualisation), and they represent powerful phantasies. Radical splitting between the good self/good object pair and the bad self/bad object and consequent lack of integration of the self has also been described in borderline patients by Kernberg (1975) where the predominance of bad object experiences may create a persecutory nightmare, with all good experiences being totally contaminated. He also describes narcissistic patients whose disturbed sense of self arises from a pathological fusion of ideal self, ideal object and actual self-image. There is a terror of mediocrity and dependency. The idealisation of the analyst hides the patient's spiteful aggression. Splitting and dissociation may also signal an attempt to control the object in such situations.

The healthy aspect of splitting makes possible the cognitive ability for *differentiation* while also being the means by which the good object is protected from destruction or impingement from 'bad' internal forces. In the case discussed in Chapter 5, Caroline Garland describes a patient whose identity had been founded upon an idea of 'goodness' that was precarious and constantly threatened by the hidden 'bad'. The patient's attempt to maintain an absolute split between good and bad through continuous projective and introjective identifications had eventually collapsed into psychosis, following which she sought analysis. Subsequently, following a session in which the analyst had made a mistake, obliging the patient to tolerate the idea of both good and bad existing within a single individual, it became possible to explore the painful developmental issues that had formed the roots of her earlier self. A greater capacity for integration in herself and her objects – most importantly the parental couple – created the beginnings of a real foundation for a mind and identity of her own.

In Klein's view, the basis for splitting is linked to the infant's own aggression (prompted in part by the real experiences of frustration imposed by external objects) which gives rise to the experience of its objects as bad and dangerous persecutors. The phantastic nature of these imagos is a result of the distortion by the infant's own aggression and sadism. As the terrifying persecutors are now dreaded

AN OUTLINE OF THE KLEINIAN MODEL

but are nevertheless installed within the ego through projection and re-introjection, so the good internal objects must be protected and kept apart from them. Splitting, a denial of the full reality of both *self* and object, is the means by which this is accomplished. Like early idealisation, splitting at this stage is necessary for the infant's sense of safety and security. Klein states:

> I believe that the ego is incapable of splitting the object—internal and external—without correspondingly a splitting within the ego taking place. Therefore the phantasies and feelings about the state of the internal object influence vitally the structure of the ego.
>
> (1946, p. 101)

In normal development, the ego will become more coherent and organised, and ambivalence tolerated: good and bad aspects of the object, now seen as a whole object, and equally important for us here, the good and bad aspects of the *self* as belonging to the 'same' self, can be recognised and accepted. This represents a move from paranoid schizoid to depressive functioning. Early fears for the survival of the ego shift to fears on behalf of the object. The preservation of the good object is thus equated with the survival of the ego (Klein, ibid.).

We know from clinical experience that moments of integration can be fragile and precarious. When faced with increased pressure from either persecutory or depressive anxieties, the patient may intensify the use of projective identification as a means of evading these fears, where communication between parts of the self and with the reality of the object is disrupted or closed off. Such contact can be experienced as threatening to the integrity of the ego. Klein writes:

> …as far as the ego is concerned, the excessive splitting off and expelling into the outer world of parts of itself considerably weakens it. For the aggressive component of feelings and of the personality is intimately bound up in the mind

with power, potency, strength, knowledge and many other desired qualities. It is, however, not only the bad parts of the self which are expelled and projected, but also good parts of the self.

(ibid., pp. 8–9)

While there is a natural developmental drive towards *integration*, there also exists a tendency towards *disintegration*, and the forces that move to fragment the individual are not only defensive but also ultimately anti-life and anti-development in outcome if not in aim. Such defensive manoeuvres lead to the sort of psychic disunity and discontinuity we see in patients who do not have a secure sense of identity, and furthermore, it is our view that it is integration and the establishment of a secure internal object that creates the environment for healthy identity development. This increased integration corresponds to a development from paranoid schizoid towards depressive position functioning. There are, however, important obstacles to this shifting, developing process.

As we know from Freud's work, the link between identification and narcissism is critical. This type of object relationship, as we would now think of it, circumvents the recognition of separateness; the object is omnipotently incorporated and a separate identity denied. A number of chapters here are concerned with the obstacles to identity development posed by narcissistic identifications and object relationships, as this reveals itself in the course of the analysis as resistance to dependency and feelings of smallness. Defences may arise to cope with anticipated shame. Herbert Rosenfeld (1964) has pointed this out in his paper *On the psychopathology of Narcissism* where he describes how the self omnipotently enters and takes over the qualities of the object/mother experienced as desirable; identification by introjection and by projection occurring simultaneously. These patients often show a particular attitude to knowledge: information is 'already known', incorporated, while the existence of an object who can offer anything is denied.

AN OUTLINE OF THE KLEINIAN MODEL

In line with Rosenfeld's argument (and a significant link to certain cases presented in this book), Sodre (2004) discusses extreme shifts in identity, describing in detail how omnipotent and destructive phantasies where there is massive projective identification into the object completely disrupts the process of sorting out 'who's who'. She reminds us of the distinction between projective identification used for purposes of empathy which enables us to emotionally and imaginatively identify with another's experience and that form of 'massive projective identification' we associate with pathological object relations. This can lead either to confusion and 'loss of a firm sense of self' or to

> an extreme rigidity in character, where artificial new boundaries are created between subject and object, but are then tenaciously adhered to. In this case the new boundaries between what is 'me' and what is 'you' have to be maintained as a fortress against the threat of the return of the split-off projected parts of the self.
>
> (pp. 55, 56)

She suggests that these manic mechanisms and violent projections lead to concrete pathological introjections, a rigid defence against dependence and separateness.

To allow the object a separate identity is to give it value, thereby recognising the subject's own dependency and need (followed perhaps by gratitude). Being able to develop a separate sense of self therefore means confronting one's smallness, dependency, vulnerability and envy of the object. The breast is not 'already possessed'.

Steiner (2011) suggests that at this moment of recognition, of emergence from a narcissistic organisation, the patient is particularly vulnerable to humiliation. To be 'seen' in one's smallness threatens shame and can prompt the individual to hide, to return to his or her psychic retreat. We suggest that the dynamic equilibrium between the paranoid schizoid and depressive positions which Steiner explores in his earlier work (1992) can be usefully recruited to understand not only mental attitudes to objects but questions relating to the maturity of identity, that is a 'mature' identity would require development away from the more schizoid fragmented states associated with the paranoid schizoid position, towards a working through of depressive anxieties and an increasing shift towards symbolic thinking. This move towards symbolic functioning however depends upon the ability to tolerate separateness and loss, that is, to face mourning. This I think is borne out by a number of the cases described in this book.

The avoidance of a separate identity often leads to defensive idealisation of the self and object in a symbiotic union. When the patient is in the grip of narcissistic idealisation (often relived in the transference), splitting is fiercely reinstated between not only a good and bad object but between an idealised and a terrifyingly bad object. Typically, the self-idealising patient feels that they are in possession of the breast, having 'become' the (ideal) object. As Rosenfeld notes this highly idealised self-image often dominates the analytic situation, and the patient rejects and denies any interpretation that interferes with it. This type of dynamic is illustrated in the patient described in Chapter 6 by Sharon Numa where mourning is evaded by clinging to a 'transference illusion' as described by Britton (1998), which protects the patient from a painful transference situation. In the case described, the patient powerfully endeavours to maintain an idealised view of the analyst and of the lost object with whom she is identified. Her formidable defences against loss and psychic truth were organised within an illusory fairy tale 'dream world' in which nostalgia and idealisation of the mother/baby analyst/patient relationship were critical in maintaining the split between her ideal world and a painful, frightening psychic reality. The author suggests that this intense splitting was driven by the premature loss of the idealised object, later compounded by the actual death of her mother. In the course of the analysis, the patient was gradually able to re-own aspects of the self that had been split off, which opened a path to real mourning and a recognition of separateness, therefore allowing a more credible basis for the patient's identity.

Klein points out that idealisation is bound up with the denial of psychic reality which is only possible through the feeling of omnipotence – a characteristic of the infantile mind. The threatening bad breast/object which arouses intense persecutory fears can only be eliminated by an ideal object, which, added to the infantile longing for an inexhaustible breast, leads to the development of the phantasy of an ideal breast. There is a painful process of what Winnicott referred to as 'gradual disillusionment' which can threaten to make the patient feel diminished and small.

Sodre (2012) also offers an important insight into the relationship between the 'ideal' and questions of size, power and illusion. She suggests that confrontations over power can often be seen to develop as a result of humiliating disappointments in relation to an idealised object. When the patient has created an idealised phantasy in which he can control an ideal object and identify with it, any response that challenges this may lead to a feeling of catastrophic collapse. The Fall is too great from a merging position of 'I'm the breast and the breast is me', to 'I need the breast, which is not me'. This often seems to lead to a realisation that 'it is not uniquely mine either', which is equated with the conviction that 'I am not loved at all'.

Sodre further argues that this disillusionment opens up a gap between the self and the object; a gap that to start with is filled by Chaos, leading to panicky feelings of falling into a terrifying unknown. Normally, the mother's love saves the day since it creates a link and is felt to rescue the baby from the abyss. But if this fails and the pain, humiliation and fear are unbearable, the 'horizontal' gap between self and breast becomes a 'vertical' gap, with only two positions, triumph or humiliation. The longing for love is then replaced by a longing for power. The patient inhabits an up and down universe in which strength fuelled by hatred is idealised and love is seen as weak and contemptible. The patient is seduced by the belief that to become 'Big' via massive projective identification with the Idealised Bad Object takes seconds, whilst growing up is always partial, insecure and takes time and hard work.

If we think about identity stabilisation in terms of a move from fragmentation to integration, we can see that the 'rescue' through a loving object relationship as Sodre describes would be crucial in helping the child (and the patient) to gain, or to regain, some cohesion in the sense of self. There is a danger in the analytic situation emanating from either the patient or the analyst that if handled poorly, the patient will feel so humiliated that he or she reaches again for a dynamic of power and omnipotence (Steiner, 2015). Perhaps Dante's 'return journey' (Chapter 4) is also the tale of a journey of 'rescue' by recovering the lost good object.

Drawing on Milton's work *Paradise Lost*, Steiner (ibid.) describes the courage required to make that 'return journey' – back to an ordinary relationship, which requires mourning the loss of omnipotence. He links this question of the 'fall' with Mahler's work described above: the delicate moment when the child experiences the thrill of conquering the world, as yet unaware of its smallness which he is about to discover with consequences for confidence and security of the self. (We might also recall here Erikson's work on mastery and achievement.)

Klein makes it clear that with respect to splitting, alongside the expulsion of dangerous substances (excrement) out of the self and into the mother (in states of hatred), split off parts of the ego are also projected into the mother. She explains: 'In so far as the mother comes to contain the bad parts of the self, she is not felt to be a separate individual but is felt to be **the** bad self' (1946, p. 102).

Klein has shown that just as the identification of the mother with bad self can lead to the prototype of an aggressive object relationship, so the identification based on the projection and expulsion of loving parts of the self influences object relations. Chapter 7 by Phil Crockatt offers an example of how the prototype of a 'bad object relationship' where good parts of the self have been lost and 'bad' aspects of the self became confused with aspects of the object is played out in the analysis. The author describes the difficulties for his patient in developing and holding onto her own identity in the face of exposure to the mental illness of her mother and elder sister who were experienced as forcing a version of herself into her that had more to do with their own repudiated problems than with an accurate perception of the patient. This experience of 'intrusive' objects left the patient with deep confusions about her identity. The author suggests that the violent behaviour that broke out in the analysis was part of the patient's attempt to eject and return her ill object's 'alien' projections to their rightful location while conveying to her analyst the experience of being invaded. He suggests that this patient hoped to find in her analyst an object that could help her sort out what belonged to her and what belonged to her object.

Of course, no identity can be considered 'complete' in the sense of 'closed', but the invasion of personal psychic boundaries by primary objects, on the one hand, or the loss of parts of the self through the excessive use of projective identification, on the other hand, are situations we know to be associated with a weak ego and poor integration.

Pertinent to identity development and the central question of integration is the nature of the superego. Klein suggests that to understand the severity of a relentless harsh superego, we need to grasp not only the frightening demands of phantasied bad internal objects but also the exacting and strict demands of the good internal objects. In melancholic states, for example, we can see the cruelty of good loved objects within. If in the course of analysis we can help to reduce the severity of the patient's superego, a sufficient degree of integration may take place, allowing them to internalise a good object, or recover the lost good object. However, the secure internalisation of the good object is menaced not only by bad internal objects but also by the greedy devouring aspects of love. Identity development relies on the internalisation of the object with relative safety so that the sense of self can grow in coherence over time and command some resilience in the face of anxieties internal or external.

The importance to identity development of an available containing object cannot be over-emphasised as can be seen by its appearance and centrality in all the clinical cases in this volume; it is perhaps a 'necessary condition' for being able to internalise a good object, upon which identity stability depends.

The concept or theory underlying the nature of thought and thinking is described by Bion in terms of containment, the transformation of experience, the process by which indigestible, inchoate, almost sensory-somatic beta-elements become thinkable mental contents through the object's 'alpha function' which reduces anxiety and brings relief. The libidinal mother offers love but for Bion *this* maternal function provides the infant with a model for understanding, for managing difficult emotional states, while simultaneously facilitating thought itself. In *Learning from Experience*, he gives his own definition:

> Melanie Klein has described an aspect of projective identification concerned with the modification of infantile fears; the infant projects a part of its psyche, namely its bad feelings into a good breast. Thence in due course they are removed and reintrojected. During their sojourn in the good breast they are felt to have been modified in such a way that the object that is reintrojected has become tolerable to the infant's psyche. From the above theory I shall abstract for use as a model the idea of a container into which an object is projected and the object that can be projected into the container; the latter I shall designate by the term contained.
>
> (1962: 90)

As noted earlier, we make use of Bion's container-contained model for understanding the early phases of identity development, in an attempt to clarify the qualities of the primary object that can be said to most promote healthy identity development as well as to underline the primitive nature of what often needs to be contained, when for example fears of annihilation arise in the infant, or when

AN OUTLINE OF THE KLEINIAN MODEL

fragile moments of ego integration suddenly feel imperilled. These states of intense anxiety can arise once more with force during an analysis when existing, early structural 'fault lines' in the personality come under pressure. Crucially for identity, if things go well, it is possible for the child (or patient) to identify with an object who can tolerate anxiety and aggression. 'Unacceptable' parts of the self may be associated not only with destructive impulses but also with loving ones. 'Good enough' containment provides a model for identification with the mental function of containment and of thought itself. This opens the path towards a more whole and coherent personality where good and bad self, good and bad object are accepted, ambivalence tolerated and the individual as a result has a more mature and realistic sense of self.

Containment, we suggest, also implies the *object being able to accept the child* in the round, both good and bad elements, ultimately being able to recognise the individuality and separateness of the child (rather than, for example, seeing them as a narcissistic extension of the parent). One might say that just as the child needs to accept that the good and bad parent is one, the parent needs to accept that the good and bad child is one (this is in one respect the theme of Chapter 7). The qualities of the object felt to be favourable to identity development therefore encompass both a capacity to contain states of fragmentation and, in addition, over time to recognise the *child's* identity and uniqueness, which will affect the process of introjection. In situations where even ordinary aggression cannot be tolerated, the need for the child to split and use primitive defences in a more extreme way is reinforced, partly in order to protect the good object.

In 'The Lost Child' (Chapter 8), Judith Jackson describes her work with a patient in whom a sense of identity was almost absent, despite his fifty years of age, a situation she links to a possible failure of maternal reverie and alpha function. His recurrent childhood experience was of literally waiting and waiting for his mother to pick him up (from school, from sports events and so on). This failure to be 'picked up' created the experience of being lost in time and space with an object who appeared to be equally lost and who had little capacity for containment. There seemed to be no solid point of orientation for him. The patient often lost his belongings, lost track of time and rarely had a solid grip on who and where he was. Through the containment offered by the analysis, he was able over time to 'gather' himself, reduce fragmentation and develop a sense of himself as existing as a person with a mind in the mind of the analyst/object. He felt more present in the here and now and became able to imagine himself in the future. This case not only demonstrates the role of the analyst in facilitating the patient's experience of a 'continuity of being' (Winnicott) by recovering her capacity for proper containment – having survived her own experiences of 'being lost' with this patient – but also offers support for the idea that the experience of continuity in time made possible by the mental function of the primary object is significant for identity development.

In describing Bion's hypothesis of the links between Love (L), Hate (H) and Knowledge (K), Britton (1992) states that if the child can introject an object capable of receiving and containing its projections, he or she is:

> provided with an internal object capable of knowing and informing. In other words, the person who internalises such an object is capable of self-knowledge and communication between different aspects of themselves. They can experience themselves and think about themselves.
>
> (1992, p. 107)

The idea of the 'container' in Bion's theory also has implications for the use of the body in relation to identity. Indeed, Freud's early well-known statement 'the ego is first and foremost a bodily ego' draws our attention to the central, primitive importance of the body in our sense of who we are, what 'belongs' to us. In fact, it was Viktor Tausk who in 1919 originally pointed out that the body self is the *first object of the self*. It lies at the border of the concrete and symbolic, a point I have already referred to with respect to Chapter 3 by Susan Lawrence whose patient retreated to a cerebral enclave, attempting to deny the reality of his physicality. It was through the work of the analysis that the patient could begin to 'think' his mental states (rather than projecting experiences into his body), in a more integrated way.

The borderline between the physical and mental qualities in some patients is, indeed, highly confused. Patients with somatic presentation or hysterical symptoms prompt us to examine the process of transformation of 'beta' to 'alpha' elements, (or its failure) particularly where her body becomes the main expressive organ, and the capacity for developing true symbolic thinking necessary for linking emotional experiences and parts of the self is restricted. As we know from the work of Esther Bick and other writers mentioned earlier, the body lends itself to somatic experiences that represent projection and introjection, expulsion and evacuation, particularly where the capacity for symbolisation has been undermined. Developmentally, the infant may rid themselves of painful states of mind as if they were bodily parts of the self, which are projected into the object's body but may then be re-introjected in a confused muddle between the bodies of self and object.

We see in the clinical account in Chapter 9 given by Anne Amos a fragmented patient who relied on the beauty and physicality of the body as a defensive carapace to provide a sense of self. In reading about this patient, C, one is reminded of Mahler's point concerning the phase of greatest narcissistic investment in the body, prior to a recognition of the self's true 'size'. C's body had itself been her 'identity' and functioned rather like a phallus in its invincibility, its effectiveness and as an object of admiration. As this carapace broke down in the face of ageing and marital difficulties, the patient became overwhelmed with anxieties which were expressed in illness and fear of illness. A more hysterical picture emerged as the analysis progressed, which seemed to offer an escape from reality while allowing her to maintain a semblance of object relating. A downgraded maternal object involved with a cruel neglectful father was revealed together with the excitement this engendered. Primitive identifications were repeated in the analysis before the patient could begin to confront this internal oedipal couple and later develop a capacity for greater symbolic functioning and separateness from the object.

Perhaps for such patients where the body is often the locus of psychic activity, the development from the concrete to the symbolic use of the 'skin' as container allows them – perhaps for the first time – to give meaning to their affective states. As Britton (1992) notes, a 'self' without meaning is merely an empty vessel.

Sexual and gender identity confusion arising from confused identifications and dis-identifications is discussed, among other significant elements, both in Chapter 2 by Amos and in Flynn's complex male patient described in Chapter 12. (A man who attempts to build an identity based on an aggressive dis-identification with the abandoning father while longing for a strong paternal presence.) The role of the actual father in identity development – in supporting the boy's male identity, or enhancing the girl's self-esteem – is present in many of the cases here, often as an absence, pointing to the importance of mental structure in identity development and the 'third position' which facilitates self-reflection and observation as well as sexual identity. An alternative object to whom one can turn would, of course, be particularly important if maternal containment fails.

Winnicott's work on the true and false self puts forward the view that our instinctual selves (id impulses) reflect our 'real selves'; the true self is by nature amoral and asocial because a good enough caregiver has allowed the infant the luxury of expressing all it feels (by way of desire, aggression and so on) without having to be concerned for the object, while the original 'false self' is an adaptation to the external world, as disillusionment sets in. This, however, only takes on a pathological form if there has been a serious failure of attunement (as with a depressed cut-off mother) or a premature awareness of the object's needs, which may result in an inauthentic compliance, a pathological false self.

Both Helene Deutsch (1942) and Greenacre (2011) were interested in certain 'inauthentic' identities (the reader will notice elements of 'inauthentic' identities and fears of fraudulence in various cases). Deutsch discusses cases where the individual's 'relationship to the outside world and his own ego appears impoverished or absent' (p. 301). The patients Deutsch describes are often unaware of their disturbance and do not 'know' about this impoverishment, but **others** become aware of a disturbing sense of unreality and an emotional deficit in these individuals. In these 'as if' personalities, she notes that their lives may seem to run along as if they are complete: they are often intellectually intact, appear to offer friendship, or empathy, but while 'outwardly he conducts his life as if he possessed a complete and sensitive emotional capacity' this is in fact empty form, a kind of mimicry, together with 'a highly plastic readiness to pick up signals from the outer world and to mould oneself and one's behaviour accordingly' (ibid., p. 304).

This is clearly important for the issue of identity and its pathology since one could say 'any object will do' as a bridge for identification. As patients, they can also mould themselves to the analytic process, but underneath, there exists a feeling of emptiness and dullness. Objects are invested in, discarded and replaced as the environment demands. Deutsch is not only speaking of a false identity and disturbances of affect but problems of structure of the personality since these individuals equally discard moral principles; there is an 'as if' morality, with deep confusion over good and bad; they adopt convictions that belong to **others** and can often 'attach themselves to groups (for example religious groups) to give content to their inner emptiness or establish validity for their existence by identification' (ibid. p. 305).

Deutsch suggests that the reality of instinctual forces of the oedipal situation has never been registered or expressed, so there is no working through of identifications or proper superego development. This link between identity and morality seems to me a very important point. Both ego and superego remain weak: instead, there is 'obedience' to the external environment, but clearly, such patients can only maintain their position through continuous splitting.

The 'Impostor' (Greenacre, 1958) is a somewhat different personality although there are similarities. It is worth quoting Greenacre's opening paragraph as a pithy description of this fraudulent type of individual:

> An impostor is not only a liar, but a very special type of liar who imposes on others fabrications of his attainments, position, or worldly possessions. This he may do through misrepresentations of his official (statistical) identity, by presenting himself with a fictitious name, history, and other items of personal identity, either borrowed from some other actual person or fabricated according to some imaginative conception of himself. There are similar falsifications of that part of his identity belonging to his accomplishments, a plagiarizing on a grand scale, or making claims which are grossly implausible. Imposture appears to contain the hope of getting something material, or some other worldly advantage.
>
> (p. 359)

As Greenacre notes, while we do not often see a full-blown case of such misrepresentation of identity in the consulting room, we do see aspects of this. She points to a constellation of factors in well-developed clinical cases of imposture: the intensity of the 'family romance', the intense circumscribed disturbance of the sense of identity (a kind of infarction in the sense of reality) and the defective nature of the superego in respect of both conscience and ideals. Greenacre seems to be describing an ever-changing process of acquisitive identification. Nothing is ever denied the omnipotent self, nothing is given up since every 'identity' is accessible and there is no painful separation from the object.

AN OUTLINE OF THE KLEINIAN MODEL

Taking account of what has been said about splitting and projective identification, we suggest that the internalisation of the good object and the beginning of secure identity development are closely related to the acceptance of the psychic reality of separateness, the recognition of the 'facts of life' which include loss and death and the relinquishing of omnipotence (Money-Kyrle, 1968).

In his 'Formulation on the two principles of mental functioning' (1911), Freud charted the move from the pleasure principle to the reality principle, from narcissistic hallucinatory gratification to engagement with the external world, a step towards reality. The recognition that there is more satisfaction to be gained from reality than from illusion plays a major part in this development.

The Oedipus complex is the matrix in which these momentous struggles relating to loss, the relinquishing of omnipotence and facing reality take place and it is the surrendering of the child's oedipal illusions which ushers in a more mature resolution of the intense inner conflicts, and a shift towards identification with the same sex parent. Wounded by oedipal defeat, the normal child will, of course, preserve daydream and fantasies of fame and heroic victory to fill the gap between the self he desires to be and the self that he is and this plays a role in restoring self-esteem. Nevertheless, the child now gains an idea of their 'size' in relation to a parental couple; giving up oedipal illusions brings a sense of loss but also the potential for growth as the 'bit by bit' acceptance of reality Freud speaks of, in turn, makes possible the sorting out of what belongs to the self and what to the object. The process of mourning, allows pivotal distinctions to be made between phantasy and reality as well as between self and object.

In his 1926 paper, Sándor Ferenczi laid out the stages in the development of the sense of reality extending on Freud's idea. He charts our development through four stages, from the period of unconditional omnipotence, magical thinking and magical gestures by which the maternal object is (magically) controlled, to a final stage of the acceptance of reality. There is a move from concrete to symbolic linguistic and thoughtful activities. The infant can begin to influence the mother through words and language. In stressing the role of omnipotence, Ferenczi prompts us to think about how deeply we resist the reality of helplessness, and yet only by confronting our dependency on a separate object can we move towards true personal identity. Important in the consideration of identity is the understanding that only with a shift from concrete to symbolic thinking can the good object be properly internalised.

Both Chapters 6 (Numa, previously discussed) and 10 (Hadary) address the question of failed mourning and its relation to idealisation. Orna Hadary describes a female patient who was imprisoned in a melancholic internal relationship with her dead mother. The chapter gives an account of her process of development from holding on to an idealised maternal object to separation and separateness. It involves a necessary shift from concrete to symbolic thinking. This patient attempted to overcome her difficulty to mourn her dead mother through a belief that the analyst was 'in fact' the ideal mother, one who knew her needs and was expected to anticipate and fit in with them. This more concrete means of escaping reality also presented a countertransference challenge since the patient put pressure on the analyst to 'fit in' with her ascribed identity as a closely attuned 'mother' rather than as an ordinary analyst. Through a process of mourning, the concrete omnipotent phantasy turned into a symbolic connection with the maternal object which allowed the patient to regain the freedom to live her life and develop her personal identity.

The question of identity raises both the issues of structure, i.e. the relative harmony or conflict between the ego and the superego (since this fundamentally affects the individual's sense of self as well as self-esteem), and the subjectivity of the experiencing self. The process of identification alters the structure of the subject's ego and superego, while projection alters the perceived qualities of the internal and external object. Generally speaking, we are offered some protection from overly harsh self-scrutiny and criticism by the positive evaluation of ourselves (albeit partly illusory) by those we care for and who care for us. In narcissistically fragile individuals, there is greater susceptibility to criticism, which is also true where we find a harsh superego. As we know, the stability of the sense of self is threatened by the loss of love, which may lead to melancholia with unstable identifications. Such anxiety and fear about the loss of love must present an obstacle to identity stability.

On the question of organising structures, we look to Freud and Klein, both in terms of the role of triangulation and the oedipal configuration, but also specifically to the question of the quality of the superego. We know that an overly harsh and dominant superego is felt by both Freud and Klein to be anti-development. Bion (1959) and Steiner (2006) write about the power of the primitive superego to obstruct the development of the more mature superego of the depressive position. To quote Steiner:

> The judgemental quality of the observing object is central to Freud's formulation of the Oedipus complex where the father was seen as the representative of power and authority exercising judgement and threatening punishment. Praise or blame, and reward or punishment, are functions of the observing object and come to be incorporated in the classical formulation of the superego. The critical role of gaze becomes apparent when we recognize that humiliation is an important part of the threat coming from superego figures.
> (Steiner, 2006, p. 941)

In studying identity, we have found this to be extremely important, and as Steiner notes, that importance is often underestimated. The role of shame, being seen, feeling exposed to the gaze and even the understanding of the analyst can stir a patient to retreat from facing object loss and separateness if the threat of humiliation is too great and felt to emanate from a critical disparaging superego/observing object.

The superego is always prone to regressive tendencies in the direction of re-externalisation, or 'to a brittle rigidity which permits no further enrichment and growth' (Loewald, 1962, p. 266). In such a situation, we may use others to support our weak unhelpful superego or confine ourselves within narrow limits.

Britton (2003), following Bion, takes up a further important aspect: the ego destructive superego. He stresses the importance of fighting off the autocratic tyranny of a malignant superego, and the need to seek the 'emancipation of the ego'. The concreteness of *judgement* which can be seen in certain patients creates an obsession with right and wrong, prohibitions and laws, which perversely destroys symbolic functioning. Following these authors, Chapter 11 by Sharon Numa explores the effects on a patient's identity development of a restrictive, rigid, imperious and omnipotent ego destructive superego made particularly dangerous and powerful by its association with the murderous Nazis of the holocaust. The patient's identity development was paralysed through both guilt and shame (she believed herself to have a 'fatal flaw' and felt functionally inadequate). She was a melancholic patient identified with a mother in perpetual mourning, imprisoned with an internal object who could not allow her to 'live' and have an identity of her own.

One of Richard Wollheim's extensive contributions to psychoanalytic thinking has been his attempt to provide a framework for an account of 'personal identity', and what it means to be a person. In his book *The Thread of Life* (1984), he describes as fundamental the *process* of a person leading a life over time, characterised by interactions between the past, the present and the future. This resonated with our interest in time, continuity and memory as significant elements in the formation of a sense of self.

Wollheim differentiates between a person's current transient 'mental state' and his underlying persistent mental disposition (dispositions refer for example to beliefs, desires, emotions, memories and fantasies). He argues that when the influence of the past, stored in dispositions, is exerted over the person, it is exercised indirectly, through present mental states with their varying degrees of 'vivacity'. He links this to Freud's model of conscious, preconscious and unconscious activity – all located in space or place, that is, within a body. Wollheim argues that the ability to think of oneself in the past and to imagine oneself in the future gives the sense of something being the 'same' over time.

The first object also comes to exist in time in the coming and going of the breast and mother. There is loss and recovery and we know that where this experience cannot be held in mind, problems of various kinds may develop – this is vividly illustrated in the case described by Judith Jackson referred to earlier where the patient's experience of himself *in* time and *over* time, in space and in mind, is remarkably tenuous. Wollheim argues that time, continuity, memory, fantasy and unconscious phantasy all give meaning to the person's sense of themselves. (This can perhaps be linked to Winnicott's idea that a 'good enough' mother provides *continuity of being*.) Wollheim sees the most significant of these being 'iconic' states which depict certain central narratives in relation to objects. These iconic states both arise from mental dispositions and influence them. Dennis Flynn's account in Chapter 12 is informed by both Wollheim's ideas on personal identity and Bion's work on thinking. The author describes a male patient with repeated traumatic failures in object relating, who reached a turning point in his life some two years into his analysis. Despite being locked within his rigid character structure, he began to raise the question: *who am I?* Flynn connects his patient's profound identity problems with his inability to 'think' his life as a continuity of experience – his relation to the thread of life being disrupted by excessive projective and introjective processes. Progress in the analysis was painful as the patient began to make links of understanding, links with deep emotional experiences of isolation and anxiety. This led to a reduction in his excessive splitting and projective activity so that the question of 'who he was' could be thought about within the analytic experience.

Wollheim's is an account that aims to contextualise the experience of subjectivity, affirming the importance of continuity and discontinuity in time while emphasising the role of past and present unconscious phantasy in the development of the self. His focus on time and memory resonates with the work of the psychoanalyst Hans Loewald (1962) on the temporal aspects of ego and superego.

Loewald, like Wollheim, looks at psychic structures as existing in time and developing in time; not time as a linear continuum but in 'psychic time' where there is a dynamic relationship between the psychic past, which reappears in the present (for example, in the transference), while in actuality being in the past. The psychic present acts on the past and constantly re-presents it and reviews it.

'Memory...manifests psychic time as activity, it makes the past present. Anticipation makes the future present' (p. 264). One of the ego's functions, Loewald suggests, is the presentation and representation of presence — creating and recreating presence, as part of the temporal aspect of its organising function. The superego he argues, as the agency of inner standards, demands and hopes in regard to the ego, functions from a 'future' position: the part of the self that looks back from a potential future, judging, rewarding or punishing accordingly. This ego's 'futurity' as represented by the superego he believes can only be developed once the oedipal objects are relinquished, once the libidinal–aggressive relationship with the oedipal figures has been partially given up and become internalised.

In this shifting landscape of identity stability, change and development, there are degrees of rigidity versus flexibility, integration versus fragmentation and the entire process is coloured by the complex interweaving of phantasy and reality. In the development of personal identity, the inherent difficulties of establishing identifications, facing the challenges of dis-identification, the loss of and mourning for the symbiotic union with the object are all mitigated if the early internalisation of the 'good' object can be securely achieved.

I will conclude this chapter with the words of Melanie Klein in *Love, Guilt and Reparation* (1937), where she refers to 'our relationship to ourselves':

> I cannot conclude, however, without attempting to throw some light upon the most complicated relationship of all, and that is the one we have to ourselves. But what are our selves? Everything, good or bad, that we have gone through from our earliest days onwards; all that we have received from the external world and all that we have felt in our inner world, happy and unhappy experiences, relationships to people, activities, interests and thoughts of all kinds – that is to say, everything we have lived through – makes part of our selves and goes to build up our personalities.
>
> (p. 338)

Moreover, she adds, should we lose contact with these experiences and object relationships, we would be the poorer for it, impoverished and empty:

> How much love, trust, gratification, comfort and gratitude, which we experienced and returned, would be lost!

The sense of impoverishment is surely acute for those patients whose sense of identity has been weakened by the loss of contact with parts of themselves.

References

Bick, E. (1968) The Experience of the Skin in Early Object Relations. *Int. J. Psycho-Anal.*, 49: 484–486.

Bion, W.R. (1959) Attacks on Linking. *Int. J. Psycho-Anal.*, 40: 308–315.

Bion, W.R. (1962) *Learning from Experience*. London: Tavistock.

Britton, R.S. (1992) The Oedipus Situation and the Depressive Position. In R. Anderson (ed.) *Clinical Lectures on Klein and Bion* (vol. 14, pp. 34–45). London and New York: Routledge, New Library of Psychoanalysis.

Britton, R.S. (1998) *Belief and Imagination: Explorations in Psychoanalysis*. London and New York: Routledge, New Library of Psychoanalysis.

Britton, R.S. (2003) Emancipation from the Super-Ego. In *Sex, Death and the Super-Ego* (pp. 103–116). London: Karnac.

Deutsche, H. (1942) Some Forms of Emotional Disturbance and Their Relationship to Schizophrenia. *Psychoanalytic Quarterly*, 11: 301–321.

Ferenczi, S. (1926) The Problem of Acceptance of Unpleasant Ideas: Advances in Knowledge of the Sense of Reality. *Int. J. Psycho-Anal.* 7: 312–323.

Freud, S. (1910) Leonardo Da Vinci and a Memory of His Childhood. S.E., 11: 59–137.

Freud, S. (1917) Mourning and Melancholia. S.E., 14: 237–258.

Freud, S. (1918) The Wolf Man. S.E., 17 (1917–1919): 28–60.

Greenacre, P. (1958) Early Physical Determinants in the Development of the Sense of Identity. *J. Amer. Psychoanal. Assn.*, 6: 612–627.

Greenacre, P. (2011) The Impostor. *Psychoanal. Q.*, 80 (4): 1025–1046.

Kernberg, O.F. (1975) *Borderline Conditions and Pathological Narcissism*. New York: Jason Aronson.

Klein, M. (1935) A Contribution to the Psychogenesis of Manic-Depressive States. *Int. J. Psycho-Anal.*, 16: 145–174. Reprinted in *The Writings of Melanie Klein* (vol. 1, pp. 262–289). London: Hogarth Press, 1975.

Klein, M. (1937) *Love, Guilt and Reparation*. Reprinted in *Love, Guilt and Reparation and Other Works 1921–1945* (pp. 306–343). London: The Hogarth Press and the Institute of Psycho-Analysis, 1975.

Klein, M. (1946) Notes on Some Schizoid Mechanisms. *Int. J. Psycho-Anal.*, 27: 99–110. Reprinted in *The Writings of Melanie Klein* (vol. 3, pp. 1–24). London: Hogarth Press, 1975.

Loewald, H.W. (1962) The Superego and the Ego Ideal. *Int. J. Psycho-Anal.*, 43: 264–268.

Mahler, M.S. (1972) Rapprochement Subphase of the Separation-Individuation Process. *Psychoanalytic Quarterly*, 41: 487–506.

Money-Kyrle, R. (1968) Cognitive Development. *Int. J. Psycho-Anal.*, 49: 691–698. Reprinted in *The Collected Papers of Roger Money-Kyrle* (pp. 416–433). Perthshire: Clunie Press, 1978.

Rosenfeld, H. (1964) On the Psychopathology of Narcissism: A Clinical Approach. *Int. J. Psycho-Anal.*, 45: 332–337. Reprinted in *Psychotic States* (pp. 169–179). London: Hogarth Press, 1965.

Sodre, I. (2004). Who's Who? Notes on Pathological Identifications. In E. Hargreaves and A. Varchevker (eds.) *Pursuit of Psychic Change* (pp. 53–65). London: Routledge, New Library of Psychoanalysis.

Sodre, I. (2012) quoted in Steiner, J. The Use and Abuse of Omnipotence in the Journey of the Hero. *Psych. Quart.*, (2015) 84 (3): 695–717.

Steiner, J. (1989) The Aim of Psychoanalysis. *Psychoanal. Psychother.*, 4(2): 109–120.

Steiner, J. (1992) The Equilibrium between the Paranoid-Schizoid and the Depressive Positions. In R. Anderson (ed.) *Clinical Lectures on Klein and Bion* (pp. 46–58). London and New York: Routledge.

Steiner, J. (2011) *Seeing and Being Seen: Emerging from a Psychic Retreat*. London: Routledge.

Steiner, J. (2015) The Use and Abuse of Omnipotence in the Journey of the Hero. *Psychoanal. Q.*, 84(3): 695–717.

Tausk, V. (1919) On the Origin of the "Influencing Machine" in Schizophrenia. Internationale Zeitschrift fur Psychoanalyse. Translated by D. Feigenbaum into English (Psychoanalytic Quart. 1933).

Winnicott, D.W. (1953) Transitional Objects and Transitional Phenomena – A Study of the First Not-Me Possession. *Int. J. Psycho-Anal.*, 34: 89–97.

Winnicott, D.W. (1960) Ego Distortions in Terms of True and False Self. In John D. Sutherland (ed.) *Maturational Processes and the Facilitating Environment* (pp. 140–152). London: Hogarth Press, 1965.

Wollheim, R. (1984) *The Thread of Life*. Cambridge MA: Harvard University Press.

2
IDENTIFICATION AND PATHOLOGICAL IDENTIFICATION
Implications for identity

Anne Amos

In *The Language of Psychoanalysis*, Jean Laplanche and Jean-Bertrand Pontalis (1973) wrote that in 'Freud's work the concept of identification comes little by little to have the central importance which makes it, not simply one psychical mechanism among others, but the operation itself whereby the human subject is constituted'.

It is indeed rare to find a psychoanalytic paper that does not refer to the concept of 'identification'. And, in the day-to-day work of analysis, the psychoanalytic endeavour is, in part, a sorting out of 'who's who'. We often ask ourselves 'in the transference, who do I represent for the patient?' We understand that the analyst is identified by the patient as a figure in his inner world and the patient reacts to the analyst as if she is that figure. Equally we might ask ourselves who is the patient identified with when he recounts something to us. Understanding identifications is the everyday subject of psychoanalytic enquiry.

In contrast identity, which tends not to be thought of as a psychoanalytic topic, is more often thought of as something that is social or on the surface, what other people see or what we consciously claim about ourselves. As psychoanalysts, we would, I think, see identity as something much more closely aligned to 'Ego' which has both conscious and, importantly, unconscious aspects; it is a sense of self, and a sense of oneself in relation to others; a relationship within ourselves and in relation to the external world. Any one individual's identity could therefore be thought about as being formed from the highly complex and complicated myriad of identifications which have been built up from birth. Sometimes these identifications or some aspects of these myriad of identifications become rigid and restrictive and our personality and development is compromised, which can be thought of as pathological identification, leading to a restricted and/or skewed identity.

Identification – a brief summary

Theoretically, Sigmund Freud first described the Oedipus complex and its resolution as the little boy's identification with his father and the girl's with her mother. Perhaps though, it was in 1910 in his study of Leonardo da Vinci that Freud described identification as a deeply unconscious event when Leonardo surrounded himself with his young apprentices and looked after them as much as he would have liked his mother to look after him. By spelling out Leonardo's unconscious identification with his mother, Freud showed how he became the object of his own desires. Leonardo was also, simultaneously loving himself, as he saw himself in his own apprentices, they were, in his unconscious mind, an aspect of himself. It was in this paper that Freud also introduced the concept of narcissism, which, put simply, is a loving of oneself.

It was, though, in 1917, in 'Mourning and Melancholia' that Freud made the brilliant and ground-breaking observation that we become the person who has left us as a way of denying that loss; we unconsciously identify with them. Identification can therefore be a way of not separating as with Leonardo and his 'loving' mother; he rather became her, or an aspect of her. But moreover, instead of feeling aggrieved and reproachful to someone whom we love for letting us down by leaving us we, ourselves, unconsciously take on the identity of that figure who has failed to love us sufficiently and attack ourselves as a means of attacking that figure. In melancholia or depression, there is no taking on the work of mourning – grieving for the person who has left us or the experience that cannot be ours – instead, the conscious feeling is of grievance and lack of self-worth. This clearly has implications for our own identity, in terms of our sense of self and how others see us. Someone whose depression is to the fore is often one track minded, keeps returning to points of grievance, seems unaware of any anger but annoys people around them and yet takes all responsibility for all that goes wrong onto themselves. We might say their personality is thin, but their view of the world holds a powerful grip on them, they seem restricted by the burden they carry, dominated as they are by unconscious identifications, rather different to the ones seen on the surface.

Anna Freud (1936), following her father, described the defence mechanism of 'identification with the aggressor', where rather than feel small and vulnerable and subject to an external threat, usually from an authority figure, we take on the characteristics of that aggressor. She connects this with the early stages of superego development when the child is developing a moral authority, a sense of what one 'ought to do'. More recently, a similar defensive, even life-saving, process is described as Stockholm syndrome where prisoners become loyal to their captors. Even, once released, the captives remain loyal to the beliefs and sentiments of their captors and will not betray them. This is also seen in survivors of torture, sexual abuse, human trafficking and other cruelties.

Forming identifications by introjection and projection

Returning to Freud himself, he describes this identification with the abandoning object happening in two ways. First, in a passive way, 'the shadow of the object falls upon the ego', and second in a more active way, 'the ego wants to incorporate the object into itself, and in accordance with the oral or cannibalistic phase of libidinal development in which it is, it wants to do so by devouring it' (1917, pp. 249). It is the latter that Melanie Klein was to take up in her theory of human development.

IMPLICATIONS FOR IDENTITY

For Klein, it is through the process of incorporation or introjection that we take into ourselves our experience of figures from the external world that form the internal objects that build our inner world and is the basis of personality. Internal objects are formed by the unconscious mechanisms of projection and introjection and these capacities are integral from birth, we are 'hard wired' to introject and project. These processes of projection and introjection are essential to emotional life, operating rather like breathing or eating and excreting in physical life. This assumes, by logical deduction, a primitive ego and constant mental activity, which in Kleinian terms is unconscious phantasy, running from birth, coterminous with physical development. While this view of a rudimentary ego existing from birth remains one of the controversies surrounding Klein's work, it roots the processes of identification and identity development at the deepest layers of the mind.

From birth onwards, the ego develops and strengthens by introjecting or incorporating good experiences – a good breast – the prototype of all experiences of love and care. The undeveloped ego, unable to cope with anxiety, gets rid of or projects bad or threatening experiences, even though they don't entirely go away and continue to threaten. The delicate, early ego protects itself by splitting off the bad and persecuting experiences from the good and sustaining internal objects. This is the normal paranoid schizoid position as described by Klein. During normal development, in reasonably good circumstances, the infant's hating and aggressive feelings are contained by an understanding and responsive parent that enables these feelings to be detoxified. For Klein, the ego develops around this good object, and the identifications with the good aspects of the mother become the basis for future helpful identifications.

Identification with a good object and experiences, around which the self-forms, takes place by the process of introjection, sometimes called incorporation or internalisation but also by projection of the bad object and experiences. This latter process is often called projective identification which is confusing as projection is an attempt to dis-identify with what we project. These different terms have added to the difficulty in understanding the complexity of the process. I think by adding the word 'identification' to the word 'projection', Klein is underscoring that the processes of projection are as important in building up who we are as introjection is and that this happens from birth and is not a superficial, semi-conscious or social process.

Klein writes vividly:

> Together with these harmful excrements, expelled in hatred, split-off parts of the ego are also projected on to the mother or, as I would rather call it, into the mother. These excrements and bad parts of the self are meant not only to injure but also to control and to take possession of the object. In so far as the mother comes to contain the bad parts of the self, she is not felt to be a separate individual but is felt to be the bad self. (*Hence, the use of the term 'identification' in 'projective identification' – my italics*). Much of the hatred against parts of the self is now directed towards the mother.
> (1946, p. 102)

And, describing the same process of projection in less primitive terms:

> Projection has many repercussions. We are inclined to attribute to other people – in a sense, to put into them – some of our own emotions and thoughts; and it is obvious that it will depend on how balanced or persecuted we are whether this projection is of a friendly or hostile nature. By attributing part of our feelings to the other person, we understand their feelings, needs and satisfactions; in other words, we are putting ourselves into the other person's shoes. There are people who go so far in this direction that they lose themselves entirely in others…..At the same time excessive introjection endangers the strength of the ego because it becomes entirely dominated by the introjected object.
> (1959, pp. 252–253)

IMPLICATIONS FOR IDENTITY

As Klein has described, projection is a means of getting rid of unwanted, painful feelings or terrifying feelings of anxiety that threaten the early self but equally she says we can project good feelings (for a full discussion of this, see Chapter 11). But it was Bion (1962) who understood projection as operating in two ways both as a means of ridding the self of unwanted feelings but also, vitally, it is a means of communication, from one person to another. This is a crucially important observation as it opens up and makes sense of human interactions. It is a theoretical model which gives analysts the means to study, in the consulting room, the unconscious identifications of their patient and how these play out in his mind and in his life. Of course, it is only a means of communication if there is a figure able to receive, process and detoxify these feelings by understanding, which we call 'containing'. Likierman (2001) writes that 'the most intense and disturbing parts of the self are only accommodated after they have journeyed through the minds of others, and after the infant has thus externalised his ego's relationship with its most disturbing aspects'. By journeying through the mind of another the infant, or the patient in analysis, then has the possibility of introjecting and identifying with a figure who can contain and tolerate his most disturbing aspects.

There are further important developmental aspects to this, which are dependent on the state of mind of the recipient of the infant's projections. While in normal or good circumstances, the mother picks up on her baby's distress and can understand and respond appropriately, this is not always the case. Some mothers are not able to take in their infant's experience – Bion thought this drives the infant to project with ever greater force, which he called 'evacuative projective identification' and thought this led the infant to then introject and identify with a 'projection-rejecting object', which destroys any capacity to make meaning of experience. Another experience for the infant is not just an uncontaining mother, but a mother who projects and perhaps swamps the infant with their fears and anxieties or who are actively invasive and abusive.

Gianna Williams (1997) has shown how in this situation 'no entry' defences are used by the infant and may be significant in anorexia, for example (for a full discussion of this, see Chapter 7).

Pathological identification

While in normal development, the processes of projection and introjection enable a complex myriad of identifications to build in the personality in analytic treatment we observe and experience when these processes have become fraught and entrenched. Sometimes, identifications in the mind are fixed and concrete in nature, absolute and unyielding, and other people or aspects of the human experience can then be totally rejected. People like this are rigid, highly defended, maintaining a position with certainty and conviction.

Racism is just one example of this. In a detailed study of 'Internal Racism', Fakhry Davids (2011) writes of the ubiquitous, unconscious nature of the us-them split, often along easy to recognise social/biological lines. The internal fuel that maintains this consensus and conviction, in any one social milieu, is the unwanted mental content that is projected and thus keeps the 'other' other. He makes a further important point that because the external environment and its institutions support this them-us split, the individual can then evade guilt and responsibility at an individual level. In other words, there is no need to introject and own that which one has projected and rejected. This capacity to identify with some aspects and dis-identify with others, as in the example of racism, hardens and limits the personality. This leaves the ego, or self, weakened and the personality restricted and threatened.

In analysis, we have an opportunity to engage with patients whose identifications and dis-identifications seem fixed and rigid, often being convinced of their own self sufficiency and denying of their dependency and vulnerability; blaming others, convinced of their own view of the world leading to a restricted and depleted emotional life. We might consider that their identifications are caught in the paranoid-schizoid position of emotional development, caught as they are in a psychic retreat (Steiner, 1993), unable to develop and expand their capacity for identification. This can be and is looked at in different ways. We can study the way in which the self and object relate to one another, looking at how the processes of projective and introjective identification (or projection and introjection) operate, but we can look at a more static picture and see how the ego or self is left, often impoverished and depleted, while simultaneously the unwanted aspects of the self are projected to be disowned.

Merged states

When the self and the other are merged, one has totally incorporated the other, so there is no boundary or separation between self and other, 'you are me' or equally, 'I am you'. This is where there has been either total projective identification and/or introjective identification. These terms are confusing partly as the end result clinically can be the same for both. Ultimately, it is a merged state that we are talking about. Theoretically and clinically, it can be difficult to work out which is which, or which way round, as both processes can occur simultaneously. Different analysts have used different terms to try and unpack the confusion: Ron Britton (1998) uses the terms acquisitive projective identification (I am you) in that we claim other people's characteristics for ourselves. For example, according to Freud, Leonardo da Vinci claimed his mother's mothering. In attributive projective identification, however (you are me), we attribute an aspect of ourselves to another, for example, Leonardo looked after his young apprentices as if they were his young self. The latter may or may not evoke a response in the other.

Ignes Sodre (2004) in 'Who's who? Notes on pathological identification' describes the complexity of projective and introjective processes and their implications for the identifications of the patient. She describes a case of Herbert Rosenfeld's where his analysand has a dream of watching and admiring a famous surgeon operating on a patient. The surgeon was concentrating so much that he lost his balance and fell into his patient. He could only revive himself by administering an oxygen apparatus that was nearby. Sodre links this to a saying in Portuguese to describe someone who thinks they are superior – 'He thinks he's got the King in his belly', where the King/surgeon have literally been swallowed whole. The subject has become the object and even superior to the original one, by swallowing it whole. The self has become so much bigger than the object by this taking over the functions, power and strength of the object.

Sodre's second case is of a patient who becomes the idealised bad object. She shows how she realised that the patient became a distorted version of his analyst; he introjected his analyst's capacity to see him and distorts this in his mind, doing this Sodre suggests, with hostility or maybe jealousy or envy. He then relates to his analyst from a very superior and powerful position, as if he is her, treating her with the cruelty and disdain he feels towards her or imagines she feels towards him. These are early, unconscious identifications in the patient that are enacted in his analysis and are technically very challenging, such is their absolute nature. The analyst is inevitably caught up and as Sodre notices, it is so easy to find oneself in the position of trying to give back to the patient these horrible projections – 'it's you who are doing this to me', which are inevitably rejected by the patient as his experience is it is his analyst who is doing it to him. Getting out of these sorts of impasses in analysis is extremely challenging and I will return to this later when describing the first of my clinical examples.

Impoverishment of the ego

Leslie Sohn (1985) takes Klein's ideas of identification and describes an extreme situation where the *identificate* is formed, which I understand to be as opposed to a true internal object. This means there is no good or true internal object to help the patient organise his mind enabling him to take in more but, instead, the patient does not seem able to introject and comes to believe he has become the desirable one. It has an excited, manic, omnipotent quality and enables the patient to get rid of feelings of need for a containing, good object to help with feelings like dependency, desire, jealousy and envy, with which his weakened ego cannot cope. Sohn describes this vividly in psychotic patients who have been 'good children', but as they grow and are increasingly faced with the need to take in in order to manage in the world, for example as students and learners, they increasingly fail to do this until they can no longer manage and anxiety swamps them and their ego fragments into psychosis. A young university student I assessed for psychoanalytic help, following a psychotic breadown, related to me as if we were two reasonable and logical human beings but his charm and intelligence were paper thin and he was quite unable to cope with relating to anything that would threaten this such as seminars at his university, gatherings with his peers and certainly essay deadlines and exams. His identity was not based on complex identifications with internal objects, which carried depth and a certain robustness, but instead on a charming and reasonable identificate. This seemed to me to be like a remnant of his pre-psychotic mental state to which he was desperately clinging.

Two contrasting clinical illustrations follow showing how aspects of identification are played out in psychoanalytic treatment and the implications of this for the patient's own identity.

Clinical example – patient A

In his analysis, A struggled with integrating deep aspects of himself, his primary identification, thus leaving his identity restricted.

A professionally successful person, A, had been recently appointed to run his own scientific laboratory. He had been in five times a week analysis with me for some years but struggled to maintain close relationships and had broken off contact with his actual parents many years earlier as they had been cruel, neglectful and abusive. As a young teenager, A had made a suicide attempt but after that set his mind on working hard and escaping from his family. He was focussed and successful. In the analysis, A thought I was a warm person but that being an analyst made me cold and rigid which he hated. He was always anxious that I didn't believe him when he described his parents' cruelty and would somehow blame him for it. In fact, a powerful cruelty would break out in A's analysis from time to time and I felt I knew something of how horrendous it was for him when he was at the mercy of an unreasonable, erratic, mad mother or a harsh, cold, all knowing father who together formed a cruel couple where any understanding and love was utterly unavailable.

In these outbreaks, A would treat me just as he described being treated by his mother. With great distress, A would tell me how upset he was that I was such a very disappointing analyst who just didn't understand. A insisted that he so much wanted to appreciate me, but I just let him down by not being kind, not understanding that what he really needed was love. I knew exactly how it felt to be the child whose mother was full of angry reproaches, how it was to feel you could never please your mother and that she was furious with you in an erratic and frightening way. I could also be the victim of A's father too when A would be to give me long, reasoned, logical discourses on how I ought to behave as an analyst, what precisely I had done wrong and how I ought to improve myself. Certainly, this figure had no idea how to listen, definitely knew best and his law was absolutely cold and cruel. What made it worse was sometimes it was 'mother' who was speaking to me then all of a sudden it was 'father', making a confusing and very lonely experience; a pale reflection, I suspect, of A's childhood experience.

A tried to solve this situation by having no contact with his actual external parents, but in the outside world, he would still meet people who he experienced like them: in his work place, in relationships and, of course, as I have described, in his analysis. This would provoke and frighten him. He also needed his analysis to help with what, by now, had also become an internal situation.

At his workplace, A had for some months found a senior colleague helpful and supportive in achieving important changes but this, in ways that are too detailed to explain here, changed so that A ended up being instrumental in having this colleague sacked.

A felt this colleague was a bully which A had not previously fully appreciated, and similarly, A had been accused of being tyrannical in achieving this sacking, an accusation that he felt was unfair. A rather similar situation had also occurred with some new friends who had invited A on holiday with them; all had gone well and enjoyably on this holiday until A experienced one of the friends as forcing him to eat food which he did not want, making A feel indignant and angry. At about this time A had a dream where his actual father appeared

> A was going to view a shop that was for sale, opposite A's place of work with his father, in anticipation that he, A, might buy it. His father had direct access to the building via a scanner, like the ones used at airports and prisons. When it came to A's turn to go through the scanner his father stuck his dirty finger nails into A's eyes. He was aggressive and A also felt very frightened of an infection.

I think the dream captures, like the two recent events, a sense of hope and human contact – A felt he could have a supportive colleague, friends to go on holiday with and even a shop to buy, representing his increased capacities. But each time this goes wrong, a bully emerges to spoil the opportunities in the form of a cruel aggressive father, blinding A and causing infection, intruding right into A's eyes. The dream and these events all capture something coming back at A, a terrifying projection returning which destroys A's capacities to see and appreciate those around him, including his analyst.

A second dream followed a short while later:

> A and A's younger sibling were at their parent's house. They were children and a tyrannosaurus rex was asleep there so they had to creep around so as not to wake the dinosaur. They hid in the attic cupboard in the wall in their parent's room and were absolutely terrified, unable to move for fear of disturbing tyrannosaurus rex.

A's association was to being accused of being a tyrant at work. A did insist, though, that it was the formerly supportive colleague who was the actual tyrant. I was, in a way that was very familiar to me, under considerable pressure to agree with A's version of who was the tyrant. It certainly could not be A and if A felt I thought this was the case, I was not understanding his point of view. In a familiar way, we were back in a monstrously cruel world with A and his analyst both terrified of awakening this monster, a persecuting tyrant that spoiled all good contact, was impossible to accommodate and had to be expelled.

Another dream:

> There were lots of ill people in beds, like an old-fashioned hospital ward, and they knew they were in danger from a red reptile but they kept quiet about this. They spoke with the woman in charge of the ward but she turned into a lizard at night.

A connected this with recently reading about the primitive brain but also said that monsters appear in the darkness. I thought A was increasingly feeling that these monsters were actually inside him and was more in touch and desperate about the way he saw himself treating people who gave to him, including his analyst. The ill people in bed represented A's vulnerability and need for analytic treatment to cope with the monsters inside him – primitive identifications with cruel figures – but the analyst too becomes a frightening reptile at night. This conflict was unbearably difficult for A. The pain of feeling a more human, imperfect contact with the inevitable feelings of doubt, responsibility and guilt was too much to bear and then it is easier to retreat into a more familiar and restricted world of cold, archaic figures. Much as with the colleague, the dismissal had to be justified by the other's behaviour; they deserved what they got, reminiscent of Sodre's description of the impossibility of trying to reverse the projection was clear. At these times, A was so merged with me as the bad persecuting figure that no separation seemed possible or any element of triangularity that would allow another view. Mostly, the tyrant that would break out, A experienced as me (and sometimes despite my best intentions I did inevitably enact this figure) which I think was upsetting for A as he found himself caught in the repetition of his early experiences. At this time in his analysis, however, I think it began to feel to A that the tyrant might be inside him and that was a truly terrifying proposition.

For A, his identifications are fixed and concrete, linked to the earliest experiences with hated cruel primary figures. These primary figures in the mind are of course some sort of combination of A's actual external objects, his parents as he perceived and experienced them, and the place they have come to occupy in his internal world. A's identity has not been formed on the experience of introjecting and identifying with good internal objects that have loving and containing capacities, but more on projecting bad experiences that felt very concrete and now have to be got rid of. My capacity to detoxify these particular experiences was limited when I too became and was experienced by A, as cruel and rejecting, especially when I didn't fit in with a particular view of the world that A, at those times, demanded. This leaves A with a concrete, brittle and precarious identity, unable to introject and identify with true or good enough internal objects, dependent on an identificate to process life's difficulties.

Fluid identifications – patient B

In contrast with A, B's identifications did not consume him in a rigid way him but were more fluid. He was able to identify and dis-identify with the figures around him.

B was a melancholic who was referred because of attacks on himself. He had an urge to chop off his fingers and pull the skin off his face. He had been anxious and depressed for many years. As a younger man, he had taken himself to a bridge with a shotgun with the full intention of killing himself but heard a distant voice calling his name. He realised the voice was his own, but for a long time, he had been in the full grip of a cruel and destructive figure who hated him and his failures, linked in particular to his failure with the family business that he had inherited. I understood B's parents to have been remote and neglectful figures with his mother being particularly cruel at times and his father stern and punishing. B had been sent to boarding school aged 8 and from his teens had very little contact with his parents – preferring to be anywhere other than at home with them. As a child, he was always in trouble with his parents and his teachers and constantly failed to achieve in any area of his life. B came for three sessions a week.

In the first session after his second, long summer break, he talked at some length about his wife's frustrations with their two small children. He was clearly trying to control his criticism of her impatience with them. In particular, he was annoyed when she went outside to smoke, her need to smoke took priority and she would just walk out and leave the children to him. He continued describing his understanding of smoking as he used to smoke a lot and he knew small children can be very annoying and irritating. He, himself, insisted that he was very relieved at a recent family event to be able to leave and be by himself away from the noise and turmoil. From his history, I knew B's own mother was an alcoholic, a fact which was in the main denied by the family.

It was not too difficult to see that B was trying to be sympathetic and putting himself in the position of the mother, in other words to identify with the mother (and analyst) who finds her children too much and much prefers alcohol/smoking or summer holidays. I could interpret to my patient his wish to protect me from his annoyance about leaving him over the summer and his wife preferring smoking to being with the children, just like his own mother. He laughed but with a sense of recognition and relief as he said, 'Thought you might say something like that'. I think he was relieved to have his familiar analyst back after the summer, but I was also simultaneously being slightly dismissed.

However, on returning to his next day's session, he described what had happened when he arrived home after the previous day's session. It was the children's bedtime and his wife was furious and told him what had happened – she had told the children it was time for bed, the younger daughter had absolutely refused to go upstairs and she, his wife, had just gone on up with their elder child, promising to read her a story. The younger child didn't appear and his wife went back downstairs, calling her but couldn't find her, finding herself cross but increasingly worried. She eventually discovered the downstairs cloakroom locked, but her daughter did not respond to being called and spoken to. She ended up getting a ladder up to the window from the garden to look through the window and she could see her daughter was in there, hiding. My patient told me all this with some exasperation but mainly with pride at his daughter's determination. My patient's identification with his daughter was now plain for me to see. Like his daughter he hides away, becomes self-sufficient when he feels really angry with the adults in his world and is punishing them for their neglect of him as well as enjoying a degree of triumph.

This short example captures the fluidity of B's identifications as they shift between the neglectful mother and with the child who is going to inflict punishment on that mother. He identifies both with the abandoning mother, but does not become her. When I notice this defensive identification, he seems relieved as he does not need to become her but can let himself feel more in touch with how much he wants to punish her. For B, at this particular point in his treatment, his identifications are fluid. They are identifications with capacities and feelings, not identifications that are concrete and absolute with cruel, primary figures. B can feel like an angry little girl or a mother who is fed up mothering. He has not become the actual cruel, erratic, neglectful mother, nor is he consumed with the wish of the angry, jealous little girl to actually lock himself away but comes eagerly to his analysis to talk about it.

B identifies with his analyst who is interested in the children and their feelings and his analysis can become a good object around which his identifications can grow. While B may be projecting into his little girl he could also take this back and think about his own experience, he could allow his analyst to see that she was negligent for leaving him and that he was jealous of his sibling who went with mother. Most importantly, he let me see his wish to punish me and to go off by himself. There is a clear connection with his past difficulties and a chance to work through these in his analysis rather than become stuck in withdrawn depression and self-destructive violence, identified with the reproachful internal figures that thought he should end his life and that had made him so ill.

Conclusion

While A and B were not at the same stage in their treatments, from these small clinical vignettes, I have tried to show how A's identity was restricted as his unconscious identifications with bad figures threatened him and his good objects did not feel strong enough while B, from a restricted and melancholic mental state, began to be in touch with aspects of himself that expanded his identity and did not threaten or persecute him to such an overwhelming degree. Strikingly, both A and B had erratic, cruel and remote parents but had dealt with this very differently. In his life, A had defended himself mainly using projection, ever fearful of being accused of bad things like being cruel, angry, lying and so forth. B had introjected and unconsciously identified with the cruel figures who he experienced inside himself and constantly berating him. Both of these are defensive solutions or pathological identifications with bad internal objects. The question to how much this relates to the actual parents remains inevitably open, but I suspect that in particular A's experiences of cruelty began very early in his life.

Neither A nor B were able to separate themselves from their primary identifications with bad objects that persecuted them, and this was fundamentally what brought them to analytic treatment. To preserve his own sense of himself, A projected his bad objects, but in his analysis, he felt threateningly merged with them and, as in his dream, was blinded by them, hence the use of the term 'projective identification'. Unlike A, B felt himself to be his bad objects and used his treatment at this point at least, to identify with his analyst who seemed to have understood and given room to his 'badness'.

In analysis, as in life, the patient needs, as Klein first said, a good internal object around which the self can develop. If the analyst can contain and detoxify the bad projections, the analysis can become the good experience which the patient can introject and around which the patient can then develop. The patient is then strengthened to take back the projections, to separate and face the pain of mourning. It is an internal good object, that is sufficiently robust, as opposed to an identificate, that enables the patient to take back some of what has been projected, usually with hate and anger. The question always remains as to whether the internalised analytic function is sufficiently integrated to enable the patient to separate and mourn, including of the analysis itself. Ultimately, it is the strength of his internal good objects that enables healthy movement in the processes of introjection and projection.

Trying to understand unconscious identifications are the 'bread and butter' of psychoanalysis. Inevitably, as analysts we become part of our patients' inner worlds and experience what is unbearable, too frightening or too persecuting for them, we play our part in these identifications. At the most extreme end, when identifications are pathological, processes of projection and introjection become extreme, thereby limiting and restricting the personality and sense of self.

Bibliography

Bion, W. (1962) 'A theory of thinking'. *The International Journal of Psychoanalysis*, 33: 306–310.

Britton, R. (1998) *Belief and Imagination: Explorations in Psychoanalysis*. London: Routledge.

Davids, M. F. (2011) *Internal Racism: A Psychoanalytic Approach to Race and Difference*. London: Palgrave MacMillan.

Freud, S. (1910) 'Leonardo da Vinci and a memory of childhood'. In *The Standard Edition of the Complete Psychological Works of Sigmund Freud*. Ed. J. Strachey *(SE)* (vol. 11, pp. 63–197). London: Hogarth Press.

Freud, S. (1917) 'Mourning and melancholia'. *S.E.* 14: 73–102.

Freud, A. (1936) *The Ego and the Mechanisms of Defence*. London: Hogarth Press.

Klein, M. (1946) 'Notes on some Schizoid mechanisms'. In *The Writings of Melanie Klein* Ed. Roger Money Kyrle (vol. 3, pp. 61–93). London: Hogarth Press.

Klein, M. (1959) 'Our adult world and its roots in infancy'. In *The Writings of Melanie Klein* (vol. 3, pp. 247–263). London: Hogarth Press.

Laplanche, J. and Pontalis, J. B. (1973) *The Language of Psychoanalysis*. London: Hogarth Press.

Likierman, M. (2001) *Melanie Klein: Her Work in Context*. London: Continuum.

Sodre, I. (2004) 'Who's who? Notes on pathological identification'. In *In Pursuit of Psychic Change: The Betty Joseph Workshop*. Eds. E. Hargreaves and A. Varchevker (pp. 53–65). London: Brunner-Routledge.

Sohn, L. (1985) 'Narcissistic organization, projective identification and the formation of the identificate'. *The International Journal of Psychoanalysis*, 63: 201–213.

Steiner, J. (1993) *Psychic Retreats: Pathological Organisations in Psychotic, Neurotic and Borderline Patients*. London: Routledge.

Williams, G. (1997) 'Some reflections on some dynamics of eating disorder: "no entry" defences and foreign bodies'. *The International Journal of Psychoanalysis*, 78: 927–941.

3

THE CEREBRAL MIND VERSUS THE BODY MIND

Containing and recovering unknown parts of the self

Susan Lawrence

He is always thinking, thinking, Where? In his head? Or in his stomach?

(Bion 1987,p163)[1]

When I was writing this chapter, I wondered what it might mean psychically to have a complete sense of self, to be centred in all of oneself. I think often patients come to analysis because they cannot develop a full or undivided sense of self, and they are aware that this is causing them to suffer. In this chapter, I will examine how a cerebral enclave can act as a defence to such suffering as a result of severe splitting in infancy.

The unconscious rejection of knowing either our internal states or our experiences of the environment prevents us from being fully grounded in our full psychic reality. It can prevent us from having a three-dimensional sense of ourselves. Awareness is perhaps experienced as too painful or unacceptable. So either through choice or necessity, a part of the self is not taken in or recognised; it may even be attacked. In addition, there can be feelings or experiences which remain unprocessed in a raw state which we can only express through symptoms or actions, rather than thoughts. Much of this rejection or denial of parts of the self is accomplished through splitting. Melanie Klein, in her 1946 paper *Notes on Some Schizoid Mechanisms*, first understood how vital the process of splitting good from bad and hate from love is to a baby's psychic development and how the infant uses splitting to defend the good from the bad. She wrote:

> In early infancy, anxieties characteristic of psychosis arise which drive the ego to develop specific defence mechanisms. In this period the fixation points for all psychotic disorders are to be found.... I enumerated various typical defences of the early ego, primarily the mechanisms of splitting the object and the impulses, idealisation, denial of inner and outer reality and stifling of emotions....

For the infant without a good enough maternal environment, idealisation in phantasy is a way to hold on to a sense of goodness when the frustrations, pain and anger of reality cannot be borne. Klein makes clear that this denial of reality occurs through psychic omnipotence. It is a central belief of Kleinian analysts, including the authors of this book that 'the internalisation of a good object is crucial to a relatively stable sense of identity. This is facilitated by an experience of continuity of good experience, as well as by the infant's innate resilience' (See Introduction). Excessive splitting thus hinders the formation of a solid identity.

Bion In A Theory of Thinking in 1962 linked the propensity for psychic splitting in infancy to the infant's own innate capacity to bear the frustration presented by reality, i.e. lack of resilience. He writes:

> Suppose the child to be extremely intolerant of frustration: the danger is that it will strive to deny frustration and to continue to deny it until its appreciation of the world of reality is itself impaired.

The denial of the self and of reality can include many aspects of psychic life and lived experience. It can include not only a banishing from awareness of unbearable feelings such as fury or pain but also an interruption of all sense of relationship or dependence on others. There can indeed often be a reversal of this in fantasy. It can also result in a blocking of the perception of many aspects of reality which are beyond bearing, e.g. the self's continuity through time, the existence of other people, the everyday frustrations of life in a human body and in an imperfect world.

The denial of these parts can leave a person with a characteristically thin sense of themselves and of their identity, as in the instance of the patient I will discuss here. To the extent that a psychic enclave is maintained with manic, omnipotent mechanisms, there may be an illusion of immense power, of being everywhere, unlimited by the constraints of reality that bind others. However, to the extent that the perceptions of the organism, the feelings and the location in time are rejected, a person may be left feeling denuded of the ordinary emotional richness of the self, which can be experienced as a nothingness. The ordinary thoughts that give meaning to everyday experience do not come to mind. They are replaced with phantasies of omnipotence and omniscience.

In some patients, the body plays a central role in these profound splits. Body sensations have a special role in creating the experience of solidity because, if these are acceptable, a feeling of having a body with an inside provides an internal space in which the phantasy of internal objects can exist. All this contributes to the stability required to establish a sense of identity. Emotions are commonly experienced as bodily functions for example, through physical tension, the meaning of which may be unrecognised by the patient. Integration of identity also includes finding meaning in the bodily symptoms that arise. In addition, the body may hold and express what has not been brought into thought. Bion highlighted the situation of the infant whose feelings and projections cannot be contained by the mother and whose unprocessed bodily and psychic impulses, beta elements and the precursors of thought are not transformed by the alpha function of the infant's mother. These infantile fragments therefore never come into mind but express themselves as psychosomatic symptoms. Subsequently, Ron Britton added two other ways in which b-elements might be evacuated: '…firstly into psychosomatic or hypochondriacal symptoms; secondly into perceptual hallucinations; or thirdly into action' (Britton1998)

All three of these were manifest in the analysis of the patient who I am going to discuss, and all three created for him a frustrating and bewildering sense of a fragmented self, with bodily phenomena that had no thought or meaning attached.

I am not just discussing here the projections by the infant into the mother. There is a constant interplay, a field, of projection and introjection between the baby and mother. It is therefore also important to consider projections from the mother, received by the infant, either directly or through acquisitive projective identification. A number of authors, including Britton (1992), have noted how mad, hostile or catastrophic maternal projections can create a feeling of dissonance in the infant so that there is a sense of an alien object that is 'not them' internally.

All of this raises questions as to the role of an analysis in enlarging the sense of self for such a patient and the function of the analyst. I have set out some initial thoughts about this here. The analyst's role in these instances may often be to raise awareness of the rejected parts for the patient and to help give them meaning. Given profound splits, strands of the countertransference can exist in parallel, and perhaps their temporary sojourn in the analyst's mind provides a starting point for bridging and integration. We might hypothesise that the analyst becomes the containing mother who might contain the split-off fragments and bring them into thought. The evacuated parts and elements can, at times, be felt by the analyst in the countertransference in unusual ways. Hartung and Steinbrecher (2018) suggested that the body serves as an intermediate store between the psyche and outer reality. They looked at the unconscious communicative process between the analyst and the analysand and, in particular, how psychosomatic symptoms can spread to the analyst's body.

The patient, who may be able to use and internalise the concrete presence and containing function of the analyst to lessen their anxiety, then faces the challenge of relinquishing this concrete object and transforming her into a more symbolic object internally and mourning the loss, in order to fully consolidate an independent psychic identity.

The patient that I present below, who I have called Paul, came to analysis feeling that his entire survival and sanity depended on denying a large part of himself. He had maintained a very narrow brittle base which was increasingly inadequate and fragile as he progressed through adult life stages. This involved identification with a highly idealised parental self and a cerebral mind kept well above all ordinary experience. His analysis, which was long and difficult, revealed the profound split of his body from his mind, amongst other splits, and I will discuss how the unprocessed elements left him with a highly fragmented sense of self and, at times, a conviction of being inhabited by alien objects. This was reflected in the quality of our sessions together, in which his states fluctuated markedly and where the intensity of unconscious disturbance created a profound sense of dislocation and discontinuity, which is perhaps reflected for the reader in the descriptions below. When the patient began to feel that he could rely on my capacity to contain his anxiety, the analysis allowed him very slowly to reclaim some split-off parts of himself from his body back into his mind and make some moves towards a greater sense of integration. This leads to an experience of a more continuous, fuller identity. Here, I consider the first three years of our work together below.

The patient's situation

Paul was an aeronautical engineer who came to analysis suffering from anxiety and panic attacks so intense that he could not sleep or live normally. He could not manage to be alone and was having unbearable suicidal thoughts: 'I wonder how people live with these feelings, I have a continuous feeling something is going to happen'. Catastrophe seemed close by and he had feelings of intense claustrophobia. At the consultation, I was struck by how this desperate situation was conveyed in a flat tone and almost as if it were funny. Having had no previous analytic treatment, the patient quickly built up to five times a week analysis.

Paul initially conveyed his mother to me as very anxious but 'loving unconditionally' and 'super protective', but it became clear to us both that his mother had always been rather ill and full of intense fears of disaster. He told me about a particular memory of his mother of a time when she did not want him to go on a school trip as she was convinced the plane would crash on the way, but he decided to go anyway. He had painful memories of her collapsed on the floor weeping during his childhood and described an urgent need to sustain his mother, in a childhood experienced as full of deprivation.

The patient was physically very ill as a child, suffering very badly from asthma and severe food and pollen allergies. He was hospitalised a number of times for poor breathing so that doctors insisted he stayed indoors, where he was constantly with his mother. In contrast, it felt to Paul like his father had little interest in his sickly son and seemed very absent, either physically when at work or mentally when there.

The analysis

The defence in the cerebral mind

It felt unbearable to Paul to be in his own mind in a normal sense, he felt he needed to maintain a position above it, where most ordinary thoughts and perceptions could be disowned and denied. His own feelings and spontaneous reactions to himself and others seemed intolerable. He described his distant cerebral state as being 'on his planet', which was a psychic enclave of hyper rationality, extreme vigilance and continuous thinking. He also wanted to perfect himself and drove himself to achieve this ideal state relentlessly: reading, working and interrogating his choices continuously. By this means, he felt he could keep the catastrophe of being overtaken by what he felt to be his bad side at bay. He only had some vague awareness of this other aspect of himself, but he described it as 'a monster'. His planet was intended to be a place of no desire or feeling and no relationships, a refuge.

In some parts of his life, he was and remained highly successful, well regarded by colleagues and employers. He provided generously for those around him, for his parents, his friends, for colleagues at work and, in the analysis, for me. Like an idealised mother, he could provide but was not provided for. This was a major element in his sense of self initially.

Paul believed that he would have to conduct his own analysis and was initially frustrated that I would not give him the theory for him to do this: 'I always want to fix things, get the theory and fix things'. The position of being a patient dependent on an analyst threatened his defensive structure profoundly. Understandably, he was worried about his planet, his protected place of retreat being taken from him and being left feeling powerless and unreal. He hoped initially that the analysis would reinforce his idealised cerebral structure, which he believed allowed him to function and which held out the promise of a different future.

He brought many dreams, which expressed vividly a phantasy of manic phallic dominance, with its fragility and ultimate emptiness. The dreams often had a hallucinatory quality which evoked the sense of the evacuation of unprocessed b-elements as described above with Bion and Britton. Much of his psychic life, including his dreams, was involved with fictional characters in video games, where he could project and identify more comfortably than with me. There was R, a hero survivor who had been mutilated, with one eye, who, nevertheless, was going to rescue the world. These states, where the game, waking consciousness and dreams all seemed to merge, expressed Paul's painful situation most poignantly – expressed his identification with a kind of schematic idealised masculine or paternal figure, a child's version of a super human oedipal partner for mother, which could not be sustained. The dream images conveyed graphically how Paul used his intellect to maintain a defensive split off area, which I have called a cerebral mind, where he could be like an ideal and idealised parent who could sustain everyone, and where he conquered all despite his handicaps. It seemed to be that he relied on this cerebral structure as a way of organising himself, as an attempt at self-containment, which avoided the anxieties of maternal containment. He was taking flight into an all-observing, ostensibly objective state as a refuge against the anxieties of subjectivity.

At the start of the analysis, I think his sense of self consisted almost entirely of this phallic cerebral part which provided for all.

The body mind

It was apparent that there were also important parts of my patient that could not find verbal expression. There was a remarkable split between Paul's cerebral mind and what I came to call his body mind, including his physicality, but also most of his ordinary thoughts and perceptions, including all needs and wants, etc. These were split off and fragmented.

His body expressed powerful feelings vividly in movement and symptoms. His feet moved continuously and he cracked the fingers on both hands making a sound like a gun shot. As sessions continued and his affects became less distant, he would talk to me of how he felt he was on his planet, while at the same time he would clearly be crying and his fingers would be cracking. His parallel sense of himself was very disturbing to him, and from quite early on he told me about this very succinctly: 'My body is quite detached from my mind. It feels like I have to look after it like everyone else. So my feelings are not in my mind'.

If I tried to explore these embodied feelings, my extremely intelligent patient had no thoughts. He could not elaborate on what was happening and they had no meaning for him. In Bion's terms, one could say that Paul had thoughts but could not think them. They were just a somatic representation. His body was crying if not screaming.

THE CEREBRAL MIND VERSUS THE BODY MIND

We began to realise that alongside the hyper rational adult, there was an internal baby that had never been able to express his feelings and was in pieces. These fragmented parts had never been contained by a maternal object. The baby existed in parallel to himself in Paul's mind, he often talked of this child in the third person and had dreams of putting babies aside in corners, while surrounded by zombies. The patient's inability to project and be contained had prevented him from forming an integrated, solid sense of himself, and he feared being plunged into chaos.

For the first two years, as he moved deeper into the analysis, he had a huge array of somatic symptoms. These included a large number of panic attacks that left him unable to breathe so that he feared he would die, a closing throat, pain in his shoulders or stomach or all over his body. He appeared to be allergic to many foods and at times to the air we were breathing. There was also considerable action outside our sessions. In the first two years of treatment, he would frequently phone me, usually suffering from a panic attack, telling me he could not breathe, that nothing seemed real, or that it felt as if a hand was at his throat strangling him. This felt to the patient like he was literally in pieces, and intensely claustrophobic, and he was very anxious that he would go mad or die. I was vividly reminded of his childhood asthma. I understood that Paul had not felt able to 'breathe out', to project normally into his mother, or express his enormous rage to her, as he could not to me and that these were b-elements being physically evacuated.

In a more ordinary way, his 'body mind' was also where his basic needs, e.g. for relationship, to be held and loved, were relegated and split off, together with his normal thoughts about everyday external life. Ordinary perceptions of reality, e.g. that I had builders in, that other patients existed, that it was freezing cold in the consulting room, were denied and unnoticed. His past and his present outside the consulting room seemed out of mind, with no links possible, while he took refuge in a cerebral state which promised to restore an ideal state in the future.

He found it hard to describe those around him and talked about people in groups or anonymously. This gave the sessions an insubstantial, rather philosophical quality, where both in the session and in my patient, ordinary links and thoughts were lacking, and he was left with little depth in his sense of self or his identity. A pathological organisation had been created which effected a profound split between the cerebral and the emotional in my patient, at the cost of him not feeling solid or whole. His experience was thin and the three-dimensional feeling of solidity that arises with the integration of body and mind was missing.

The split crudely represented male and female, his maternal and paternal identifications. His inability to resolve the oedipal situation meant the bringing together of the split was linked to a catastrophe he attached to the mother and father coming together as a parental couple. He could not master the oedipal anxieties and continued to relate to each parent with marked separation much of the time.

A clinical illustration

I am going to present below an extract from a number of sessions that occurred in a one-week period early on in the analysis and then discuss this in relation to the issues of identity facing this patient.

Friday

The patient arrives very anxious and angry, he says he feels very physical, his anger is in his body and he wants to express it. (I feel alarmed and I imagine violence.)

He goes on to tell me about his dreams, in the first he is advising the US president, going with him and a number of other people around the world, including the Middle East. In the second dream, he is racing around a mountain, like flying, on a motor cycle.

He links the middle east to violence and terrorism.

I describe his high manic state and say that he has taken off from his session before the weekend in order to protect himself from his

THE CEREBRAL MIND VERSUS THE BODY MIND

rage at being dropped by me for the next two days. He does not dare come down to earth, where he might face a war, like in the Middle East.

He tells me he can't bear ordinary life. (He feels very remote to me, and I feel quite useless to him.)

Monday

The patient is angry and withdrawn. Over the weekend, he tells me he had another panic attack in Sainsbury's supermarket, and I link this to his anxiety over the weekend and our separation.

Tuesday

His one evening session, P comes in looking quite disoriented and rigid.

He tells me he feels he is not there. He is in a bad state of mind, his body is all hurting, especially his right arm and shoulder. (I think perhaps he is wanting to punch or write.) Every time he panics, he feels he cannot breathe.

He tells me he has given up work for the week. He feels he is stealing his employer's money as he cannot work.

During the day, he had spent time playing games and reading, feeling there was something else he should attend to, in himself. He cries bitterly for much of the session and says he only feels safe to cry with me. He says it feels like a car hitting him, I talk about his feeling overcome by waves of anger and pain. (I feel concerned for him.)

He talks about feeling horrified by his state and says that he would like to disappear under the waves. Just before the end of the session, he tells me he thinks he is going to panic. He tries to leave but looks so anxious and stiff that I suggest to him to sit down and he sits on the floor. He is clearly desperate and says the floor is what he feels he deserves. (I am struck by how he is physically completely transformed…the session runs over for a few minutes. After a while he gets up and leaves. He thanks me for my time and I feel very moved.)

Wednesday

He tells me he might need a psychiatrist, and he is worried about going mad. I interpret that he feels he needs to bring a father figure in as he believes his mother analyst is unable to cope and will be overwhelmed by him. I link it to the phone call he took from the GP during his session the week before. I ask him if he feels he needs drugs, and it is clear it is the figure of the psychiatrist that he wants, not the drugs.

I tell him I don't think his state is getting worse, but that I think he is anxious that he will be completely taken over by his anxiety. (I don't feel consciously very worried, but I wonder whether I am defending against my own anxiety.)

Thursday

He seems more stable.

He tells me two dreams, starting by saying the second is not important.

In the first dream, he is in a tall thin building, maybe like a school, like Hogwarts. There are many people, friends or peers, there, and he is sleeping on the ground floor. A man arrives and goes to the roof, and the patient tells me he himself is now not in the dream. The man can control everybody's minds. The patient thinks this is important, perhaps because the man is a part of himself, his super mind. He doesn't think this is a good thing.

I say I agree perhaps he is the man who gets high up in the tall building when he hates being ordinary with his friends on the ground floor. Although he starts on the ground, this super part of him takes possession of a magical Hogwarts phallus which can control his mind and everyone else's. There is a long pause.

I say it is also like our session, where he takes control and decides the other dream is not important and discards it.

He tells me the second dream. He was in B, there are more beautiful places, but it can be fun to go there with friends, there are a series of lidos, they came to the last one, a private one, where once you were inside it was surprising, there was a theatre and everyone was very dressed up, and he felt like a child, he couldn't eat or drink in there, etc. He says he thinks it is some random thing.

I say I think it is like his analysis, a drama of his internal mind played out here in my consulting room, where he neither eats or drinks.

He tells me he went to a neuroscience conference, there was a talk about how you could see the effects of schizophrenic drugs on brain scans. The speaker said psychiatrists were a waste of time. He feels his job is a waste of time. He would like them to measure his brain having a panic attack.

I tell him that I think you believe you will feel better if you are observing a scientific investigation rather than being a person having a panic attack in your analysis. I add I think he feels he is getting too dependent on his analyst mother and expects to pull me into the drama, and then he feels we need a father, we need a psychiatrist or some scientific investigation.

He tells me the psychiatrist will give him drugs, he doesn't want that. But with friends, he has a difficulty; if he says he is not alright, they suggest he tries other things, he doesn't believe their opinions much. They don't understand anything about analysis.

I reply that I think it is easier to feel his friends have doubts rather than to tell me he does.

He says: No, he feels he is realising he is going to have to stay in his treatment for a while. But, he feels quite calm today. Where is his anger and sadness? It is like he has lost them although it is a relief.

I say it is Thursday, we are in middle of analytic week and he feels steadier. (I wondered about him being really calm and of being cut off.)

He replies: I need more Thursdays.

Friday

The patient seems quite steady and calm. (I feel relieved.) He talks about how he feels the controlling God/supermind in his dream is a flight from himself, how he likes to feel in control and is horrified at the other parts of himself. They are hard to think about.

Discussion of the material

I think this week of clinical material illustrates some of the processes in containing the patient. In the first Friday session Paul's dream of rushing around on high expresses his defence against his need of me before the weekend. In the dream, he felt he could become anything or anybody, an advisor to the US president, perhaps the US president himself, anywhere in the world. He feels his identity to be untethered and unlimited, with a defensive mania. In similar sessions, previously, he had talked of becoming a neuroscientist, perhaps as a similar but more high-powered and masculine counterpart to my flakier occupation as an analyst. I felt the dream showed how he needed to cling to his defence, the president or mountain, as a phallic cerebral identification, which was supposed to provide a sort of organising self-containment but failed to do so.

On Monday, he seemed to be in a state of high anxiety and anxious withdrawal, leading to a state almost of depersonalisation which made him panic. I think his anxiety about the containment not feeling sufficient was rising during these sessions, and he felt at his most fragmented responding by withdrawing from me and from his own feelings.

On Tuesday, his anxiety came to a head, and he could no longer split off the terrible grief and pain that was lodged in his body and longed for expression. His body brings him down to earth, literally to the floor. He has hardly any thoughts but feels he is literally imploding. He recognises he is stealing the employer's money, which I took to mean he understood he was not valuing me in the analysis and that he was much more in touch with his need for me. He seemed to feel safe with me and have some confidence.

I think this regressed collapsed state was associated with his mother, and in the analysis, it became a powerful way of forming a link with me. It seemed that the ill body he brought to me, where there was a risk of suffocation and death, was the main connection he could form with me. His ill body, his mother and me got absolutely merged together in the transference. He only needed his analyst mother when there was something terribly wrong with his body which he could not cope with. In the session, all the embodied feelings of infancy come flooding back until he felt he would – and half wanted to – drown in them. In talking about wanting to disappear under the waves, I think he was referring to the anxieties about humiliation that that his needy vulnerable state evoked.

At the same time, I think he was enacting and identifying with the child he believed to be in his analyst mother's mind, and the anxieties about himself which I believe were projected into him as a small child. He believed that I needed him to be sick, that I wanted him to share my fantasies of catastrophe about his physical and psychical state, and not to be the admired potent boy but a child patient who was handicapped and rendered impotent with a myriad of ailments.

This infant internally felt like 'a starving alien' to him. To bring this about, he had effectively to castrate himself psychically, ending up imprisoned in a female passive position, helpless on the floor, legless, where it seemed there was no father available for identification. Understandably, he felt desperate about this situation although he perceived, at the same time, that he might expect some support from me in a way that differed from his previous experiences.

Wednesday's session highlights another difficulty for my patient in the analysis. He began by asking whether he should have a psychiatrist and then the material on Thursday about brain scans shows how he feared that he would overwhelm me and that we needed an oedipal third, the psychiatrist to protect us.

On Thursday, he returned to the same theme with the discussion about brain scans and his projection of his doubts about me into his friends. He was ambivalent, psychiatrists might be useless and it was clear that he felt he was getting something worthwhile in his analysis. I had not collapsed and had given him some understanding which he valued. But perhaps, he worried that the care I had given him might be envied. If he had the containment he wanted with his mother analyst, would he and I be vulnerable to attack?

He begins to move back into the manic cerebral defence. In his first dream. The man in the dream who can control everybody's minds arrives at the top of the thin building and wipes out my patient as the ordinary boy sleeping at the bottom of the building who is with his siblings/classmates. I think the thin building, which might topple, suggests the thin sense the patient had of himself in this state of mind. In the session, I felt he does something similar to the high man, eliminating what I might feel is important. I think by the end of the session, he had some understanding of the situation and the disjointed thin sense of himself that this created.

On reflection, I felt the second dream on Thursday expressed an idea of him inside the space of my consulting room, almost inside the womb, where he needed neither to eat nor to drink. At the same time, the possible perils for him of containment are apparent that he might become too caught up with the mother and need a father psychiatrist to limit him and protect us both.

This material indicates how essential a solid internal state of mind in me was for the patient to feel contained, and to be able to allow himself to make contact with all the fragmented parts of himself that he had cut off, without expecting us both to drown.

The position Paul wished to maintain was founded on a brittle pathological structure which was breaking down irretrievably, but which felt to him like the only possible stable sense of identity, even if a very denuded and limited one. The patient himself soon recognised that his structure was collapsing and that despite his best efforts to retreat to his enclave, he could not rid himself of the need for relationship and dependency that I and the analysis offered. This was a source of desperation for him as he felt the likely outcome was to be engulfed in maternal chaos and castration. The psychic parents could only be experienced separately at this point, he could not achieve the oedipal resolution necessary for there to be a couple, which might have allowed him to both experience his feeling states and understand them. The only other way seemed to him to reject his internal perceptions and the external world totally: at times, he clearly wished to lose himself

THE CEREBRAL MIND VERSUS THE BODY MIND

completely in a psychotic withdrawal. The process is seen above of withdrawal, an increasing sense of containment and then renewed withdrawal was a cycle that was repeated many times at this stage of the analysis.

Discussion of the countertransference, the struggle for containment

The countertransference with this patient was remarkable as it developed in layers that ran in parallel, reflecting the profound splits and fragmentation within the patient.

The cerebral enclave in my patient evoked a polarity of extreme countertransference feelings in me. These were of being the expert answer to all his problems, the all providing breast or his ego ideal, on the one hand, and of complete uselessness and despair, on the other hand. It was hard for Paul to tolerate any sense of separation between us, and I, as an idealised mother analyst, was to be installed with him on his planet, with no psychic distance between us. He assumed he did not have to tell me things as I already knew them. He was in almost total projective identification with me and believed I was in the same state. I had a feeling of intense closeness and had a sense of having almost telepathic communication with my patient. He let me know we were going to have the perfect analysis, as a totally fused couple of a genius patient and a genius analyst, controlled by him internally.

At other times, it seemed that he did not expect anything of me and believed he would have to conduct his own analysis while providing money and sustenance for me. He feared I would only deplete him. I then felt like the hopeless, despised part of 'no use' that his cerebral mind was intent on getting rid of, like a rejected child cast aside by a judgemental father or observer. After a while I understood that these were the projected counterparts to the cerebral part of my patient's psychic structure.

My countertransference to the split-off 'body mind' aspects of my patient was much less easy to articulate and more fragmented.

In sessions, I was subject to inexplicable feelings and frustrations. Often, the pace was very slow, and I felt constrained as if all I could do was passively wait and observe, a relegated castrated analyst. In some sessions, I felt viscerally his extreme fury, which had no apparent basis in the session. I was aware of receiving intense projections of catastrophe, believing that the patient would collapse into a psychotic state where I could not reach him. Paul himself began to believe he was too much for me that I would send him to a psychiatric hospital, and I was wondering if this might come about. For a time, I had anxieties like a terrified paranoid mother, convinced that he needed a father psychiatrist and that the analysis would cause him to break down irrevocably. I think it was my capacity, after some work and consultation with colleagues, to resist being overwhelmed by these projections and then to begin to contain them and give them meaning for him which gave the patient a sense of sufficient parental structure to allow him to draw back from a more disastrous psychotic collapse.

Alongside these feelings, it became apparent that at times I also introjected some of the raw b-elements that remained unprocessed. It was only with hindsight that I realised how closely my symptoms mirrored my patient's and how they intensified in his session. I acquired, for example, a sniff and a cough which immediately worsened when I saw Paul and mysteriously vanished with other patients. I became aware that this was a state of projective identification, where my body had taken in some of the unprocessed unthought beta elements that he was dealing with.

Development in the analysis

Slowly, in the analysis, the psychic situation began to change although it was very hard and painful for the patient. He was anxious that I was going to drag him down to an ordinary existence which he dreaded, where he feared being deprived of all power and plunged into chaos.

As he became more aware of his fractured psychic state, the new sense that there were other parts of himself was very disturbing to him. One evening he told me 'I think there are too many different mes inside…I don't understand how I wasn't aware of the other parts, why am I like this? And I don't know what to do'. He also had growing evidence about still other fragments of himself less able to be articulated, and involving profound feelings and impulses, which he had no words for.

For the first three years, his reaction to me and to the analysis was often one of claustrophobia and hatred although well controlled. He spent weeks in states of extreme anger as he gradually became more aware of his feelings and began to make often distressing links with the past. The physical embodiment of his feelings gradually subsided and the allergies, breathing difficulties, etc. became much more sporadic. His emotions became much more present in his mind. Only after a long time did his anger become less terrifying to him and more manageable. The sessions became somewhat more normal, peopled by those around him, his ordinary life in the present, and more manageable, more neurotic anxieties. His ordinary memories of the past began to appear as links in the sessions. Externally, over this period of time, both his work and his relationships became more stable.

Some concluding thoughts on the naming and structuring function of the analyst

Before coming to analysis, I believe that Paul had managed to function by inhabiting an enclave of cerebral hyper-rationality, which was a defensive identification with an ideal omnipotent paternal figure. In the beginning of treatment, this constituted almost his entire sense of himself and his belief of being able to survive psychically, with some minimal separation from his mother's mind. His phantasy was also specifically that these cerebral capacities would be able to save mother and then in the transference, me. In the transference, we could be together as an ideal analytic couple on his planet forever, but ordinary feelings, thoughts or dependence, in other words many aspects of internal and external reality, were split off and eliminated from mind. I think this felt necessary to protect the patient from anxiety about chaos. Paul soon came to recognise how impoverished and denuded the cerebral position made him feel, and how little substance or confidence it provided: 'I usually feel I can be anything, but it means being nothing'.

The split-off parts of himself were to some extent projected, but much remained largely unprocessed and totally out of mind. We can perhaps understand much of his extensive somatic illness, collapse and the acting out that occurred in analysis as raw b-elements that could only gradually be brought into mind through an experience of containment. I think my central task was to act as an analyst mother, with a mind and alpha function, containing and then transforming the beta elements into thoughts. (For more on this, see the introductory chapter above.) Initially, this involved my actually perceiving his feeling states in his body and giving them a name so that he had some awareness of them and could integrate them into his sense of himself. It also involved tolerating some extreme projections. Paul did not perhaps believe that I, unlike his mother, could provide sufficient containment and thought that I would collapse. The somatic symptoms I developed early on, which he may have felt responsible for, may have heightened his doubts as to my robustness, and he certainly felt the need to look after me.

My eventual capacity to both tolerate and give meaning to the projected fragments depended on my internal world and in particular on my capacity to provide psychically a firm oedipal configuration for the patient. My professional training and support were very helpful in this. Eventually, his anxiety seemed to lessen, and over time, there was some sense he could internalise me as an object who understood him and cared about him.

For the three years in question, Paul remained highly dependent on my physical presence to contain his psychic splitting and frequently projected much of his ego function into me in a state of identification. Over time some greater separateness seemed possible, and he felt able physically to move house further away, to understand that he might disagree with me, to become aware of my actual relationships with others. All of this helped to expand and consolidate his capacity to contain himself. It took a considerable further time before the patient was able to disidentify with me and not to need my concrete presence, to truly have a solid sense of himself and his identity as distinct from that of his analyst.

Over a long period of time, his bodily communications and ordinary feelings came more to mind and the psychotic elements of his personality seemed to mitigate. Thinking about this patient brought to my mind how Bion said in 1978: 'There can be such a thing as too much cerebration, the cerebral hemispheres used to the detriment of the sympathetic or autonomic nervous system… and so the marriage between this patient and himself has never really been consummated' (Bion 1987 p. 166).

In Bion's terms, very slowly in the analysis, the patient began to be introduced to himself, to consummate the marriage of the parts of body and mind. I believe this enabled Paul to extend his sense of himself and establish a more stable and continuous sense of identity.

Note

1 Quotation reprinted with kind permission of The Marsh Agency Ltd.

References

Bion W. (1962) 'A Theory of Thinking'. In *The Complete Works of Bion*, edited by Chris Mawson (2014) (vol. XI, pp. 236–238). Karnac.

Bion, W. (1987) 'Clinical Seminars, Sao Paolo'. In *Clinical Seminars and Other Works* Ed. Francesca Bion (pp. 141–241). London: Routledge.

Britton, R. (1992) *Keeping Things in Mind* (vol. 14, pp. 102–113). London: Routledge

Britton, R. (1998) *Naming and Containing, Belief and Imagination: Explorations in Psychoanalysis* (vol. 31, pp. 19–29). London and New York: Routledge

Hartung, T. and Steinbrecher, M. (2018) 'Somatic Pain to Psychic Pain: The Body in the Psychoanalytic Field'. *The International Journal of Psychoanalysis*, 99: 19–180.

Klein, M. (1946) 'Notes on Some Schizoid Mechanisms'. *International Journal of Psychoanalysis*, 27: 99–110.

4

ORIENTATION, DISORIENTATION AND IDENTITY DEVELOPMENT

An illustration from Dante's *Divine Comedy*

Giovanna Rita Di Ceglie

Introduction

The dynamics of orientation and disorientation have been the subject of my reflection over the last few years. In this chapter, I explore their contribution to identity development. I will argue how in situations of psychic disorientation emergence from it is linked to finding or re-finding a new point of reference, which might, in turn, lead to the formation of new layers of identity.

I will illustrate this process by focusing on aspects of the poetic psychic journey of Dante Alighieri in *The Divine Comedy* which begins with the description of an experience of disorientation from which Dante then emerges as he makes his ascent to see and be seen by God as the supreme orientating object of both his internal world and the culture of the Middle Ages. This immense poetic, philosophical and psychic project, mainly written during his exile, gives Dante a renewed sense of identity, which is rooted in his infantile experiences, and integrates all aspects of his identity, his religious and philosophical identity, his identity as a poet and his 'national' and political identity as a citizen of his beloved Florence.

Orientation, containment and the development of thinking

Orientation and disorientation between mother and infant, and between patient and analyst in clinical work, have been the subject of one of my previous papers (2013). In that paper, I viewed orientation as an important dimension of containment in the development of thinking. I explored how mutual orientation between the mother and infant creates the condition for a mutual positioning in space and time in order to find one another. I described this as being part of the processes of containment of early splitting and projections, their transformation and re-introjection as described by Bion's with his model of the container/contained. I explored containment and orientation in relation to the Greek object called 'symbolon' as a metaphor for early negotiations between mother and infant as well as between analyst and patient in the psychoanalytic process.

In this chapter, I explore the link between early experiences of reciprocal orientation and an early stage of identity formation, based on the infant's capacity to *identify* the object as the privileged, first *reference point* progressively experienced as unique. This is simultaneous to the experience of being *identified* as such by the object. This provides a sense of belonging and attachment to that primary object which will, when things go well, lead to a sense of ownership of the body, of the mind and of one's own history. It is not easy to articulate how this primitive link between mother and infant is formed. It is such an extraordinary time experienced by the new born as well as by the mother. What I am emphasising here is the first psychic and physical attempt of the new born to find an orientating object.

Chris Mawson (2019) in his exploration of the centrality of anxiety in psychoanalysis highlights the infant's existential, ontological anxieties threatened by the unbearable experience of non-being and links it to Freud's notion of 'the specific action' on the part of the mother towards the infant as the foundation of being and thinking. Esther Bick (1968) linked the new born's 'catastrophic anxieties' to the unintegrated state in relation to the development of the skin. Bick describes how the new-born infant searches for a containing object through the perception of light, voice, smell, sound and touch, which can hold parts of the personality together not yet differentiated from parts of the body. Bick seems to refer implicitly to the sense of disorientation and lack of a sense of gravity of the new-born baby due to the immaturity and fragility of the skin. The skin as an *organ*, as a concrete container, is at the boundary between the inside and the outside and this is particularly interesting in relation to the notion of identity which is at the boundary of the inner and the external world. Reflecting on Bick's paper, I wish to emphasise here the importance of the perceptual apparatus as a whole for the infant to feel and hold on to an object as the first point of reference in order to feel 'in one piece'. I believe that it is this need for a primitive sense of unity and of existing as a unity that makes the new born to exercise the capacity to orientate themselves in the world around them. They come to know the self in the process of knowing the world. The whole perceptive apparatus, from the very beginning of life, has the function of ensuring that the attachment to the mother as the point of reference is not lost. These experiences are subjected continuously to internal and external demands leading to complex movements in and out of disorientation.

These early struggles are the beginning of what Damasio (2000) calls the 'autobiographical self'. They are imbued since the very beginning by unconscious phantasies (Isaccs, 1948) and will influence, as mental images are memorised, the forming of the root of identity, with subsequent layers of experience and phantasies progressively attaching actively to it. Klein's notion of an early self and of an early awareness of the object, as well as her insistence on the infant's tendency towards integration, is consistent with research in developmental psychology.

Daniel Stern (1985) from a developmental research perspective has informed us that infants from the earliest days of life have the mental capacity to apprehend the object and the environment and are capable of translating perceptions of the object across different perceptive modalities. The new born can also see what is within 8 inches from his/her eyes and it is interesting that this is the exact distance between the mother's eyes and the baby at the breast. The recognition of the mother by the new-born infant occurs well before this recognition is actually communicated clearly enough for the mother to register it when the baby seems suddenly to look at his or her mother as if to say: 'ah, it is you!'. The innate capacity to translate perceptions across different modalities seems to have the function, among many others, to maintain a continuity in orientation towards the mother as the privileged reference point and to protect the infant in dealing with the inevitable discontinuities in contact and orientations. This capacity contributes to provide the infant with what Winnicott (1960) described as a sense of *continuity of being*. I think that these very early memories of experiences of reciprocal recognition and a reciprocal sense of belonging and ownership constitute the powerful infantile social root of later layers of identity.

The early movements to reach for the breast as well as for the mother's gaze represent a kind of journey for the new-born infant which involves innumerable repetitions of successes and failures, accompanied by moments of despair, hope and bliss of different intensities. These early experiences can be seen as a kind of paradigm for the psychic work involved any time we are faced with new challenges and crises in the course of life. I will illustrate this paradigm through Dante's poetic journey through *Hell*, *Purgatory* and *Paradise* as representations of states of mind dominated, respectively, by fear, hope and bliss.

Disorientation, orientation and identity in Dante's *Divine Comedy*

Elliott Jaques (1965) saw in Dante's masterpiece the working through in his mid-life crisis, of his infantile depression, anxiety and guilt leading to greater integration and creativity in mature life. In this chapter, I will focus on the centrality of the experience of disorientation. *The Divine Comedy* provides an illustration on the theme of disorientation/orientation in relation to identity and, in particular, to the inner recovery of the primitive link with the life-giving object experienced as the first orientating object through mutual recognition and sense of belonging.

The illuminating project of *The Divine Comedy*, in my view, enabled Dante to deal with disorientation. It gave him a renewed sense of purpose in describing with painstaking precision the human tendency towards disorientation away from the supreme orientating object represented by God. Dante begins his poem with a description of his disorientation upon reaching midlife:

In the middle of the journey of our life[1]	*Nel mezzo del cammin di nostra vita*
I found myself in a dark wood	*Mi ritrovai per una selva oscura,*
for the right way had been lost.	*Chè la diritta via era smarrita.*
Ah! how hard it is to tell of this wilderness	*Ahi quanto a dir qual era è cosa dura*
so thick and asper that	*Questa selva selvaggia ed aspra e forte,*
just thinking of it brings the fear back	*Che nel pensier rinnova la paura!*
So bitter it is that little more is death.	*Tanto è amara che poco è più morte.*
	(Inferno, Canto I, 1–7)

We do not know what the origin of such a state of disorientation described by Dante is about. He writes:

I cannot really say how I entered there	*Io non so ben ridir com'I v'entrai,*
so full of sleep was I then	*Tant'era pieno di sonno a quel punto*
when the right way I left	*Che la verace via abbandonai.*
	(Inferno, Canto I, 1–3)

Dante is not telling us about the external circumstances or what he might have gone through at that time, but it is not too improbable that he is referring to his state of mind following the experience of being banished from Florence.[2] It is not hard to imagine the sense of loss and despair of Dante when, exiled from Florence under

103

threat of a death sentence, he lost his home, his possessions, his political status and his identity blemished with terrible accusations. It must have stirred in him a sense of dreadful uncertainty and confusion in a political situation rife with rivalry. It was, furthermore, at a moment when he had hoped, by interceding with Pope Bonifacio VIII, that his political party could bring some form of peaceful stability to Florence. However, Dante's sense of disorientation, one might speculate, also extended to his religious identity. We know that Dante after the death of his beloved Beatrice immersed himself in the study of philosophy and theology and thereby became acquainted with other religious orientations. Earlier doubts might have resurfaced in midlife and may have been reinforced by disillusionment at the corruption, greed, fraudulence and betrayal of God's representative on earth. His identity as a poet might also have been shaken by the exile, having had to leave everything behind.[3] Dante's disorientation seems therefore to have affected the three layers of his identity profoundly: as a poet, as a political leader and as a believer in the salvific spiritual function of the Catholic Church. As mentioned earlier, we do not hear, in that first tercet, a single word which might refer to the external reality of the exile as being the cause of his disorientation. Dante writes that he let it happen 'by being full of sleep' maybe referring to his own sense of responsibility for being in a state of profound crisis and depression.

'Mi ritrovai in una selva oscura' which literally could be translated 'I found myself being *again* in a dark wood' reveals, if we draw attention to the unconscious use of the word 'ritrovai' (Black, 2017), the repetition of an earlier experience of disorientation, confusion and dread. The first tercet is extremely powerful in its simplicity. It is evocative of an infant left in a dark room with no one to turn to and progressively losing hope, giving up and drowning in despair. Dante also uses the verb 'ridir' which means 'to say it again'. Indeed, in the *Vita nova*, written during his adolescence and probably completed four years after the death of Beatrice, we have a most detailed description of Dante being in a feverish state of mind. He endures visions of the most terrifying nature where the whole world seems to come to an end at the thought of Beatrice's death and his own death, followed by the vision of her dead body taken care of by some women. These dreadful visions, through the naming inside himself of Beatrice (he felt ashamed to say her name aloud) and the comfort he received by the women beside him, turned into visions of a mystical nature where death, peace and goodness prevail, a paradisiac world of angels with Beatrice now partaking of a divine world. It is interesting that the point of salvation from death in this instance is linked to the capacity to retrieve the link in his internal world with a good loved object. Beatrice did die and Dante describes in the *Vita nova* that a man appeared, 'pale and faint' (scolorito e fioco), announcing: 'Haven't you heard? Dead is your woman who was so beautiful'. (*Che fai? Non sai novella? Morta è la donna tua ch'era sì bella.*) (Vita nuova, 2002) It is interesting to notice that 'Bella' was the actual name of Dante's mother. It is probable that Beatrice's death brought back memories of an earlier disorientation after the death of his mother when he was five years old. Dante concludes the *Vita nova* hoping that he would live long enough to say of Beatrice 'what was never said of any other woman'.

It is not unrealistic to speculate that Dante's love at first sight for the nine-year-old Beatrice, who greeted him when he was nine, represented the realisation of an unconscious deep-seated longing to re-experience being seen by his mother's loving eyes again. Where would the extraordinary power of Dante's experience of seeing and being seen by Beatrice come from if not from the powerful desire to experience again some of the earliest exclusive experiences with his mother which had been cut short at such a young age. And how could we think of Dante's description of his despair at the withdrawal of Beatrice's 'saluto', her approving and loving greeting, if not as the rekindled experience of having lost forever the love from the object and his own capacity to love, bringing the experience of disorientation described in the first tercet so close to death.

I wish also to refer here to Dante's sense of persecution in relation to the mother and later Beatrice as the perfect, unique, idealised object who contains all the goodness of the world. At the same time, the gaze of this perfect object could also destroy him and make him feel less than perfect, unworthy of her and of his father's gaze too. The father would unconsciously be perceived as disapproving and intolerant of his son's secret passions and longings. Dante in the *Vita nova* anticipates his hope for his soul to join Beatrice in contemplation of the quintessential goodness of God in paradise. Writing about Beatrice gave Dante a sense of purpose, a reference point out of disorientation which possibly relieved him of the unconscious sense of guilt for having abandoned her, or not protected her from death. We see the emergence, out of disorientation and loss, of his poetic identity by making use of symbol formation (Segal, 1957) linked to his determination to repair his early link with a maternal object. This wish we will see as being connected with having to appease his own envy, split off and projected into the terrifying vision of the she-wolf which stops the arduous work of reparation.

Dante wishes that we could experience with him what it felt like to be in the dark wood: dark, bitter and impenetrable. In a powerful simile (Canto I, 22–27), Dante tells us that he felt like someone who, having just made it out of a tempestuous sea to the safety of the seashore, looks back terrified to 'the step' towards death. To my reading, here he is clearly referring to the intrapsychic force which moved him towards an un-retrievable state of psychic death. We will soon learn that this psychic force dragging him down, 'where the sun is silent' (dove il sol tace), is envy. Dante's description of the she-wolf as the beast 'weighed down by its leanness' is a powerful illustration of Klein's notion of early splitting and projections used by the infant when prey of extreme mental states under the aegis of life and death instincts. The she-wolf, which impedes Dante from pursuing the 'right trajectory' and which is so central in the experience of disorientation, is evocative of the infant's moving away from the frustrating object towards another direction. Dante describes the she-wolf in this way:

So cruel and evil is her nature that her greed is never satiated	*E ha natura sì malvagia e ria, Che mai non empie la bramosa voglia,*
and after the meal is hangrier than before	*E dopo il pasto ha più fame che pria'.*

(Inferno, Canto I, 97–99)

Dante, prey of terror at the sight of the she-wolf, screams: 'have pity on me' (miserere di me) to what looks like a human figure.

The encounter with Virgil as a newly found sense of direction

While I was precipitating down to a low place,	*Mentre ch'i rovinava in basso loco,*
In front of my eyes appeared the one who because of	*Dinanzi ali occhi mi si fu offerto*
a long silence seemed faint.	*Chi per lungo silenzio parea fioco*
When I saw him in the big desert I shouted 'have pity on me'	*Quando vidi costui nel grand deserto 'miserere di me', gridai a lui,*
Whoever you may be either a shadow or a real man.	*'Qual che tu sii, o ombra od omo certo'.*

(Inferno, Canto I, 61–66)

By screaming 'miserere di me', Dante makes an extraordinary move, he turns physically and psychologically towards a potentially life-saving object retrieved from the inner depth of his internal world. This object, which is not yet fully recognised, takes us to the theme of the orientation of the new born latching on, under the aegis of the life instinct, to the first object on sight. Virgil reveals then his own identity to Dante and this evokes in Dante the memory of his own identity. It is as if he is saying: 'by telling me who you are, I am reminded of who I am'. Dante movingly feels reconnected with his former self as a poet through seeing and being seen by Virgil. This process of recognition is fundamental to identity development.

Oh among other poets' honour and light, profit me from the long study and great love which made me search for your book. You are the one from whom I have taken the beautiful style that has brought me honour.	O de li altri poeti onore e lume Vagliami 'l lungo studio e 'l grande amore Che m'ha fatto cercar lo tuo volume. Tu se' lo mio maestro e 'l mio autore… Tu se' solo colui da cui io tolsi Lo bello stile che m'ha fatto onore.

(Inferno, Canto I, 82–87)

The reconstitution of three layers of identity

Through the encounter with Virgil who can be considered the embodiment of a poetic identity, Dante finds relief from disorientation through reconnecting with his own identity as a poet. Virgil functions here as a mirror in which Dante can recognise himself as a poet immensely indebted to Virgil. Later in *Purgatory*, Dante will make Stazio, another poet, say that Virgil's Eneid had been 'his mother', the symbolic breast who nourished Dante's creativity. Dante reacquires his capacity for poetic creativity following its breakdown and this enables him to tell the story of his own search for a new home, just like Eneas, the hero of Virgil's epic work, left the ruins of Troy carrying his father in search for a new home. The capacity to tell the story of this search is linked to the reacquisition of his own capacity for symbol formation (Segal, 1957). This enables Dante to put in poetic images his own recognition of envy in the struggle during his poetic journey and seems to tell us that he was able to proceed only when he was able to recognise how much he owed to Virgil.

Dante's identity as a poet reaches an even stronger confirmation during his journey through Limbo. Here, Dante is recognised and accepted as a poet by a family of the other great poets: Homer, Ovidio, Orazio and Lucano. Virgil is greeted by them with the following words: 'Let's honour the highest of poets' (onorate l'altissimo poeta?). This is followed by Virgil's introduction of Dante to them. Dante proudly writes:

And I was the sixth among so much wisdom	sì ch'io fui sesto tra cotanto senno.

(Inferno, Canto IV, 102)

Limbo is a kind of oasis in hell, a place reserved for those who pursued the highest achievements based on knowledge and intelligence. But, there is something missing. They are in limbo because they were born before Christ and could not be baptised to acquire a religious identity. But also, as we learn from Virgil in Purgatory canto VI, for lack of faith. They are defined as 'those who are suspended' (color che son sospesi) and *defined* as 'neither sad nor happy'.

Dante says that he is the sixth, among the family of poets. There is a sense of acceptance of his debt to his predecessors without disregarding his own talent. The reestablishment of his poetic identity and poetic project at first felt to be lost in the dark wood of his despair is through the encounter with Virgil as his guide, the basis, for the reconstruction of the other two layers of identity: the religious and the political one. The starting point of this reconstruction is Dante's re-connection with the memory of Beatrice who prompts Virgil to be Dante's first guide (thanks to the intersession of a group of female saints in paradise gently reproaching her for not having noticed that Dante was in great trouble and in need of help).

Remembering and being remembered by the loved internal object seems to be simultaneous to the restoration of his symbolic capacity. Virgil is supposed to guide him out of disorientation by orientating him through hell and purgatory. Beatrice becomes his next guide from the earthly paradise onwards up to the point when she will leave him with the ultimate goal of seeing and being seen by God.

Through the reacquisition of his symbolic function, Dante has created a structure where he can elaborate memories, desires and phantasies and beliefs. *The Divine Comedy* is a containing structure for his creative imagination and endeavour. It is also a way of ordering his inner world by creating an orientating map of the human psyche with a specific goal: to become worthy of his ultimate encounter with God, not as an end in itself but as the confirmation of what is divine in human nature (Ryan, 1993). In other words, through the journey which is a poetic and psychological journey, he constructs a religious identity which is highly personal, albeit within the sets of belief of the Middle Ages and, sometimes, in plain contradiction to them.

Hell is dominated by despair and cruelty. What is lost is not just the good object but the idea of goodness itself so that what is described as a punishment by an unforgiving divine justice is also a representation of a state of mind where relentless punishment, sadism and revenge central to the feeling of severe depression dominated by the harshest superego. There can only be a sense of timeless immobility and isolation in such a state of mind. The damned are described as

swearing against God and their parents,	*Bestemmiavano Dio e lor parenti*
the human species and their time	*L'umana specie e il loco il tempo e il seme*
and space and the seed of their species and their birth.	*Di lor semenza e di lor nascimenti.*

(Inferno, Canto III, 103–105)

I quote these tercets as an extraordinary illustration of a state of mind oriented towards evil and Satan as the embodiment of the anti-life force standing against the life-giving object, against God as the creator of the universe, and against the parents and their creative intercourse, against the time and place of origin. It is a powerful description of a world which as Dante and Virgil progress into the ravine becomes progressively lurid and sadistic. It is the concrete representation of the psychic state of mind described by Meltzer (1966) where the bottom and its idealised content become the newly found orientation.

Dante's poetic identity had been put to the test in his description of hell, so much so that when approaching the bottom of the abyss, he wonders how he could manage to use the same language used to address his mother and father (Inferno, XXXII, 9). It is as if the words themselves felt contaminated by the description of horror. We can infer from this that Dante felt that words could be used more at the service of projective identification than communication. The role of projections into the hostile territory of hell acquires a concrete aspect at times as when, for example, Virgil in negotiating how to proceed through it, suggests that they take the 'right breast' (la destra mammella)!

Purgatory is the place where hope emerges and with it a sense of struggle with conflicting ambivalent feelings. Hope is recovered but not without conflict. There is a sense of greater freedom and choice compared with the immobility and isolation of hell. There is considerable physical pain, but psychic pain for the damage done emerges as well as trust in forgiveness as expressed in the following tercet by the soul of Manfredi, King of Sicily and killed in battle:

Horrible were my sins:	*Orribil furon li peccati miei:*
But infinite goodness can hold in her harms	*Ma la bontà infinita ha sì gran braccia,*
Anyone who turns towards her	*Che prende ciò che si rivolge a lei*

(Purgatorio, Canto III, 121–123)

There is a psychic constellation in Purgatory which favours the reparative processes described by Klein as part of the working through of the depressive position. The active turning towards the breast imbued with phantasies of infinite goodness is already the beginning of reparative process linked to the active forgiving of the object which, in turn, is experienced as forgiving towards the infant.

Right at the beginning of *Purgatory*, in the Ante Purgatory, we encounter a description of disorientation. The newly arrived souls at the seashore at the foot of Purgatory's mountain are disoriented. They ask Virgil and Dante for directions only to discover that they too don't know where to begin to ascend. The experience of disorientation is recurrent throughout Purgatory. However, disorientation is now more bearable because there is a desire to search for the 'right' way. The desire to ascend *is* in a way 'the right way' that had been lost in the disoriented state of mind dominated by envy and greed. The mountain of Purgatory as a representation of the difficulties and ambivalence towards the feeding breast is still arduous and the infant does not quite know how to approach it but is more reliant on the inner strength of his desire and on his greater trust in the kindness of the environment.

Dante needs to invoke the Muses at the beginning of *Purgatory* to resurrect 'the dead poetry' to describe his newly found orientation upwards as opposed to the one downwards towards hell. He declares unashamedly of belonging to the Muses (I am yours, I belong to you). We are soon then made to witness Dante's moving and futile embrace with the soul of Casella, a musician who in real life had composed music to the lyrics of a Dante's canzone 'Amor che ne la mente mi ragiona' (Convivio, trattato III, canzone seconda). Dante asks him to give him the comfort of his beautiful voice and Casella begins to sing it, enchanting Dante, Virgil and the crowd of newly arrived souls. They are soon scolded by Cato, the guardian of Purgatory, for letting themselves be distracted from the task ahead. I found this temporary diversion of orientation at the foot of the mountain of Purgatory evocative of the infant who, having recovered some hope after the return of the breast, indulges and plays with it delaying the complex process of reaching for the nipple to feed from it.

The ascent towards the summit coincides with a progressive repair of Dante's skin which bears on his forehead the stigma of sins (Canto XII). The reparation of Dante's skin seems to be the metaphor for the intrapsychic reparation of the fabric of the self and the object in taking responsibility for the damage caused (Klein 1940). In *Purgatory*, there is pining for reparation and longing to be remembered on Earth in a good way. *Purgatory* is also where loss is an inevitable experience. Virgil as an external good object will eventually leave Dante. Dante describes the moment when, apprehensive about his anticipation of seeing Beatrice for the first time, recognising the signs of his old passion turns towards Virgil, 'like a little child runs towards his mam' (come l' fantolin corre alla mamma), to realise that Virgil is not there anymore:

Virgil had left us emptied of him,	Ma Virgilio n'avea lasciati scemi
Virgil the sweetest father	di se', Virgilio dolcissimo patre,
Virgil, whom for my health I turned to	Virgilio, a cui per mia salute die'mi

(Purgatorio, Canto XXX, 43)

Virgilio, the sweetest of fathers, disappears leaving Dante full of tears. Virgil who had wiped the tears from Dante's cheeks through his concern for him is now causing new tears, a renewed sense of loss which reminds him of the tears shed by Eve when expelled from the Garden of Eden.

The experience of mourning is central in *Purgatory* as it allows for the repair of symbolic functioning and dreaming. This capacity is also thought to be central in identity development. Where mourning cannot be worked through, concrete solutions are favoured with the short-circuiting of the experience of the psychic pain of loss (Di Ceglie, 2012).

When Virgil disappears, Beatrice appears as Dante's new guide in his new journey towards and through paradise. Beatrice's eyes are veiled at first. She calls Dante by name. This is the first time that Dante is addressed by his name as it marks a moment of recognition of the reality of his identity. Beatrice tells him that he should not cry for Virgil's departure but for other reasons. She asks him to look at her, twice repeating that she is Beatrice. She is stern and reproachful and Dante says that he felt like a child under the gaze of a severe mother. Dante experiences such a sense of shame that he cannot look at Beatrice as she carries on reproaching him for having turned away from her love after her death, orienting himself towards the wrong path of worldly pursuits. It follows a moving process of contrition, guilt and penance before Dante can look at Beatrice' eyes.

Steiner (2011) has explored the significance of shame and embarrassment linked to the anxieties of seeing and being seen by the analyst in the momentous process of beginning to acknowledge the reality of separateness, difference and dependence on the analyst. Indeed, the encounter with Beatrice represents a momentous psychological shift in Dante's journey. If with Virgil, we see the restoration of Dante's poetic identity, with Beatrice, we see the beginning of the strengthening of his religious and highly moral identity which will guide his poetry and his political endeavour. Only through the painful process of working through his personal inner 'purgatory' under Beatrice's gaze and words, will Dante then become capable of unashamedly bearing her radiant loving eyes as a source of inner joy and internal paradise.

in her eyes was burning a smile	chè dentro gli occhi suoi ardeva un riso
such, that I thought with mine I was touching the pick	tal, ch'io pensai co' miei toccar lo fondo
of my grace and my paradise	della mia grazia e del mio paradiso.
	(Paradiso, Canto XV, 34)

Paradise represents the process leading Dante up to a mystical experience through the mediating function of Beatrice as his guide. It is interesting to notice that in *Paradise* too there is an initial reference to disorientation, but this time, Dante refers to the disorientation of the readers. Dante is aware of the possibility for them to get lost in their desire to follow him. He is concerned of engendering disorientation in crossing waters never crossed before by anyone and even suggests the readers to turn back to their familiar shores! (Paradiso, Canto II, 1–6).

Dante encounters several saints in paradise and ultimately Saint Bernard of Clairvaux, who intercedes with the Virgin Mary who, in turn, allows Dante to experience the contact eye to eye with the source of all goodness, intelligence, knowledge and love.

The experience of mutual orientation between God and Dante is felt to be real in the mystical moment of the process of recognition of the goodness of the object. It enables Dante to feel part of that goodness. This experience of total bliss, which he cannot articulate in words, is compared by Dante to the experience of the infant at the breast who has a similar experience, feeding at the breast and maybe seeing himself reflected in his mother's eyes. The experience not articulated verbally remains unconscious. The mystical moment of reciprocal orientation with God, whose gaze he could now tolerate, albeit for a fleeting moment, gives Dante a renewed sense of belief in the goodness of life, in his own goodness and in what is divine in human nature (Ryan, 1993). This will inspire both his poetry and his extraordinary work of integration and ownership of his identity as a poet as well as a citizen of Florence albeit exiled. It brings resolve to continue and tireless search for political solutions to bring peace for Florence and Italy. Dante was aware of how infantile processes can influence political life when in *Purgatory* he compared Italy, seized by blind greed, to 'the starving child who refuses the breast' (Paradiso, XXX, 139–141).

With the process of recovering his poetic identity, by coming out of the dark wood, his religious identity is also recovered. Dante's political identity also remerges in exile and supports him in making sense of his previous experience and of the vicissitudes of his political life in his troubled Florence. The process of political recognition of Dante's own political and Florentine identity first occurs in meeting Farinata Degli Uberti, a former enemy belonging to one of the powerful families of the Ghibelline faction. With a few words, Dante conjures up the image of Farinata as a towering figure in contrast to the defeated humiliated rival of the battle of Campaldino. The process of reciprocal recognition between the two old enemies is moving. Farinata first recognises Dante from his Florentine accent and invites Dante to spend some time with him. Contemptuous of hell, Farinata battles with Dante a battle of words. The quick-witted exchange between the two is briefly interrupted by the sudden awakening of another entombed contemporary, the father of Dante's best friend Guido Cavalcanti who was an atheist and the Ghibelline faction. Dante seems to identify with Farinata as they both share the experience of exile from Florence and love for their troubled city. He asks Farinata if he knows anything about Dante's own sentence of exile and if he can say something about his future. Farinata says that heretics in hell cannot see things when they are far into the future, but they also cannot see anything concerning the near future. This is only until the end of the world when then there will be for them complete blindness of knowledge, no lighter but eternal darkness. This last prophecy of what is to come for the heretics leaves Dante in a state of loss, bewilderment and confusion. A reminder of his confused state of mind and loss of orientation, similar to that of being in the dark woods when depressed, feeling lost and without hope or faith. In this episode, we can see how Dante's political and religious identities merge into one another. Both identities are shaken by the threat of confusion and the loss of orientation towards the good object as the desire to search for it feels rather precarious.

Virgil comforts him by telling him that he will receive some enlightenment about his future from the one 'whose beautiful eyes see everything' (Inferno, X, 131). Beatrice in Paradise will encourage Dante to express his wishes to know about his future from his great, great grandfather, Cacciaguida. Cacciaguida predicts that Dante will not be able to return to Florence but that as an exile he will be able, with the help of others, to be still actively involved in determining the course of events for Italy. Dante's reconnection with his past history is an interesting turn. Dante, in his ascent towards God, cares a lot about his future life on earth and wishes to reach out to a sense of unity and continuity of his remote genealogy. Simultaneously, we find in the Cacciaguida's episode a most poignant description of a past happy, peaceful life within the city walls of Florence, in contrast to the moral decline and the disorienting and confusing present times in a city dominated by greed, arrogance and factionalism.

Splitting processes and orientation in *The Divine Comedy*

Another feature well illustrated in *The Divine Comedy* is the description of early splitting with associated projections of parts of the self into different aspects of the object. Splitting has a very important discriminating and ordering function between good and bad. This type of splitting is relevant to the maintenance of orientation and attraction towards the good object, which contains also good parts of the self as distinct from the bad ones. It is worth emphasising that the good object is felt to be *a place*, a container where the goodness of the self and the object is believed to be located. This applies to the bad object as well.

Splitting between good and bad is the matrix of *The Divine Comedy*. Hell is the representation of all that is bad. It is described as the painful bank which contains the entire evil of the universe, 'the painful bank where the whole universe's evil rests' ('La dolente ripa che il mal dell'universo tutto insacca', Inferno, Canto VII, 17–18). Virgil has the function of showing Dante how low human nature can fall. Paradise is the opposite and represents all that is good, perfect and harmonious. Purgatory is a representation of an attempt to integrate good and bad and therefore is more a representation of the depressive position. None of the souls are perfectly good or perfectly bad. I linked these mechanisms to the struggles of the new born and the mother in finding and maintaining orientation through the early struggles.

Another type of splitting between the good and bad object and between love and hatred could occur as a defence against excessive envy as it aims at blurring the good and bad, obstructing the integration of the good and bad aspects in the object as well as in the self. This failure of splitting between good and bad is often given evidence in the transference with particular patients who, when faced with unexpected and inevitable imperfections or failures of the analyst, begin to question and doubt the essential good intentions of the analyst. The counterpart is a sense of loss of the analyst as a reference point. There is no home to go to anymore, nor a place to put the good or the bad parts of the self which are now blurred.

We can see that the splitting at the service of discrimination and knowledge could represent the beginning of an ethical core albeit based on fear and early anxieties. With greater integration of the depressive position, this ethical core will hopefully lead to a more conscious choice of action based on concern for the other and towards the preservation of life. Dante abhors the type of splitting which does not permit a clear differentiation between God and Satan. Indeed, in the Anti-inferno, he places those souls together with the angels who, at the time of the fall of Lucifer, didn't rebel with him nor were loyal to God (Inferno, Canto III, 37–39). They are those who are truly exiled from hell and paradise alike. Hell rejects them as it would feel diminished by their presence. Dante shows curiosity to know about them, but he is soon discouraged from paying too much attention as Virgil prompts him to move ahead (Inferno, Canto III, 37–39).

Conclusion

In this chapter, I have tried to show the link between disorientation and orientation and the development of identity. I hypothesised that, consequentially, disorientation is connected to a loss of identity and a sense of confusion, while the reacquisition of orientation contributes to a renewed sense of identity.

I have used *The Divine Comedy* and interpretations of its interactions with Dante's biography as an illustration of the complex processes related to the earliest experience of orientation/disorientation of the new-born infant in relation to the mother as the first orientating object.

The apparition of Virgil as Dante's first guide in 'the great desert' (nel grand deserto) of his internal world represents the beginning of the reacquisition of contact with his needs in search of the good object felt to be lost in the 'dark wood' of his depression. This involves the restoring of his identity as a poet. Beatrice takes over from Virgil the function of orientating Dante through a process of confrontation at the service of a reorientation involving greater integration, greater capacity to bear responsibility for the damage caused by orientation towards the 'wrong base' (Money-Kyrle, 1968, p. 425). Beatrice through a chain of intercessions and mediations guides Dante's ascent to his ultimate encounter with God which I understand for Dante represents the supreme unity of knowledge, intellect and love, a life creative force orientating the movement of the universe as well as the human mind if it chooses to be inspired by it. Dante cannot describe or remember the instant of mutual orientation and recognition of this force. What remains is an impression of an experience, like a dream the content of which is soon dissolved 'like snow in the sun's light' and dispersed 'like the Sybil's words in the wind':

> *Così la neve al sol si disigilla,*
> *Così al vento ne le foglie lievi*
> *Si perdea la sentenza di Sibilla.*
> (Paradiso, Canto XXXIII, 64–66)

Dante, finally, re-emerges from the fleeting experience, seeing himself reflected in the eye of God, to the reality of his own identity whose desire and will are now oriented by the same force of love that moves the sun and the other stars. Dante concludes his journey by saying:

Here my fantasy power had no more,	*All'alta fantasia qui mancò possa:*
as love which like a well-balanced wheel	*Ma già volgeva il mio disiro e 'l velle,*
moves the sun and the other stars	*Sì come ruota che igualmente è mossa,*
was already directing my desire and will.	*L'Amor che move il Sole e l'altre stelle.*

(Paradiso, Canto XXXIII, 142–145)

It is not possible to cover the philosophical and theological complexity enclosed in Dante's poetry of the last canto of Paradise. Christopher Ryan (1993) interprets Dante's vision of his own image in the second of the three circles as 'a momentary flash of intuition' with regards to the unity of human nature and God. However, it is the relational nature of the experience which is striking and which I wish to emphasise. God is often described through the *Comedy* and, in particular, in *Purgatory* as 'a pleased maker', 'lieto fattore', at the contemplation of the creation of the human soul. The soul is compared to a 'like a little girl' happily and freely wishing to orientate herself to 'ciò che la trastulla' 'towards the play that entertains her'. Dante unequivocally takes us with this simile to the childhood moments of playful, passionate exchanges with the parents. The following quote from Klein well describes the unconscious processes involved in those playful exchanges:

> We find in the analysis of our patient that the breast in its good aspects is the prototype of maternal goodness, inexhaustible patience and generosity as well as creativeness. It is these phantasies and instinctual needs that so enrich the primal object that it remains the foundation of hope, trust and belief in goodness.
>
> (Klein, 1957, p. 180)

Klein describes the creative function of unconscious phantasies which enrich the good nourishing and needed object who, in turn, generates and confirms in the infant a belief in his own goodness. The final verse of the Comedy 'the love that moves the sun and other stars' is evocative of the infant who can then move from the parental lap because its goodness is felt, at least for the time being, inside himself. It represents the final confirmation of Dante's re-orientation towards his own creativity experienced as the direct emanation of the original project of creation and becomes the enduring core of his identity.

Notes

1 All Italian to English translation of Dante author's own.
2 What seemed to have happened during 1301–1302 is that the French King Charles de Valois had asked the Pope Bonifacio VIII permission to invade Florence. Dante as part of the White Guelf party which ruled Florence at the time was against this plan. It was decided that Dante as ambassador for the Guelf government (*priorato*) went to Rome to negotiate with the Pope an alternative solution. Unexpectedly, the Pope detained him there and gave permission to the French King to join forces with the exiled Black Guelfs to enter Florence, terrorise the city and overthrow the White Guelfs who were then exiled under death sentence.
3 It is alleged that some cantos of *The Divine Comedy* written before his banishment which Dante might have thought as lost were later brought back to Dante in 1306 by a relative (Pasquini, 2015).

References

Bick, E. (1968). 'The Experience of the Skin in Early Object-Relations'. *The International Journal of Psychoanalysis,* 49: 484–486; also in *Melanie Klein Today* (vol. 1). London: Routledge (1988).

Black, D. (2017). 'Dante's 'Two Suns': reflections on the psychological source of *The Divine Comedy*'. *The International Journal of Psychoanalysis*, 98: 1699–1717.

Damasio, A. (2000). *The Feeling of What Happens*. London: William Heinemann.

Dante Alighieri. (2002). *Vita Nuova* (p. 44), edited by E. Sanguineti. Garzanti.

Di Ceglie, G.R. (2013). 'Orientation, containment and the emergence of symbolic thinking'. *The International Journal of Psychoanalysis*, 94(6): 1077–1091.

Di Ceglie, D. (2012) 'Identity and inability to mourn'. *The Skin I Live in. The International Journal of Psychoanalysis*, 93: 1308–1313.

Isaacs, S. (1948). 'The nature and function of phantasy'. *The internatiol Journal of Psycho-Analysis*, 29: 73–97.

Jaques, E. (1965). 'Death and the mid-life crisis'. *The International Journal of Psychoanalysis*, 46: 502–514.

Klein, M. (1940). 'Mourning and its relation to manic-depressive states'. In *The Writings of Melanie Klein, Vol. 1: Love, Guilt and Reparation and Other Works, 1921-1945* (pp. 344–369), edited by R. Money-Kyrle. London: Hogarth Press.

Klein, M. (1957). *Envy and Gratitude and Other Works* (vol. III, p.180). London: The Hogarth Press.

Mawson, C. (2019). *Psychoanalysis and Anxiety: From Knowing to Being*. London: Routledge.

Meltzer, D. (1966). 'The relation of anal masturbation to projective identification'. *International Journal of Psycho-Analysis*, 47, 335–342.

Money-Kyrle, R. (1968). 'Cognitive development'. In *The Collected Papers of Roger Money-Kyrle* (pp. 416–430), edited by D. Meltzer and E. O'Shaughnessy. Clunie Press.

Money-Kyrle, R. (1971). 'The aim of psychoanalysis'. *International Journal of Psycho-Analysis*, 52: 103–106.

Pasquini, E. (2015) *Vita di Dante*. Milano: RCS Libri S.p.A.

Ryan, C. (1993). 'The theology of Dante'. In *The Cambridge Companion to Dante* (Chapter 9, pp. 136–152), edited by Rachel Jacoff. Cambridge: Cambridge University Press.

Segal, H. (1957). 'Notes on symbol formation'. *The International Journal of Psycho-Analysis*, 38: 391–397.

Steiner, J. (2011). *Seeing and Being Seen: Emerging from a Psychic Retreat*. London: Routledge, The New Library of Psychoanalysis.

Stern, D.N. (1985). *The Interpersonal World of the Infants: A View from Psychoanalysis and Developmental Psychology*. New York: Basic Books.

Winnicott, D.W. (1960) The theory of the parent–infant relationship. *International Journal of Psycho-Analysis*, 41: 585–595.

5

A MIND OF ONE'S OWN

The growth of identity in an adult patient

Caroline Garland

Introduction

This paper is about a patient who began her analysis with no sense of who or what she was. I describe an early stage, a first step, in the development of a relatively stable sense of identity where beforehand there was none. None, that is, that could be regarded as having developed organically, called her own. Instead, this patient had a mode of 'good behaviour' that derived from a fear of what would happen to her or to her objects if she were to be 'bad': rebellious, bad-tempered, self-willed, defiant, greedy, oppositional – anything at all that could be construed as negative. When the pressures on her good behaviour became too great, she turned suddenly 'inside out'. Then, the badness was revealed to be overwhelming, in the form of an extreme and violent destructiveness. In a state of desperation, it was projected out massively and located in an object that had once been felt to be entirely good. The outcome for her was a psychotic breakdown.

I say 'relatively stable' because I am not assuming that a sense of identity is impregnable: it can be affected, distorted and altered by extremes or excesses of various kinds, whether ill-fortune (illness, war, torture, forced migration, senescence) or good fortune (winning the lottery, great fame, great success). Identity develops and is achieved as the individual develops: in ordinary circumstances, one might think of it as the emotional concomitant of physical growth and development, proceeding in parallel with it. In this patient's case, the two were radically separated, and in the same way and to the same extent, her own notions of good and bad remained separate. Any sense of a depressive capacity and consequently any ability to mourn the loss of an ideal object were absent in her functioning. Her terror of being excluded forever from human contact was behind her refusal, or inability to allow negativity into her own behaviour. It cost her a great deal. Life was lived through a series of massive projections and projective identifications. She remained lonely and somewhat baffled by her inability to have the kinds of ordinarily robust contacts and friendships she could see others engaged in.

In the development of a secure sense of identity, an analysis is valuable. One might almost say that this is what analysis is for. In the case of my patient, and during her analysis, two factors led gradually to a greater grasp of reality, and consequently to the development of a stable sense of her own substance and identity, as opposed to the tattered patchwork garment she hid under. The first was a reduction in her tendency to conduct her life through a series of projective and introjective identifications, all concerned with maintaining an absolute distinction between good and bad. The second was her gradual recognition and toleration of the existence of an Oedipal couple. I discuss this development in the later part of the paper, taking the view that the gradual recognition and tolerance of and for that couple, and the consequent differentiation of the self from these primary objects, is necessary for the establishment of an identity – a mind of one's own.

This patient's anxiously defensive 'good' behaviour, although entirely genuine in its efforts, came across as rather different from the mixed, ragged nature of 'goodness' as we ordinarily encounter it, or, indeed, attempt to be it ourselves. In my patient's case, the demand for perpetual good behaviour in self and others was part of an attempt to deal with conscious anxieties of a psychotic kind. She engaged in a frantic attempt to preserve a belief in self and objects as devoid of any real badness when, in fact, both self and object were unconsciously felt to be brittle and unstable. Once a flaw was (reluctantly) perceived, this patient's doubts proliferated rapidly. Objects became feared and hated persecutors, full of malevolent destructiveness. And almost immediately, the patient's view of herself followed the same course. Thus, a situation in which she was unable to maintain a view of those around as good (sane and well-intentioned), or to maintain her belief in her own capacity to keep the world in this state, carried the potential for a feared descent into madness. What was it that had led to this particularly precarious sense of self?

I hope to show how a very early separation and loss had led to a radical split in psychic structure, between absolute good on the one hand and absolute bad on the other hand. This split was fundamental to my patient's pre-analytic character and functioning. Before it could be recognised and understood, the 'good' was overwhelmed and destroyed by the 'bad', in the severe breakdown she suffered. I am going to describe the stage in her analysis with me when this structure first became apparent, gradually and painfully, both to me and to the patient.

Background to the referral

In the patient's childhood experience, there had been a serious and prolonged attempt on the part of the maternal grandmother to install a sense of goodness and badness that was absolute: the presence of one meant the other no longer existed. I describe the outcome of this upbringing, where it was not only a defence but also clearly linked to states of intense anxiety. These anxieties began to be seen in the patient's analysis, in particular within the transference/counter-transference relationship. I shall try to describe the stage in the patient's analysis when there were the first signs of a more realistic sense of her own and her objects' goodness *and* badness, which led to the hope of her developing a less brittle and more integrated psychic reality.

The analysis with me began four months after she was discharged from a psychiatric hospital having suffered a severe breakdown, a paranoid psychosis. This had developed some time after an earlier analysis had come to an end.

The patient, Dr M (whom I call Marie) was in her middle 40s. She was a Consultant Paediatrician in a London teaching hospital, one of a team specialising in the treatment of neonates. When she broke down, she was compulsorily removed from her post and put on sick leave. There was then a lengthy assessment for fitness to take up her position again, during which her work was carefully monitored until, roughly two years after the onset of her illness and eighteen months into her analysis with me, she was considered fit to practice once more.

Marie was a pretty woman, small, neat and well-dressed, with long dark curly hair that she twisted up on top of her head. She was a good patient – she attended regularly and on time, paid her bills at once and expressed gratitude for being helped through this analysis to get back on her feet. However, in the countertransference, I became aware of a high level of tension in myself surrounding each of her sessions. I noticed that I felt I had to do more than be careful with her: I had to *get it right*. I felt anxious about the possibility of a further breakdown.

Part of the problem was that for a long time behind the surface 'brightness', I felt Marie was quite seriously depressed and anxious. And, it seemed that real emotional contact was missing, not only because of her depression. The paranoid psychosis had centred on Marie's former analyst, Dr Y, and it had been terrifying. So she, quite explicitly, did not want to become emotionally involved again and tried to maintain a distance. This was very different from the analysis with Dr Y. My impression was that a silent idealisation of the relationship had existed between them, which had been mutually and tactily agreed upon – that she was the perfect patient and he the ideal analyst. In this setting, she developed a deep and blissful love for Dr Y with powerful unspoken sexual feelings. This state of affairs appeared to have been left untouched and unexamined before this first analysis ended, apparently successfully. Within a few months of the ending, Dr Y issued social invitations to her. His rationale was that 'It will help to resolve the transference'. He asked for her help in referring for medical treatment the child of one of his other patients, and this was followed by an invitation to his next birthday party. Marie became afraid. She had lost her ideal analyst/analysis. He had been replaced by an ordinary man who was behaving in a way that alarmed her. He was no longer without flaw. She asked him not to contact her anymore.

Rapidly over the course of the next few weeks, her image of him deteriorated. From the ideal and adored figure of her analysis, he became a cynical and ruthless philanderer, and still more sinister, a dangerous terrorist who was about to destroy London. Increasingly isolated outside of her work context, talking to no one, she became convinced that she had to act, to save not only London but the whole of the wider Western world from the plan she imagined he was generating with fellow terrorists. She went to the police, who seemed to have recognised that she was ill. They contacted her medical colleagues the same day. She spent several weeks in hospital, medicated and gradually recognising the delusional nature of her ideas and the dreadful reality of her situation – isolated and now jobless.

Marie felt deeply shamed and humiliated by her breakdown. She dreaded meeting the gaze of her former colleagues. Up to that point, she had displayed a degree of omnipotence connected with a belief in her capacity to maintain extremely high standards for herself and her objects. Now, it was all gone. All her life she had tried to be good, and in fact, she was so, not least because she truly wanted to be. She was hard working and cooperative. She was generous, often putting herself out for her friends. She introduced them to each other and then, she felt, saw them getting on better together than she had been able to do with either. Then, she tried hard to conquer painful stabs of jealousy and envy, knowing that these bad feelings were unworthy. But often she felt lonely.

The history

Marie was the oldest of six children, born in southern Ireland to a family of devout Catholics. Her father was a hardworking farmer. Her mother was 22 years old when Marie was born. When the baby was 4½ months old, the mother lost her milk, felt unwell and exhausted and eventually recognised that she was pregnant again. The grandmother, (mother's own mother) who lived in the next village, took over the care of the firstborn more or less totally. Thus, for Marie weaning meant not just the loss of the breast, but also effectively of the mother herself, a radical rupture in the course of her young life. It took place abruptly, and there was no intermediate bottle-feeding: from then on Marie was strapped into a high chair and fed from a small metal spoon. When she was thirteen months old, the second baby, a boy, was born.

Shortly afterwards, the grandmother took *both* infants away with her for the next nine months, to her own house in the next village, while the vulnerable and ailing mother – who during this time fell pregnant with the third baby – was encouraged to rest and get strong once more. And although grandmother and the two children returned to the family home when Marie was fifteen months old, Marie's mother was present but unavailable to her. She was either pregnant or breast-feeding and always exhausted. Thus in terms of caretaking, the two older children remained as grandmother's charges even in the parental home. When the two children wanted contact with their mother, this was 'bad' because it might tire or upset her. It was characterised as 'the Devil'. And Marie ultimately came to believe that she *was* bad even though she behaved properly. Grandmother warned: 'The Devil is inside us always, tempting us to be bad'. If badness was spotted, or if Marie did not behave as her grandmother had required, she'd go to Hell, and Hell, she knew, was a place of eternal rejection and exclusion. She already knew she was bad because she had been sent away, which meant she hadn't been loved – because she was bad. Inside she might feel defiant and angry, but this only overlaid fear.

The children were not allowed to say 'I want'. 'I want' did not get. Grandmother believed that badness in children lay in any and all acts of independent will or desire. Her often-repeated words were 'In this house, "I want" does not exist. Even in the garden of the King, there is not a blade of grass that may say "I want"'. In other words, even if you are dying of thirst, you may not say *I want some water*. It also meant that the statement, or even the wish, 'I want my Mama' could not be said out loud.

However, neither were the children allowed to *not* want. If Marie did not like/want what grandmother had cooked, then grandmother would cook it for the next three days as a matter of principle. Marie kept quiet and swallowed what she did not want. She admired the spirit of her little brother who pretended to eat but hid the food in his pockets. (Perhaps, it is not entirely a co-incidence that he has gone on to have a more ordinary life in terms of intimate relationships.)

The grandmother was as preoccupied with internal physical badness as she was with the mental. She gave the children cod-liver oil every day and routine enemas every week. Thus, their bodies as well as their minds were in grandmother's power and control. This extended to any hint of sexuality. When Marie began to menstruate, her grandmother made her dress in corsets and bodices that concealed any growing roundness or femininity. The idea of pleasure in the existence or the appearance of the body was impossible. Sex for girls was bad, and sexual desire – which might be seen as a special case of 'I want' – was out of the question.

Grandmother's dominance in the child's life had a further consequence in terms of psychic structure. The relationship in childhood that should have been with a couple, with all the emotional and spatial possibilities of *three*, was reduced to a focus on a relationship with *one* – moreover one who had both a fierce moral agenda and enormous power over the child's development. Within the linear arrangement of this one to one, there was less room for the development of complexity or ambiguity, and the split between good and bad was, therefore, more total and maintained more vigorously. In this way, Marie had her identity as a child imposed upon her, thrust upon her, via indoctrination. It had not developed 'organically' and autonomously within the triangular space provided by a relationship with a couple, usually – though not of course always – the parental couple. Thus, the rupture in Marie's early life was followed by a restricted and restrictive upbringing, in which the split between good and bad was forcibly maintained.

The analysis

Marie's analysis with me began with a long period of routine, sensible, helpful, but to my mind somehow pedestrian work. Quite suddenly, two years into the analysis this began to change, more or less overnight. I describe two sessions in which I made mistakes, one in each session. I don't like making mistakes. Sometimes they are inevitable, however hard one tries to avoid them. They may be unforced – 'common or garden' errors. At other times, they could be called forced errors (to borrow an analogy from tennis) when for example the patient puts the analyst under pressure. Then, they may turn out to be enactments of an element within the analysis that had not been clearly recognised, helping the analyst understand something of the unconscious aspects of the here-and-now situation in the room – in this case the tension that I felt with her. My anxiety about *not getting it right* may have reflected both her need for me to be flawless and her own anxiety about making mistakes. As well I may have been getting increasingly anxious that I too could become trapped as an idealised figure in the analysis, with the risk at its end of a catastrophic outcome, as had happened before.

The patient's four weekly sessions took place from Monday to Thursday and this was a Tuesday session. Nothing seemed to me to have been out of the ordinary on the Monday.

Clinical material 1 (Tuesday)

She comments on my persistent cough. She hopes I feel better soon.
PAUSE
P: (*carefully*) Yesterday I thought you sent me away early ....
but later I realised my watch was fast ... .
Today I did not feel like coming.....I have nothing really to say.

(I was surprised, and quite worried — had I really done that? I had been completely unaware of it, which was additionally worrying)

A: I think if you felt I ended the session early you might have had feelings about it and about me, which would alarm you — so you didn't want to come today.

LONG SILENCE

(I continued) It seems hard for you to let yourself think maybe I really did end it early.

P: Well, I thought you did — till I saw my watch was fast some hours later. But I don't know what to say about it because naturally I don't want to......oh, I don't know, nothing I say is right.....*(fretful)*

I was a bit confused here, not only because of being unsure as to whether or not I had got the time wrong yesterday but also because if I had, then surely her watch needed to have been running slow rather than fast if she were to be mistaken rather than I.

PAUSE

A: But what if you *are* right?

P: *(quickly)* Well, it's not a crime. It could happen to anybody. It's not serious, that kind of thing happens all the time ….

A: You are working quite hard to manage this in a reasonable and civilized way.

SILENCE

P: Maybe I'm working hard to avoid turning you into the sort of person who sends me away early — really that's not fair, because I know you are not. It would make you a mindless, strict person who was not interested in me.

PAUSE

A: But supposing I'm a careless or a muddled person — what do you do with that?

P: *(intensely)* I'd have to remove myself. From the analysis.

A: Well, perhaps that's exactly what 'I have nothing to say' means.

P: *(agitated)* I have a terrible fear you could become that — all those things are terrible, unbearable. The worst is careless and muddled, it's confusing, it's a bit mad. At least the other is not confusing. *At least I know where I am.* But muddled – it makes me afraid that I won't know if what the other person says is right, or she might get it wrong. She is very scary for me, I don't know where I am (*upset*)...............my grandmother was always right, then she would contradict herself, say the opposite, and then that would be right too....

She continues by telling me that her former analyst had once responded to a text he had received in the session; at first denied it, and then later admitted it and apologized.

Maybe the trouble with yesterday is you are *not apologizing*, perhaps offering to make up the time or something. At least I can be a little bit angry.

A: But what's really scary for you is if the person you call 'the other person' doesn't even know she's done it.

P: If you become a muddled person *that's the end.*

I think at this point she is in touch with some elements of her breakdown: her object is thin and brittle and in danger of disintegrating altogether. At some point around here I put a pair of difficult opposites to her – muddled but honest vs crooked or deceiving.

A: An imperfect person – isn't it *that* that feels really difficult, like 'the end'? Because it seems easier to forgive Dr Y for doing something that's clearly not on than to forgive me for not even knowing what I'd done.

P: (*She becomes very agitated and begins to cry*). I am afraid that in the exact moment I discover that the person with me is wrong, and they are trying to tell me they are right, then I feel I am living in a Fascist state – I am not allowed to disagree, I have to agree and it is a kind of abuse. This kind of person – she.........

A: 'This kind of person' – that's me, right now.

P: (*sobbing*) The problem is not being angry; it's about what people *do* with my anger.... Maybe this is what went wrong in my first analysis – I didn't say, I wasn't allowed to. I was never sure if it was right or wrong to be angry. So I forgave him because he said the truth. I was a bit brain-washed, I still am, I'm trying hard not to be. In the end you convince yourself you're wrong.

Maybe you become mad – not knowing what you're supposed to believe.
LONG SILENCE
A: (*eventually, firmly*) Look. It seems to me that right now you *do* believe I ended the session early. This gives you a problem. What are you to do, to keep me as a good analyst? Then you find a solution to the problem: your watch was slow.
P: When I had the breakdown everyone thought I was mad, but I didn't, I thought *they* were (*very upset and tearful*)
A: But look, I'm trying to persuade you you're *not* mad!................... it's odd but *I think corruption is easier for you to deal with than fallibility.*
PAUSE
P: (*very small voice, hesitantly*) It's true. In some ways that's right. How strange. When I know it's corrupt, then at least I know where I am.
End of session

It seemed clear that what was most disturbing for Marie was not the thought that she was a bad person, but the thought that *I* was: careless, or muddled – or corrupt, but not admitting it. When I tried to take this up with her, and her anger and distress about it, she was in touch once more with something which to her spelled unthinkable breakdown and madness – 'that's the end'. However, as well, perhaps, her intense upset could just be seen to be the beginning of her mourning for a kind of goodness and a kind of sanity that had themselves been a bit mad or delusional in that they could tolerate no flaw, no fallibility. The fact that I did not admit to the lateness (unsure whether it was her mistake or mine at first), neither did I apologise and offer to make up the time, may even have been the beginning of a new way for her to 'know where she was'.

The following session, Wednesday, Marie arrived very punctually. She indicated that she did not want to talk about the day before. I commented that she was afraid that if she did, something would go terribly wrong in the session. She sighed. The problem for her, she said, is that if she feels I have done something that feels like a rejection, *she begins to hate me.* I become very severe, a nastily and cruelly rejecting person. She said that she does not believe in incompetence and she is very afraid of her own capacity for hate. (The presence of grandmother was palpable in these comments.)

After a long silence, I commented that she does not really trust someone who appears to be good or well-disposed to her – they are only good until the inevitable bad occurs. She is always on the lookout for the mistake that is to reveal the hidden malignancy. I wonder aloud to her if the day before she had been trying to see if I was corruptible if I would accept her explanation of the watch and thus let myself off the hook.

P: *(urgently)* But what does it mean 'good'? Does it mean 'perfect'? That's impossible! OK, if you are not perfect and you make mistakes, well it's OK – No……. *oh I am so confused ………. because what is goodness if there is always badness attached to it? I want it to be perfection, I know it's an illusion, childish.*
(*This was a crucial moment in the analysis, the revelation that there could be no goodness if anything bad were to be present as well.*)
SILENCE

P: I clung to the idea of perfection in my first analysis, it was to protect both of us – from hate.

A: And the fear of retaliation, of *being* hated.

P: That's the worst thing that can happen in my life. All my life I have tried to be good in order not to be hated. Or hating. It turns the world into a horrible place. …….it is the destruction of the whole world.
SILENCE
I think it has stayed in my brain as a part of me, a bodily thing, *I couldn't think it.* It's terribly painful – it's not a feeling, just an awful disturbance, like a storm in the brain.
I commented that being sent away early by me had felt to her like an act of hate…both the first being-sent-away-early by her mother, and this second smaller more immediate one. Actually they were the same thing, evoking the same kind of storm.

SILENCE

P: There is a strange feeling in my brain, like a sort of clicking noise…. what is it, is it things having to join up?

Here I thought the patient was close to her own psychosis: this was not an 'as if' click. It was almost a somatic delusion. It was what happens in her brain when she cannot 'think' something. There is perhaps a kind of shutter that clicks, that comes down and cuts off the intolerable experience and in this way maintains the split created by her upbringing and its fundamental discontinuity. I thought that rather than its being 'things having to join up', it was what *prevented* things from joining up – good with bad, and perhaps also, in a quite different register, mother with father, to produce yet another infant. When she feels hate, her whole world fills with hate and is destroyed. She could not conceive of *not being hated* when she herself felt hate. She lived in a post-nuclear landscape.

After these sessions, I felt I had some clearer understanding of two consecutive dreams that she had had some weeks earlier and which had seemed full of psychotic imagery.

> In the first dream she was surrounded by tiny biting creatures she could not see – she called them 'dust mites'. Suddenly one of them became just big enough for her to be able to see it face to face. It had a red angry face and teeth.

I thought that in this dream the object – the whole world – was broken up into feeling-fragments. The tiny red angry biting face, which just became big enough to see suggested the patient's increasing contact with herself as a red-faced and angry infant, with biting teeth. It was immediately followed by a second dream.

> She was in a room with her mother and her grandmother. Outside the open window the air was full of flying fish, with open mouths full of sharp teeth. One of them flew

into the room and she became very afraid. Her mother told her not to worry, the fish were on their way back to another country.

Here, the bits of her fragmented object, full of her biting feelings, had become larger and more visible – as they had also been in fact in the sessions I have reported. It was frightening to be in the same room with them but also present in this second sequence was a figure who can tell her that they were transit: they would not be there for ever. (Actually, this was probably a considerable overestimation at that point as to the extent to which she could be reassured as to my trustworthiness.)

To continue with that particular week: on Thursday, the fourth and last session of the week, she began by telling me that she had been due to have a review meeting with a senior colleague that morning, but she had overslept and only woken at ten minutes past the appointed time. She thought it was just because she was tired and needed to sleep. It had never happened to her before. I said to her that she was trying out what it was like to be fallible. Perhaps, it was a way of saying to me that it was all right what I had done, because look, here she was doing it too. Marie was dismissive of this and as well of my putting it to her that perhaps I was the person she would have liked to make wait. She spoke briskly and pseudo-sensibly in her 'Consultant's voice': 'Oh I don't know', she said. 'It was just that my alarm clock did not work'.

She was silent, and her stomach began to rumble loudly, always a sign for me that there was something indigestible going on in her mind. The silence continued, and I commented that she wanted to move away from the state of mind in which electrical storms happen in the brain, and into the ordinary world of reality and alarm clocks that don't work. She did not respond.

Clinical material 2 (March)

I now describe my second mistake a few weeks later. Marie always reminded me if I did not give her the bill promptly on the first of the month and always told me when I did so that she would bring the cheque next day – which she always did. That day the bill was ready for her on the little table by the couch but most unusually she did not take it. I put it to one side and prepared the couch for the next patient. Then, I heard her doing something right outside the door – the weather was cold and she was taking longer than usual to put on her coat, so I went to the door and gave her the bill. She smiled and said sorry she forgot it.

A few moments later, I heard her coming back up the stairs, and she knocked on the door to return it to me, telling me, still smiling, it was 'for the wrong patient'. I apologised, found the right bill and give it to her. I regretted my hasty action, and I was dreading the next session because it was quite clear that the other patient, who had had the same number of sessions, paid less for the month than she did.

The following day she was late – she dropped her coat on the waiting room floor and did not pick it up – she was clearly flustered. She said she had been in two minds about coming. Part of her did not want to. There was a long silence in which she was clearly upset. Then, she began a long story about her professional body, which had failed to support her with a grant which they had originally promised to do. She had wept as she went home, feeling she was utterly alone and meant nothing to anyone. For my part, I was sure that this story linked to yesterday's incident with the bill, but I could not, at that point, put it together within the transference convincingly enough to make an interpretation that felt right. I decided to play it straight, feeling I could not let the session end without having broached it.

A: I think that my handing you the wrong bill cannot have helped that feeling.
PAUSE
P: (*in a quite different tone of voice – matter of fact, sensible*) Well, I *was* surprised when I saw the bill – but then I saw the name and realised it wasn't for me. It's not important.

I persisted with my line of thinking, and Marie became upset and agitated. She said she feels she is overlooked and undervalued, both at work and at home, in spite of all her efforts. She thinks the Committee behaved in a mean way. I note that I am living in a nice house, am clearly comfortably off and yet I charge her more than I charge someone else. Like the treacherous Dean, I seem to her mean, refusing her the kind of help I give others. What I say makes Marie burst out:

P: I am afraid that if I start feeling all this hate, all these terrible things, I will become a *ruthless arsehole*.

This was extraordinary language from Marie. It was very different from that used by her modest, civilised 'good' self. It was followed by intense distress over the difference in fee she noticed in the 'wrong' bill, and she sobs while speaking very quickly.

Of course there are differences in what people pay, she may have been coming for a very long time, she may be very poor, she may be very needy………. I know many people charge much more than you …………. (*sobbing, angry*) …. others are more fragile, they need more care maybe…but *I have always had to look after others*, to be the good one…….

This area of great distress, rage and pain touched on much that had been fundamental in her childhood: the loss of her fragile mother, who was not robust enough to manage her baby's hatred for sending her away; the bitterness Marie then felt at not knowing how to relate to her ordinarily noisy quarrelling family so that her exclusion from it survived into adulthood; all that and the fact that she could now let me know how deep her distrust was of me – this ruthless figure who gave preferential treatment to her (analytic) sister. She became impatient in the session, fearing it would all unravel in guilt and psychotic self-doubt, and finally, as it had before, become a delusional conviction that I too was a criminal and terrorist. Exculpating her object seemed even more important than 'behaving well' herself. She was afraid that her defiance and rage, if it did not destroy her object, would engender an implacable hatred, resulting in a cold and permanent exclusion.

Discussion

Although Marie was returned to the family home and the parental couple at fifteen months, this caesura in her early life had lasting consequences. As we saw in the first session, being sent away five minutes early from the session, gotten rid of, was devastating, evoking the experience of a traumatic weaning and separation. In an infant so young, that 'storm in the brain' which *cannot be formulated as a thought* may have been the nearest she could come to recalling that early experience. It had existed as a somatic, bodily series of sensations which could not be understood, merely undergone.

Bion (1967) describes a view of how we develop our psychological apparatus for relating to the world. There is in the new-born infant a perceptual template, a pre-conception of 'a good object'. When the baby encounters the breast and is fed satisfactorily and for long enough, the preconception is made real, is 'realised' and takes on a particular shape: *this* breast, *my* mother. With this *realisation*, there is the potential for a conception, which will give the baby a knowledge of goodness, and an orientation to goodness which will serve for the rest of its life. 'This is mother – and she is mine'.

The pre-conception that was evolving in relation to Marie's mother was abruptly terminated before a stable *realisation* of 'goodness' could be established. Moreover, Marie's mother herself was vulnerable and likely to disintegrate under pressure. She had needed *her own* mother to keep her in one piece, which meant that the breast/mother that Marie encountered and took in during her earliest months was not ordinarily, solidly good. That apprehension, however, precarious it may have been, of goodness in the form of breast/mother, was replaced by a lost mother/breast and a very present metal spoon, administered by someone feeding her while she was strapped into a high chair. The feelings of fear and hatred that this evoked in Marie were characterised as, and located in the Devil: they filled her with a dread that she herself was devilish for feeling hatred. The solution to these difficulties was, from her earliest months, to construct or create *for herself* a good object, which had to be maintained as flawless, kept in one piece by her own efforts. And as I have wanted to show through the clinical material, she had a number of manoeuvres for maintaining her object in this ideal state: denial, exculpation (everyone does it), projection, forgiveness, absolution and so on. When the defences failed, as in the first analysis, the compulsory goodness – which might so easily pass for a solidly based morality – could be seen to be mostly a desperate defence of her own vulnerability. Paradoxically, one could view Marie's breakdown as a catastrophic version of the beginnings of the depressive position: suddenly, she had seen that Dr Y, her ideal object, was also mortal, fallible, no longer a god; and it felt intolerable.

Marie had never again felt she was her parents' child: she belonged to her grandmother. The imposition of her grandmother's moral system, which was effectively grafted onto a none-too-stable rootstock, and the punishments that followed behaviour designated by grandmother as 'bad', meant that her good behaviour was merely a simulacrum of true good. It could admit to no deviation or flaw. It seems to demonstrate the importance of the freedom of the will not only for the growth of identity but, consequently, for truly moral choice, and the growth of a sense of *this is what I am, this is what I think*. The outcome of not being allowed to want, and not being allowed to *not* want was a total suppression of will: of independence of body, of mind and of spirit. This was the basis for Marie's 'swallowing' everything she was told, or instructed in, by her grandmother. And I, of course, had to be constantly aware of the risk of having a 'good' patient, rather than a real one – a patient who learned what I was thinking, who swallowed whatever I had cooked up and agreed with it too readily.

Yet grandmother's rigidity, which to my mind was based on a harsh antiquated rural Catholicism rather than simply mindless cruelty, may, in fact, have held the infant in one piece during the removal from her mother. This may just have prevented the electrical storms in the brain from becoming total, recruiting the whole of Marie's mental functioning until normal development became impossible, making her effectively a psychotic infant. Of course, this rigid structure had nothing to do with a proper containment. Marie had had to be her own container: feelings of distress or longing or wanting or rebellion or envy and rivalry had to be stifled and/or hidden. In this context, an important dream happened early in the analysis. She had been with a group of international medics at a conference. On the last evening, they were all drinking and singing national songs, but she felt unable to let herself go and join in. That night, she dreamed she was in an iron box, with a small grille for a window. She could see out but could not move outside it.

I think this iron box – this strongbox, this *safe* – became Marie's version of containment. In origin, it was the grandmother: by now, it had also become Marie's own iron self-control, requiring a powerful system of splitting between good and bad, which as I have described, eventually collapsed into a psychosis. The fear, and the envy, she had felt of the group's exuberant behaviour, her sense of being unable to join in, which was experienced as being excluded, had had to be kept locked up. Inside the strongbox, she was safe – until the internal pressures became too great and it burst open, exploding into paranoia and psychosis.

So that startling phrase 'a ruthless arsehole' can also be seen to make sense. Babies are born from the vagina, and they are good: they are loved and valued and held on to by the mother. What emerges from the anus is bad – it is expelled and disposed of as shit, both literally and figuratively. When Marie was handed over to grandmother, she felt she became a shit-baby, worthless – indeed bad – and it was mother who was felt to be the 'ruthless arsehole'. This, I think, is the 'thing that cannot be thought' but which produces the storm in the brain, and the clicking noise of the shutter closing. For it was grandmother who held on to her and preserved her in one piece – even loved her in her own ferociously moralistic way. Marie did not integrate her loving and hating feelings for her mother partly because there was a readily available opportunity for a radical split to be maintained: mother was vulnerable, weak (which she was) but nevertheless good; grandmother was harsh and punitive (which she was) and, therefore, bad. Through the split, the infant Marie could preserve her love for her mother, her belief in her as good, however precarious and brittle that imperfectly 're-alised' goodness. Yet, the cost was that at a deep level she could not believe she herself to be good; she continued to struggle against feeling that she was worthless – effectively shit.

When Marie discovered that an analytic sibling appeared to be having preferential treatment, she cried out that if she allowed herself to mind this she would become 'a ruthless arsehole'. There was certainly something ruthless and about-to-expel-something-or-somebody around in the room. But I think she was protecting both me and mother from her murderous hatred when she claimed it as hers when in fact the horror for her is that she thinks she has finally detected it in me. It took a long time in the analysis before we could become confident about these very early and intense processes being experienced as thoughts – in the mind *and in the room* – rather than in the body as the rumbling tummy, the storms in the brain, the chaos or the clicking noises in her head.

As Ron Britton (1998) has described, the movement from the paranoid/schizoid position towards something more depressive is cyclical rather than linear: it has to be worked at and re-achieved over and over again. I suspect that whatever degree of integration Marie will manage may always have to be consciously achieved, rather than organically developed. This movement for her may need watchfulness, hard thought and self-discipline, rather than a secure and confident certainty that she will eventually re-find her good object, bruised but alive in spite of her hatred. It could be thought of as a new system that would have to be discovered, thought about and tested cautiously if it is eventually to install itself *alongside* the existing iron – probably titanium – moral system, with its rigidity and its tendency to split. I did not think it would ever entirely replace the original installation, which was forged in the tragedy of the loss – indeed, the destruction – of the mother's breast and the white heat of fear of the Devil. But my hope was that the original installation would shrink, occupy less mental space, as this different way of thinking about the world, this new installation, could begin to build up fragment by fragment within the analysis.

However, this 'different way' is the autonomous, organic kind of morality that normally develops under more ordinary conditions, leading to a sense of identity. It requires first a fundamental continuity in the most important relationships in a growing child's development. Second, it will include the tacit permission for the child to take part in, and to play its own part in, its third part, in the many potential roles implicit in those same crucial relationships: the passionate possession of one; the exclusion of another; the love of and also the hatred for 'the couple', with all the associated feelings of desire, rejection, triumph and despair. All this, together with the parents' provision of a balance of permission, tolerance, sometimes of course frank prohibition and intolerance, plain old irritability, forms a matrix, a field of emotional possibilities that can be explored in dream, phantasy, play and action. This is the ground in which the child's own psychological and emotional integration – an internal sense of what is good and what is bad, and what is a bit of both – may evolve: one which has not been imposed, nor is the result of indoctrination, but one which has grown and developed when the permissions and the prohibitions have been provided by the same figures who are the objects of love and of hate and have been lived out and struggled through with them.

It is within this triangular arena that love and hate may come to form a durable and confident connection with the developing sense of *what I know is good* and *what I know is bad*. Where there is the chance of an organic connection between these two polarities, and if all goes well, they will come to extend to having a sense of a difference between *what I think is right* and *what I think is wrong*.

Under these circumstances, the developing superego will be able to include permissions, satisfactions, even approval as well as prohibitions and disapproval. This will be the outcome of a relationship with the self/ego, involving a dialogue with that same self. A sense of identity means the ability to consider and assess one's own behaviour, and to make consequent choices. The ego will be robust enough to tell the superego to stop making impossible and/or destructive demands: to get off its high moral horse. It will be strong enough to keep the id in check, or at least to tell it to wait. There is then less chance of a primitive morality, with delusional ideas about absolute goodness and niceness, and a split-off and projected sense of absolute badness projected into the person of the Devil. In other words, it has a chance of being grounded in identity rather than conformity, and in sanity rather than insanity. This makes possible an expansion, a growth in the size and the strength of the ego, in a way that allows the internal dialogue within the parts of the self to grow and develop constructively.

References

Bion, W. (1967) 'A theory of thinking'. In *Second Thoughts: Selected Papers on Psycho-analysis* (pp. 110–117). London: Karnac.

Britton, R. (1998) 'Before and after the depressive position. Ps(n) − D − Ps(N + 1)'. In *Belief and Imagination: Explorations in Psychoanalysis*, edited by E. Bott Spillius (p. 31). London: Routledge. The New Library of Psychoanalysis Series.

6

FAILURE TO MOURN

Idealisation, illusion and identity

Sharon Numa

In this chapter, I focus on a particular aspect of the relationship between failure to mourn and the difficulty in developing towards a mature sense of identity – that is, the way in which the defensive use of idealisation and narcissistic illusion with its seductive promise of perfect harmony between self and object disrupt the process of mourning and, therefore, the possibility of achieving a reasonably coherent sense of identity.

For identity to be established with any degree of security, the anxieties of the depressive position have to be faced and worked through, which involves the recognition of the mother as a whole and separate object. This shift allows what Freud had noted was the ego's natural tendency towards synthesis and integration. With the reduction of persecutory anxieties, the need for splitting and consequent fragmentation of the self is simultaneously reduced. This process promotes greater integration and internal cohesion over time.

Mourning is central to this process of integration: the gradual move towards a sense of reality (Ferenczi, 1926) requires that omnipotence be relinquished and with it the 'ideal'. The recognition that the object is separate (neither possessed nor omnipotently controlled) brings anxiety, but the sorting out of what belongs to the self and what to the object makes possible a more stable and unique sense of identity, as unwanted parts of the self that have been projected are, often with difficulty, taken back; however, good parts of the self are also lost through projection, impoverishing the personality. The 'enrichment of the ego' described by Freud as the consequence of mourning the lost object is dependent upon the capacity to face the reality of loss so that the object can be remembered and 'installed' within the ego, but we could add that it also implies a degree of integration of this kind, that is, the gradual move away from what Klein described as the paranoid schizoid position towards the working through of depressive anxieties. I will be discussing a young woman, an actress who I will call Lila, who struggled to surrender her defensive omnipotence and her phantasy of 'the ideal', unable to face the painful experiences of loss and abandonment.

Vividly conveyed by this patient was her dream-like encapsulation of an idealised time, place and lost object relationship together with her need to preserve the internal object in an immobilised, perfect state. Reality was experienced as being at odds with the patient's survival so that she fought to defend against knowing about both external and internal reality. Lila created instead an alternative reality, a *fairy tale dream world*, sealed off from psychic reality, and aimed at splitting off the bad, hated maternal object together with the associated 'bad self'.

Lila's 'dream world' was an excited idealised world filled with ideal objects in relation to an ideal self, at the heart of which was an ideal mother/baby unit. The early years of her analysis were marked by a kind of manic energy, and a completely uncritical enthusiasm for analysis.

Both Freud (1917) and Klein (1935) have described mania as part of a complex pathological response to loss. I think Lila 'lost' her object (the attentive, receptive focus of the maternal object) long before her mother actually died when she was only ten years old, a tragedy which reinforced Lila's reliance on omnipotent manic defences. It seemed that there was an absence of an available containing object able to manage the infantile anxieties that arise in the face of early loss. Erik Brenman (2006) notes:

"The capacity to mourn separation and loss does not arise **de novo**. It has been built up before in a relationship with a mother …" who has "coped with the problem of frustration, greed and anxiety."

(p. 30)

In 'Mourning and Melancholia' (1917), Freud describes the melancholic solution to loss – identification with the lost object, as aiming to evade knowledge of underlying *ambivalence* towards the object. He describes 'the work of mourning' as allowing pivotal distinctions to be made between *phantasy and reality* and between *self and object*, distinctions necessary for psychic growth (and *pari passu*, essential for identity development as we argue in this book). Freud remarks that if the lost object is not only identified with but idealised, this pathological identification may indicate 'a loss of a more ideal kind'.

Grinberg (1978) further links object loss to a loss of the *sense of self*. He notes that a meaningful object tie often carries with it a particular self-image, a role or sense of self unique to that relationship. 'Faced with the loss of an object one rushes to the mirror to find out what has become of one's own image' (p. 245). I think the disruption to identity that he describes must be greater where there is a pre-existing narcissistic object relationship in which the patient attains perfection by 'becoming' an ideal self through projective identification with an ideal object. As Klein has shown, idealisation of this kind can only be sustained through omnipotent phantasies and mechanisms. Identification with the lost idealised object is one form of 'turning away from reality'. Importantly for the question of identity, it simultaneously implies the phantasy of an 'ideal self'. Holding a standard of perfection for the self is clearly an unrealistic basis on which to develop one's identity.

Even in normal mourning, there is resistance to reality: the 'bit by bit' process by which we accept the evidence of reality (that the object no longer exists) is slow and painful.

In a later paper, Freud (1924) speaks of the role of phantasy in creating a domain, 'kept free from the demands of the exigencies of life, like a kind of "reservation"' – a split-off area of the mind. Illusion may become preferable to the mental pain of psychic reality, but illusion relies in varying degrees on denial, disavowal and splitting. Healthy, more flexible compromise solutions to conflict are, thus, no longer available to the ego. The ideal object becomes split off from the persecutory object and only a part of the patient will relate to a part of the object. The integration required for identity stability becomes impossible.

Projective and introjective mechanisms often play a role in creating the sort of 'alternative reality' Lila vigorously attempted to sustain. Sodre (2004) writes interestingly about extreme shifts in a person's sense of identity caused by 'massive projective identification', linking it to Rosenfeld's (1964) work on narcissism. I think that Lila used the phantasy of unity with the object as a holding structure for the self, sacrificing the development of a unique and separate identity. Even in the absence of such massive loss of a sense of self, there are threats to identity caused by shifting, shallow identifications which are without real *meaning* to the patient but which offer a spurious and temporary sense of 'identity'. This is particularly salient in narcissistic patients such as Lila, and her profession as an actress, furthermore, provided infinite opportunities for transient identifications and for her to enter 'roles'. These were often tragic roles and I felt that on and off stage she was 'acting the pain she really felt'.[1]

Lila's beliefs and opinions often seemed fused with the latest idealised object. This problem of 'who's who', of course, presented itself in the analysis between us. Were developments in the analysis due to her identification with me or to deeper internal changes? I return to this later.

The problem of narcissistic illusions and their relation to reality has a longstanding history within psychoanalytic thinking. Narcissistic states are marked by *over-valuation*, whether of the self, the object or both. Idealisation distorts the real qualities of self and object since it confers illusory value. Such states are normal in early development and they retain a place in psychic life as Winnicott

(1971) has argued. However, tenaciously held illusions that continue to create profound splits within the person's inner world inevitably compromises integration and orientation to reality. Where the primary relationship fails, *gradual disillusionment* is disrupted with significant developmental consequences.

My experience with Lila in the analysis suggested that there had been a failure of internalisation of the good object so that facing separation and loss, as well as working through oedipal anxieties, remained highly problematic. The patient developed instead a kind of 'innocence' or literally 'ignorance' about the real nature of her objects and the relationship between them and about certain aspects of the external world – her dream world being marked by a child-like naivety and 'not knowing'.

Klein has described how the recognition of damage to the object and to the self can prompt the ongoing internal work of reparation – restoring the good object through love. The phantasy of an ideal 'innocent' self must, therefore, be given up. It is important for the question of identity that the individual comes to recognise and accept that it is 'the same me' that hates and inflicts damage as the 'me' that loves. The loss of 'innocence' is inevitable once depressive anxieties are truly faced.

However, since stability of identity will often come under pressure, it is perhaps realistic to emphasise the capacity to *regain* contact with parts of the self and with the good object when this contact is lost.

I will try to describe both the transference as I understood it, and my countertransference difficulty in challenging Lila's 'fairy tale dream world' as well as her gradual move towards greater integration.

The analysis

The romantic phantasy of innocent harmony surfaced within the analysis in the form of a 'transference illusion' with its atmosphere of specialness (Britton 1989, 1999). The only emotion that my patient seemed able to tolerate was a non-conflictual affection. She was a lively and engaging patient who would frequently point out tastes or ideas which she assumed I shared with her. Lila had a capacity for both warmth and humour. However, if I raised the issue of difference, including the inescapable difference of my being a black woman, she would feel pushed out of the special relationship and would then circumvent the notion of 'difference' in a way that retained *her* view of reality. For example, she said that my being black if anything showed that I was special; after all, how many black analysts were there? Perhaps I was the first… or the only one in the country? These thoughts were then used to confirm to my patient that we were a very special couple. However, it seemed to me more important to Lila that I was a woman and, as she believed, a mother, than the fact of my being a *black* woman. Racial anxieties did, however, emerge later in the analysis when issues of her superiority, her 'princess' identity could be examined.

Lila's world of pleasurable contact and child-like affection was a seductive one and I became, in Britton's terms, 'complacent' (2004), feeling I had a pleasant, cooperative and interesting patient, failing for some time to attend to my unease – namely, the sense of the analysis and of my own identity as an analyst being colonised by this charming patient. For in fact Lila was in search of an ideal mother, not an analyst and I was being gently prompted to fulfil that role, as described in Sandler's (1976) seminal paper on 'role responsiveness'. At the same time, she felt threatened by any idea of dependency, expressing an anxiety that psychoanalysis would change her, and in particular rob her of her creativity. Any attempt to put Lila in touch with a difficult psychic reality seemed to be experienced by her as an attack on goodness and love, as if I had made a brutal assault on her world of innocence. The patient would feel wounded and misunderstood, I tended to retreat and Lila reasserted her dream world through which prism her perceptions and observations were filtered. She both unconsciously invited me to join her in her 'dream world' – in fact, a type of psychic retreat (Steiner, 1993) – while allowing me to imagine that she had entered my analytic world. It was some time before I became fully aware of an aspect of my countertransference: my tendency to retreat and protect her from 'disillusionment'.

Not only was Lila's dream world intended to sustain an illusory safe place with an ideal mother, it also abolished the image of a cruel and damaging father whom she secretly held responsible for her mother's death. She later admitted to a belief that her mother died 'from a broken heart', a blow inflicted by father's infidelity and abandonment. This represented a catastrophic, cruel parental intercourse, a painful link that had to be disavowed. To be in touch with the psychic reality of her own triumph over the collapsed mother or hostility towards her father would mean revising her view of him and also of herself as a wholly innocent, loving and sweet daughter. This was after all her 'identity'.

The patient's history

Loss and death were important elements of Lila's family history. She was born in X where she lived for her first six years after her parents were forced to flee Europe for political reasons. She had an older sister, Teresa, who had accompanied her parents abroad. In the European town whence her parents fled, her mother's family had a long and prestigious history and were held in high regard. Lila's grandparents were wealthy aristocrats and, at one level, she saw herself as participating in an idealised historical myth. Unfortunate events subsequently led the family to return to Europe.

Lila's mother immediately set about realising her cherished project — building what she called her *dream house*, high on a hill overlooking their seaside town. This luxurious house with its swimming pool often appeared in my patient's dreams. Indeed, I believe that her fairy tale dream world became fortified in identification with her mother's 'dream house', serving as a defence against the catastrophe that followed — the reality proved to be a crumbling edifice. Before the 'dream house' was completed, her father announced he was having an affair and left to live with his mistress. Lila was eight years old. Her mother collapsed and became profoundly depressed over the next few years. She spent much time in bed, utterly crushed. My patient had memories of lying with her in bed, either soothing or 'entertaining' her mother, believing herself to be mother's only sustenance. (The entertaining little girl was clearly present in the consulting room.) Her mother was eventually found to have a heart condition and died very suddenly.

Lila described herself as mother's 'adored princess' and her mother as '*innocent, dreamy, wonderful, naïve* and *too good for this world*'. She was described by their devoted maid as 'not made for the dirty nappies of life'. I pictured her mother as a fragile, narcissistic woman: a distant, beautiful but elusive object of desire. Lila's close identification with her mother was clear.

Lila 'adored' her father; he was her beacon in the practicalities of life. She glossed over his manic tendencies and his womanising, a denial that was a source of conflict with her older sister who considered her to be 'blind'. After a number of relationships, father eventually began a stable relationship and remarried. At the beginning of her analysis, Lila was in very frequent contact with him. I noticed that he also leaned on her, often confiding in her rather inappropriately, which fostered her oedipal illusions and manic excitement.

Unconsciously connected to her oedipal ascension, Lila had underlying fears of being discovered as an 'impostor' rather as when she had 'copied' school work or 'busked it' in class.

As I got to know Lila, I noted the different levels of identification, including that of identification with her 'energetic' father which served an important defensive function, a life-line taking her away from the image of the lifeless, depressed mother in need of 'repair': however, her identification with a manic penis for purposes of repairing damage was, of course, doomed to failure.

Lila suffered a somatic collapse as a teenager and she brought a variety of somatic problems when she entered analysis (for which she often sought esoteric 'alternative treatments') which I will not address in this paper but which I thought to some extent had become linked to her identification with the maternal body, the lost object, the nagging symptoms acting as an unconscious, continuous reproach to the mother. Her somatic symptoms ameliorated over the first few years.

Lila had trained as an actress and a singer. Early in the analysis, she told me that she hated the idea of becoming a mother, declaring she would *never* have children – interesting, given her idealisation of the maternal role.

In the initial consultation, Lila told me that she had 'a happy childhood', and I registered the stark contrast to my own feelings as I listened to her moving and very sad story. However, she also said quietly and with an uncertain smile: 'Sometimes I don't know who I am'; in that moment, the sense of Lila being a lost, confused little girl made a powerful impression on me. It also indicated early on a problem with her sense of identity.

Lila sought analysis when a highly idealised relationship of her youth failed to deliver her 'London dreams'.

First phase of the analysis: idealisation, illusion and nostalgia

An inescapable feature of Lila's sessions was a mood of nostalgia, relating to her country of birth: a distant time, place and a relationship with an adored mother. Sohn (1983) argues that while nostalgia can be a normal part of working through a painful loss, excessive nostalgic retrospection can keep the object in a 'psychic limbo' where it need never be truly relinquished. Werman (1977) also makes an important and clinically useful distinction between 'normal' and 'pathological' nostalgia, the first reflecting a continuation of mourning while the latter acts as an *idealised blockade*; an opposition to the 'facts of life' such as death (Money-Kyrle, 1968, 1971).

In her sessions, Lila conveyed a sense of timeless lingering in the past, a painful yearning, which also conveyed the idea of rupture from an idealised experience. She would nostalgically ruminate about her paradise lost, her country of birth, 'a la recherche du temps perdu' (Proust (1960)). There were vague sensory memories, imprecise in terms of detail but images that romanticised her 'country' and the parental couple of that time. As Proust so well understood, nostalgia becomes tied to sensory memories, the tastes, smells and sounds of past experience. In his famous description of tasting the 'petite madeleine' in Combray, he beautifully describes how this sensory experience evokes in him 'this unremembered state'. Among her vague ruminations, Lila did point to one sharp memory – a particularly pleasurable one of 'charming all the adults at the ice cream stall', which confirmed her 'sweetness', a quality she felt her mother valued. This sweetness also entered our sessions.

Lila would quite frequently comment on details of my person – always in a natural way like a small child, in a manner that did not seem to require a response. At this stage of the analysis, despite this atmosphere of intimacy, she often seemed more alive in the past than in the here and now. I recalled Anne Alvarez's description of a patient who 'was like someone walking backwards into the future, looking longingly at a brightly lit past' (2009, p. 305). I was also struck by Lila's insistence on, and perhaps search for, a 'true self' (her words) that existed 'there and then' before the age of 5. In this she was in some way acknowledging a feeling of inauthenticity in her present experience of herself. Nayman (1991) in discussing temporality in relation to the narcissistic personality describes a similar patient:

> this man clings to a past self that feels more substantial and to which he attributes the feelings of authenticity and vitality so painfully absent from his present adult experience.
>
> (p. 484)

The relation of identity to time and continuity is an important one and has been referred to in the Introduction and in other chapters in this book. Here, I will just mention the work of Akhtar (1996) who outlines two types of common phantasies linked to nostalgia, but which he argues are in fact *defences against mourning*: 'Someday' and 'If Only' phantasies. I think both have a powerful element of illusion. He describes the former as idealising the future; they foster (often baseless) optimism, while 'If Only' fantasies idealise the past and lay the groundwork for nostalgia. While universal, he suggests that if they enter character pathology, they are ego depleting. Both, he argues, though particularly 'if only' fantasies, are accompanied by a pervasive search for the idealised lost object suggesting that underlying these positions there is a central horror and fear of facing loss, which handicaps the emergence of a sense of self grounded in psychic and external reality. In the pursuit of the ideal, deeper object relationships are sacrificed. In fact, both 'If Only' and 'Someday' fantasies appeared to be integral to Lila's dream world. Theatre with its promise of fame and recognition, being seen, provided fuel for her 'Someday' fantasies.

There was certainly a theatrical aspect to my patient's presentation and personality and, although she was not a typical 'as if' personality (Deutsch, 1942), nor was she a typical hysteric, there were elements of both within her character structure.

In the first weeks of analysis, she brought an interesting dream:

> I had to go on stage unprepared and did not know my lines or what I was supposed to do. But I just thought "I'll busk it", and I went forward. My father was in the audience sitting next to a schoolfriend of mine (who 'adored him'). He was smiling and clapping.

Lila associated 'busking it' with her schoolwork: she had often *copied* other children's work since her mother never helped her with homework. (She told me this as if it was an amusing idiosyncrasy of her mother's.) She then associated to an actor whom she worked with and admired because he had been able to 'step into a lead role' at short notice.

I am reminded of Britton's (1999) revisiting of the case of Anna O: he describes an oedipal drama where the patient ascends the stage and takes on the part of one or other of the parental objects. At the time I took up Lila's possible anxiety about what 'part', she was expected to play here with me (as if the analysis might be a piece of theatre); it seemed she was planning to manage her anxiety by 'stepping into my shoes' while being applauded by a narcissistic, father part of her, felt to support an inauthentic part of herself (the 'impostor').

As an actress, Lila was always rather blindly optimistic, an optimism frequently untempered by proper reality orientation (which occasionally led to painful narcissistic wounds). Theatre and the gaze of the audience were itself meant to afford the narcissistic supplies she craved, the search for the lost maternal focus. Phyllis Greenacre (1958) describes how being believed in by an audience can offer 'a temporary feeling of completion of identity' through the 'intoxication of being in the limelight, (which reproduces the infantile situation with the general public taking the place of the mother)' (p. 1036).

Separateness and separation

Initially, Lila barely registered separations: holidays and breaks were 'no problem' since, she would say, 'you are with me'. I thought this did not indicate a real sense of a supportive internal object, but rather a description of complex projective and introjective unconscious phantasies. She continued in my absence the type of relationship described by Betty Joseph (1989) in her essay on patients who cannot 'suffer' psychic pain. Joseph suggests that early in the analysis 'holidays and gaps can be non-experienced.... because such patients retreat into their world and keep up a type of internal eurphoric relationship with the analyst' (p. 90).

Eventually, holidays did become very painful for Lila but at this stage various excitements were recruited to 'fill her up' in the gaps. These were often situations in which partial or wholesale projective and/or introjective identifications took place, either with me or with idealised figures in her profession.

Vignette

Over a particularly long weekend break during which she was filming, Lila 'took over' an adjoining film set that belonged to a cookery programme once that shoot was over. She assumed ownership of the food on the table and invited members of her own cast to eat. She commented: 'they were like excited children', hungrily eating the excellent food, until the enactment was abruptly brought to a humiliating end by the return of the actual programme Producer who angrily threw them off the set. Lila came to her session extremely enraged and indignant.

I suggested that the extra days of the bank holiday break had pushed her into a very difficult state of mind, and to cope with this, I thought she had in her own mind 'become' the abundant breast, the 'producer', and I was no longer experienced as absent; the hungry needy child was projected into the members of the cast. This phantasy was sharply deflated when she was forced to recognise her 'size' – as one of the siblings – when the producer returned. She was affronted by the implication of his behaviour: 'Who do you think you are?'

Despite the embarrassment she began to feel during the session, my understanding of this episode seemed to help Lila as she could briefly allow contact with the feeling that she had, indeed, missed her sessions. I was able to point out the disorienting effect on her sense of identity produced by 'stepping into the shoes' of a phantasy version of me as the abundant (and possibly superior) mother.

There were occasions which puzzled me at the time when Lila would quite suddenly and unconsciously 'turn away' in a ruthless decathexis of both me and the analysis, something I understood better much later. Ambivalence was enacted, never acknowledged. Lila attended absolutely regularly but was nearly always late, particularly before breaks, but this 'meant nothing', relating this tendency entirely to her European temperament. On one occasion before a break, Lila told me that after her mother died she would not talk about it at school, in order to ensure that she 'could survive as the same me' (a false continuity of her sense of self). I felt that I would survive as the 'same' analyst, the good analyst, and she could be the 'same' good patient, if she could disavow the fact of my absence, splitting off her envy and jealousy of my family, particularly as she was convinced I was an ideal mother. I remembered that when Lila began her analysis, she was also determined that 'nothing should change her', defending the fragile identity of being a 'happy child'.

Lila did often express great sadness about the loss of her mother; she would sob curled up on the couch, significantly always wrapping my blanket around her, in a rather dramatic way, but I would tend to feel as if we were watching a sad romantic film together, rather than Lila really being in touch with the loss or indeed with an object that felt real. Freud's words echoed: 'He (the subject) may know whom he has lost, but not what he has lost in him (the object)' (1917, p. 245). Lila's episodes of tearful recollection would elide with talking about a romantic film, ruminations, for example, about *The Bridges of Madison County*, as if film and reality were all one. This was, however, a delicate situation and not always easy to judge correctly.

In a session before a long summer break in the following year, Lila arrived very late saying excitedly that she had been out with a 'very sexy, attractive' actor, P. Further material and particularly the tone of what she said made it clear to me that she was treating both her boyfriend of the time, who I will call Richard, and her analysis with careless contempt – though this of course was denied. I thought there was now an unconscious denigrated version of me as the 'boring woman at home' (a phrase she had used to describe married women stuck with children). *She* was out with an exciting man/father, justifying her actions by impatiently describing Richard as clinging, always needing to be with her, irritating and no fun. (I assume *I* was no fun, and I needed *her* to be with me.) As well as repeating a childhood scene, this mood seemed intended to reverse her experience of exclusion as we approached the break. Beneath the idealised maternal figure, Lila associated feminine identity and receptivity with a needy 'clinging' part of her now projected into Richard and myself, a part of her full of anxious, angry, messy feelings (the 'dirty nappy') which she imagined I did not want. Was the 'bored' mother/analyst a version of the depressed mother?

Clinical material

In this situation, my main countertransference difficulty was 'the problem of disillusionment'. To illustrate my difficulty, I will describe an ordinary Monday session in the second year of analysis.

In the previous Friday session, I had spoken about Lila's difficulty in knowing what was real inside her (what true, what false), perhaps questioning if I knew who *I* was. My patient was dismissive, appearing quite irritated as the session ended but smiled as she left.

Monday

Lila entered in a lively, excited way saying: 'On the way out on Friday I noticed a book on your shelf …Neruda's "Macchu Picchu"…He's one of my favourite poets! So – you like it too!' She went on to talk about having understood what I meant during that session about 'feeling real' – a phrase I had not in fact used. She 'got it' and had walked around for some time after the session: 'it was so good to feel real'. (This was clearly meant as a gift but in fact created a sense of discomfort in me.)

I said that perhaps my comments had registered in some way but had been transformed into something she could walk around with in a concrete way.

Lila seemed disappointed and I immediately experienced the familiar feeling that I had been hurtful. At these moments, I think Lila unconsciously experienced me as her critical sister but this could not be allowed to surface.

She quickly went on to talk about one of her flatmates, D., who was depressed, she had just lost a boyfriend. D just watched TV, the patient made dinner but declined to eat herself and she wasn't hungry. She offered D her thoughts on remaining 'true to herself', 'being real', seeming to have become a version of me/a therapist.

I said that I thought she had left annoyed and upset on Friday, feeling instantly that I had created distance between us, and that just as instantly this had led to an excited defensive union with me via the rather dizzying Heights of Macchu Picchu as she left my room.

(Lila laughed, then said she had not felt irritated on Friday.)

I elaborated rather carefully on how I felt she had incorporated me and my words and felt 'full', projecting into D the depressed part of her that felt excluded and abandoned both by the weekend and by what I had said.

Lila seemed to 'leave the room', becoming chatty about engaging films. I said that part of her was now outside of the consulting room engaged in a virtual reality. (I noticed she had been keen to stress that, for a change, it was D who fell into TV watching – not her.)

Lila did not respond directly but seemed more present and went on to tell me a story about E, her other flatmate, as if to prove she had genuinely felt 'real' following Friday's session. E had, in an underhand way, bought a dress on Saturday that she knew my patient had chosen for an upcoming wedding party and moreover paraded the dress for Lila's approval. She had expressed her 'real feelings' of anger. 'She admired the dress then stole it; I was furious!'

I felt sympathetic to Lila's annoyance, aware that on this occasion, she was fighting for a dress she had chosen, not 'copied'. At the same time, the material brought to mind the way she too would 'steal' or go 'shopping' for an identity (for example, in projective identification with me). Today, we were to be united in harmony, a wedding, through our shared love of Neruda while ignoring underlying ambivalence or conflicting feelings.

With some difficulty I tried to take up these various points.

Lila protested vigorously, saying she had even worked well over the weekend on a number of tasks.

I said that she now felt me as hurtful and rejecting, accusatory, rather than trying to deepen our understanding.

(The session felt stuck. I felt this type of 'scrutiny' was upsetting Lila. This was confirmed by what followed, but in a way that seemed potentially useful.)

As we neared the end of the session, there was a change of tone: Lila said she would have liked to speak to me on Saturday because her camera woman, S, had upset her by saying that her eyes looked lively until she 'zoomed in' when they looked dead. S wanted to redo the shoot in a different light.

I acknowledged how difficult she found my different light as I looked through my analytic lens, which she was afraid might reveal that the 'liveliness' she so often brought hid something much more anxious and depressed.

Unusually, Lila did not reject this out of hand and left the session thoughtfully.

I thought that the 'dead eyes' were perhaps a reflection of the dead gaze of her depressed unavailable mother who could not reflect her child and had ceased to be a source of vitality, experienced by Lila as psychic abandonment.

Despite these difficulties, there were positive developments in Lila's external life, which made it at times difficult to discern what was really going on in the analysis. I suspect at this point, Lila was acting in identification with me, rather than as yet moving towards real separateness. On the other hand, my countertransference was also shifting as I had 'woken up', recognising my own frustration with – and to a degree collusion with – her 'dream world' and its stultifying effect on the analysis. I had become more robust and perhaps unconsciously more of a 'real' object for Lila instead of the phantom object of idealisation.

From 'blindness' to insight

Gradually as Lila's trust in the analysis grew, she could begin to acknowledge the loneliness, pain and disappointment when I was absent as well as the opposite – her fear of being engulfed and lost in my identity (a projection of her own acquisitive tendencies). For a period, she responded concretely to this fear by turning down in panic those acting roles that required her to be a 'mother', lest she get 'trapped' in that maternal role.

There were, of course, shifts back and forth in the process towards greater contact with psychic reality.

At a certain point, Lila had rebuffed in a cruel way Richard's invitation to go and live in his 'poor village' in another country. This would be a lifeless place she asserted, horrified. It led to an important dream, which marked the beginning of an increased capacity to 'know about' the more cruel angry and superior parts of herself.

> I am in my house (mother's dream house) on top of the hill…it's beautiful. There's the swimming pool, it's sunny. I feel my mother is there behind me, though I don't see her. I am looking from the hill down to where lots of people are. They look very small.

Interestingly, Lila said rather sadly: 'this is a bit of a princess dream isn't it; I don't like that about me'.

I said that she felt I too had invited her to come and live in a 'poor village', in contact with a 'poor and empty' part of herself making her feel threatened and anxious, so she had retreated to her superior 'beautiful' position.

The vertical 'up and down' relations of power described by Sodre (see Introduction) showed itself clearly as Lila projected herself into an idealised breast, while looking down in contempt on the 'small people' who were 'beneath her', with whom she had vigorously dis-identified. Not seeing me/mother behind her could have meant a number of things (in someone for whom *being seen* and looking was highly important), but was she in the dream turning her back on the mother who was unconsciously experienced as turning her back on the patient (leaving her feeling small and empty)?

In the sessions that followed, I spoke to her about an area of her inner world that felt 'lifeless' like her fantasy of R's village, linking this to a dream where she was sitting in a very small room next to her mother's coffin, in stillness and darkness. I was also able to link this and later material to her recent associations to Jose Saramago's book 'Blindness', to her attack on sight and insight and to her own devastated internal landscape reflected in Saramago's description of that terrible place.

The deadness she so feared, hidden beneath her liveness was not only an identification with a lost dead mother but I thought was created by her killing off a vital, feeling and painful part of her. In this frozen state, she could neither mourn nor gain strength from being a more 'whole' self. I think Lila felt that recovering those parts of the self would mean a re-traumatisation, facing her with pain guilt and helplessness – and the knowledge that her liveliness could not keep her mother alive either mentally or physically. I understood that she feared total internal disorganisation.

We were finally able to allow space for the 'small' needy aspect of herself as Lila's fear that I and other important objects might 'look down on' her vulnerable self receded; persecutory anxieties were diminishing and there was greater openness in the analysis.

Following this period of work, for the first time, Lila described a very violent episode which took place in her mother's 'dream house'. She remembers herself as hiding beneath a table, terrified, during an assault on their maid while her mother was 'brushing her hair in her room', oblivious.

I suggested that inside *her* dream world there was also a violent reality which she, in identification with an internal mother who does not see or hear, was afraid to know anything about. I added that she feared her loving 'good self' would not be able to protect her good objects from her violent uncontrollable attacks.

Lila now told me about an experience she had in the US many years before I met her. She had been shocked and frightened by an episode of vile racism which she had witnessed. She was bewildered because she had felt identified with the abused denigrated black American. Unable to stay in the US another minute, she had enlisted the help of her father to get her back home immediately where, she was able to say with some shame, she could regain her sense of herself as a 'white' princess restoring her position of superiority.

Lila began to understand that her omnipotent princess 'identity', owning the breast at the top of a hill, involved a defensive superiority, but this made her deeply uncomfortable as she was also very kind to the devoted maid whom she loved and helped financially. In the transference, I suggested I was a well-treated, but lowly black servant dependent on her largesse. I suggested that she 'treats her slaves well'. Although Lila found this extremely difficult to think about, the fact that I seemed able to tolerate her having an unconscious denigrated version of me without retaliation was important. Racist thoughts were not at all ego syntonic for Lila, but she could at least explore aspects of this hated 'self' (perhaps a 'black' self that she had had to flee from).

Understanding had begun to take the place of a merciless internal object or superego, which, in turn, meant that Lila could begin to 'see', to face the idea of damage and guilt. Her dilemma was a painful one: how could she attack a damaged object or one that was experienced as already vulnerable, perhaps crushed and humiliated? How could she be strengthened by an object into whom these aspects of the self had been projected? Nevertheless, the process of re-owning what had been split off had begun.

From 'identity with' to a sense of identity

The path forward was not an easy one. Now in Lila's fifth year, there were periods when she became very depressed, or frightened and angry, and I was concerned. She felt I was taking away her protections, and she would be left as she now was, exposed. Her mood in these very intense sessions alternated between anguished tears, fears of collapse and fury with me. She was terrified of having a breakdown, like her mother. However, she was also always able to return for her next session, and I felt there was trust in the analysis. It was also clear that she was relieved to 'rediscover' me each time, intact, and felt sad and deeply ashamed about the many occasions on which in a split-off way she had treated me and those she undoubtedly cared for with haughty indifference. She could also understand that she treated the more vulnerable aspects of herself with a certain contempt and she could begin to integrate not only the rageful baby and child but the 'small weak' aspects of the self.

Being sensitive to Lila's vulnerability to humiliation as she emerged from her narcissistic organisation, in fact facing the collapse of her phantasied dream world, felt terribly important. Steiner (2011) likens the shame that arises on emerging from a psychic retreat to the nakedness and shame upon expulsion from the Garden of Eden, the lost paradise.

> The patient who has hidden himself in the retreat often dreads emerging from it because it exposes him to anxieties and suffering – which is often precisely what had led him to deploy the defences in the first place. However, the first and most immediate consequence of emerging from a psychic retreat is a feeling of being exposed and observed. It is here that feelings of embarrassment, shame and humiliation commonly arise.
>
> (p. 3)

Over time, Lila's objects were gaining in reality, and her intense identification with me lessened. She had begun to be much more aware of me as a separate object (perhaps, she mused, having 'different tastes and desires') an object that could, therefore, be lost, which naturally created anxiety. During this phase, I believe Lila was moving from using or borrowing her version of *my* identity towards her own separate identity. I could interpret that she now seemed to see that what I might want for her was not that she be a version of me (the narcissistic mother) but that she might be herself.

Steiner (1989) describes a two-stage process in understanding the role of mourning in identity development which I think is relevant to Lila's analysis: the first in which an object is used as a container to 'collect the disparate parts of the self which he receives through projective identification' (p. 115).

This is a necessary phase, during which the object *gives meaning* to the projected fragments, but full withdrawal of projections and reintegration does not take place he suggests until a second stage, which represents a move towards independence.

During her sixth year of analysis, the patient developed a relationship with a man, 'A', in which for the first time, she allowed real intimacy and vulnerability. Running in parallel with these developments, there was a significant shift in her oedipal phantasies. She had always consistently *turned a blind eye* to her father's weaknesses and his startling exploitation of her financial legacy from her mother. Some of the aggression she had seen as belonging to her sister now became more available to her. Lila could bear to know about another, hidden, image of a father that was seen as 'asset stripping', a man whom she felt also devalued and destroyed her mother – a painful view of the parental couple. She could allow these thoughts to exist alongside her love and gratitude to him, but the child-like idealisation was modified. She became more aware of thoughts about the possible man in my life – the existence of a 'third' outside of the special dyadic couple. Each of these stages brought sadness and feelings of loss, together with a wish to cling onto her 'dream world'.

Later material showed how an oedipal configuration had been superimposed on a more frightening mother/baby couple. A shift in her internalised oedipal situation allowed Lila to approach even more closely the many 'faces' of a more disturbing mother and a desperate child. She recovered a vivid memory from age 7:

> I was in the pool of our house. It was a lovely sunny day. My mother was standing by the side of the pool, holding a mirror – a round hand mirror – adjusting her hair. I called out because I wanted to show her I could do handstands in the water. I was shouting: 'Mummy! look at me! Look at me!' I got more and more frantic, jumping wildly trying to get her attention. She kept saying 'in a minute'…but she never did look.

This poignant memory, which produced a feeling of real pain, represented how dropped Lila felt, out of the eye and mind of the object. But, it also described the prototype of her object relationships, with its many reversals: now the frantic child, now the narcissistic mother. I could understand those moments in the past when I would feel suddenly 'dropped' as she 'turned away' from me to narcissistic excitement – her own face in the mirror. Winnicott (1956) writes: 'What does the baby see when he or she looks at the mother's face? I am suggesting that, ordinarily, what the baby sees is himself or herself', This he says, is generally taken for granted, but 'many babies….look and they do not see themselves'.

This has consequences for identity development which in its earliest phases relies on the mirroring eye of the mother.

Later, Lila was also able to tell me in some distress, that on the day of her mother's death, when she was asked to go to the hospital urgently, she had refused – continuing instead to become fixated on a virtual game on the computer. We could understand her belief that in the analysis she could only survive if I looked at my world, the analytic screen, while she looked at hers, the dream world.

Conclusion

It seemed that a premature loss of the ideal object had propelled Lila into a life-long search for this lost ideal object, a search that became greatly intensified by her mother's untimely death and the absence of an available emotionally mature containing object. Instead, Lila relied on omnipotent manic defences which created a closed defensive system – organised to evade mourning and the anxieties of the depressive position, cementing the split between her idealised 'self' and her 'bad' self. With containment came greater integration, emotional meaning and a sense of continuity and cohesion in her sense of self.

In moving towards the depressive position, Lila faced what had always been an irreconcilable unconscious conflict: the so-loved object was also hated and attacked for its betrayal and abandonment. In mourning the phantasy of symbiotic union, her identity could find a foothold in reality. A 'good enough' self, for a patient like Lila, is often shunned as a poor substitute for narcissistic perfection, but if accepted can render an imperfect but authentic self while allowing for the internalisation of a good though flawed object.

Lila was able to develop a sense of herself as a woman and enjoy her sexuality; she developed a close and meaningful relationship with A, who was to become her husband, and with whom she later had two children. The termination phase of the analysis raised many countertransference feelings, as the analyst must also be able to 'let go' if the patient's identity is to feel truly separate. Despite her sadness and anxiety, Lila was able to face and work through the process of mourning without terror of a catastrophic collapse of the self.

Note

1 Fernando Pessoa 'Autopsychography'.

References

Akhtar, S. (1996) '"Someday..." and "If Only..." Fantasies: Pathological Optimism and Inordinate Nostalgia as Related forms of Idealization'. *J. Amer. Psychoanal. Assn.*, 44: 723–753.

Alvarez, A. (2009) 'The Case of Luisa'. *Psychoanal. Inq.*, 29(4): 304–313.

Brenman, E. (2006) *Recovery of the Lost Good Object*. London: Routledge, The New Library of Psychoanalysis.

Britton, R. (1989) 'The Missing Link: Parental Sexuality in the Oedipus Complex'. In *The Oedipus Complex Today* (p 83–101), edited by J. Steiner. London: Karnac Books.

Britton, R. (1999) 'Getting in on the Act: The Hysterical Solution'. *Int. J. Psycho-Anal.*, 80: 1–14.

Britton, R. (2004) 'Complacency in Analysis and Everyday Life'. In *In Pursuit of Psychic Change* (pp. 69–83), edited by E. Hargreaves and A. Varchevker. London: Brunner-Routledge, The New Library of Psychoanalysis.

Deutsch, H. (1942) 'Some Forms of Emotional Disturbance and Their Relationship to Schizophrenia'. *Psychoanal. Q.*, 11: 301–321.

Ferenczi, S. (1926) 'The Problem of Acceptance of Unpleasant Ideas: Advances in Knowledge of the Sense of Reality'. *Int. J. Psycho-Anal.*, 7: 312–323.

Freud, S. (1917) 'Mourning and Melancholia'. *SE*, 14: 237–258.

Freud, S. (1924) 'The Loss of Reality in Neurosis and Psychosis'. *SE*, 19: 183–187.

Greenacre, P. (1958) 'The Impostor'. *Psychoanal. Q.*, 27: 359–382.

Grinberg, L. (1978) 'The Razor's Edge'. *Int. J. Psycho-Anal.*, 59: 245–254.

Joseph, B. (1989) *Psychic Equilibrium and Psychic Change: Selected Papers of Betty Joseph*. London and New York: Routledge, The New Library of Psychoanalysis.

Klein, M. (1935) 'A Contribution to the Psychogenesis of Manic-Depresssive States'. *Int. J. Psychoanal.*, 16: 145–174.

Money-Kyrle, R.E. (1968) 'Cognitive Development'. *Int. J. Psycho-Anal.*, 49: 691–698.

Money-Kyrle, R. (1971) 'The Aim of Psychoanalysis'. *Int. J. Psycho-Anal.*, 52: 103–106.

Nayman, S. (1991) 'Temporality and the Self: A Phenomenological Study of the Narcissist, the Schizoid, and the As-if Personality'. *Psychoan. Contemp. Thought*, 14(3): 479–503.

Proust, M. (1960) 'Swann's Way'. In Volume One of *Remembrance of Things Past*. Translated by C.K. Scott Moncrieff. New Mills, UK: Chatto & Windus; Originally published A La Recherche du Temps Perdu (1913–1927). Paris: Grasset and Gallimard.

Rosenfeld, H. (1964) 'On the Psychopathology of Narcissism: A Clinical Approach'. *Int. J. Psychoanal.*, 45(2–3), 332–337.

Sandler, J. (1976) 'Counter-Transference and Role-Responsiveness'. *Int. Rev. Psychol.*, 3: 43–47.

Sodre, I. (2004) 'Who's who? Notes on pathological identifications'. In *Pursuit of Psychic Change,* London: Routledge. Edith Hargreaves & Arturo Varchevker p. 82–101.

Sohn, L. (1983) 'Nostalgia'. *Int. J. Psycho-Anal.*, 64: 203–210.

Steiner, J. (1989) 'The Aim of Psychoanalysis'. *Psychoanal. Psychotherapy*, 4(2): 109–120.

Steiner, J. (1993) *Psychic Retreats: Pathological Organizations of the Personality in Psychotic Neurotic and Borderline Patients*. London: Routledge.

Steiner, J. (2011) *Seeing and Being Seen: Emerging from a Psychic Retreat*. London: Routledge, New Library of Psychoanalysis.

Werman, D.S. (1977) 'Normal and Pathological Nostalgia'. *J. Amer. Psychoanal. Assn.*, 25: 387–398.

Winnicott, D.W. (1956) 'On Transference'. *Int. J. Psycho-Anal.*, 37: 386–388.

Winnicott, D.W. (1971) *Playing and Reality*. London: Tavistock Publications.

7

IDENTITY AND THE STRUGGLE TO "BE" IN THE FACE OF DISTORTING PROJECTIONS FROM AN ILL OBJECT

Philip Crockatt

Introduction

In this paper, I describe the problems of Ms H whose difficulties in establishing her identity were, I believe, exacerbated by repeated exposure to the mental illness of her mother and her elder sister, who both forced into her versions of herself more to do with their own repudiated problems than with an accurate perception of Ms H. The experience of "intrusive" objects left her with deep confusions about who she was. Her confusions were relived in a crucial phase of a long analysis during which Ms H physically assaulted her analyst at moments when she felt misperceived and intruded into. I suggest that Ms H's phase of violent behaviour can be understood both as a constructive attempt to return her ill object's "alien" projections to their rightful location but also to get across to her analyst the experience of being invaded by another person's projections. Her hope was that her analyst might be able not only to weather the storms involved in this turbulent experience but also to help her sort out what belonged to her and what belonged to her object. In this way, she hoped both to gain a firmer sense of herself and be able to see her objects more clearly.

Central to understanding the problem of the "intrusive" object and the impact on the child are, I suggest, the phenomena of projective identification (Klein, 1946) and introjective identification (Freud, 1917). Klein focused on projective identification as an early defence of the child, and on the resulting problem of the distorted perceptions of parents. Neither Klein nor her early followers emphasised, however, the reciprocal problem of a parent actively projecting parts of themselves into their child and the consequent distorted perception of the child or on the consequent problems for the child of being pressured to introject and to take on an identity required by the parent. It is self-evident, however, that projective identifications move in both directions, from parent into child as well as from child into parent. It is also likely, given a child's dependence, that projective identifications from parent to child will be extremely influential. In "good enough" families, we assume that these are relatively benign and that parents perceive their children reasonably accurately. In families where the parents or siblings are severely mentally ill, it is likely that children will be exposed for long periods to the distorted perceptions of their ill parents or siblings.

There is, indeed, a significant literature, from the 1950s onwards, suggesting that the distorting perceptions of ill parents are a significant factor in the development of mental illness and problems of identity in children, for example, Bateson et al. (1956), Searles (1959) and Laing and Esterson (1965). Within the more recent psychoanalytic literature, Selma Fraiberg (1975) has described the experience of "ghosts in the nursery" in which an alive, present child is confused in the mind of the parent with a dead figure from the past. Rosenfeld (1983) stresses the importance of recognising the patient who has suffered "an intense intrusion of projective identification from close members of his family" (p. 265), noting that such patients often need to project violently to deal with resultant tensions. Gianna Williams (1998), through her long experience as a child psychotherapist working with the impact on children of ill parents, has described the projective activity of ill parents as "omega" function. She deliberately contrasts this with the "alpha" function, which Bion describes as the hallmark of the healthy, containing parent. Williams elaborates typical defensive manoeuvres that children use to try to deal with these invasive experiences. Paul Williams (2004) has written of the "invasive object". David Simpson (2014) has written about the problem of being the "wrong child" from the parents' point of view. Wilhelm Skogstad (2013) has described the experience of the "intrusive" object, looking both at the way an impenetrable object can be experienced as intrusive but also referring to the problems for the child when the parent is actually intrusive.

In our introduction, Sharon Numa has emphasised the view of our seminar that an essential prerequisite for identity formation is the experience of a containing parent. Containment of two kinds, we suggest, is necessary for the development of identity. First, the child needs a mother who can both stand and understand primitive, potentially overwhelming experiences and feelings. Ignes Sodre has emphasised that the emergence from narcissism, a fundamental stage in the development of a separate identity, can be experienced as arousing traumatic and paranoid, "up-down", versions of the parent child relationship. Frances Tustin (1973) has described the problem of the "explosion-producing gap between phantasy and reality" (p. 25) over which the mother needs to nurse the child. The role of the mother at this point is through her love, strength and containing capacities to help the child with his potentially overwhelming feelings of disintegration, of intense and mixed feelings of love, hate, terror and persecution. Having achieved this, the containing parent needs, second, to be able to perceive her child relatively accurately, rather than, for example, as a narcissistic extension of themselves. Extreme levels of parental narcissism, often associated with mental illness in the parent, can lead to serious failures of containment which involve distorted perceptions of the child based on parental projective identifications. Familiar examples of this problem occur in the experience, for example, of replacement babies, as mentioned above (Fraiberg op. cit.).

What happens to a child and to their identity when they are on the receiving end of distorting parental projections? I will consider three possibilities. One outcome, as Gianna Williams (1997) suggests, is that the child fights to keep the projections out, by developing a system of "no-entry" defences in an attempt to hold onto their own identity; refusing to eat, for example, but, sometimes, becoming impenetrable in all areas. A second outcome is that the child might identify with the intrusive parent, a process described by Anna Freud as "identification with the aggressor" (Freud, 1936). Through this introjective identification, the child becomes the intrusive object and may find a figure into whom he can project, mastering the original, passive experience by turning it into an active one, in the way described by Freud (1920) in his discussion of ways of dealing with trauma. Both the no-entry defence and identification with the intrusive object enable the child to keep out parental projections, but in the former, there may be a disastrous retreat from relationships, and in the latter, self and object may become confused, as in melancholia. A third outcome is captured in William's description of some children as "porous", by which she means more open to taking into the self the content of parental projections. The "porous" child introjects and takes on the identity ascribed to him by the parent, often with a sense that this self-sacrifice is required in order to help an ill parent maintain their sanity or psychic equilibrium. In practice, all three ways of dealing with the experience of being intruded into by parental projections are likely to co-exist in the same child or may be employed at different times. In the case to be described, I will suggest that Ms H. was a "porous" child in her early life, but as she grew up and then during her analysis she began to fight vigorously to keep alien projections out, both through developing no entry defences and through identification with the aggressor.

The implications for identity formation of these experiences are profound. The "porous" child internalises what Williams describes as a "foreign body", a version of the self-suffused and confused with elements of the object. Ron Britton (1998), describing the same phenomenon, refers to the introjection of an "alien" internal object in patients whose parents were seriously psychiatrically disturbed. The consequent problem for the child in developing their own identity, and subsequently for patient and analyst, is to disentangle what is self and what is object in the experience of intrusion. It has been noted that this sorting-out process may involve the patient re-projecting the "foreign body" into the analyst in as violent a way as it was projected into the child (Grinberg, 1962; Rosenfeld op. cit.; Williams op. cit.). I will suggest that this is what, in essence, happened in the analysis to be described and that Ms H's violence was not only an expression of negativity, or illness, but had a vital role in establishing her identity.

Clinical material

The patient's history

Ms H aged 23, at the start of the analysis, had one sister, five years older. Her mother was an ill woman, abandoned as a teenager by her own mother. She had struggled with drug problems and perverse sexuality but was "rescued" by the patient's father, a successful lawyer who was himself depressed, and at that time was undergoing intensive psychoanalysis. On meeting Ms H's mother, he left his analysis, probably, we could speculate, locating his problems in his disturbed protégé, and started a family. The patient described her early years as relatively good but suffused with an idealised feel. Her mother believed herself to be the perfect mother of perfect children. As the children grew, however, she returned to her old ways, drug-taking and becoming sexually promiscuous. When the patient was 9, her father gave up trying to "cure" his wife, and the parents separated, the two girls going to live with their mother. They were exposed to parties at which drugs were consumed and perverse, sexual behaviour took place. The patient has a memory of being sexually abused at the age of 12 by a male partner of her mother's. When she told her mother she said that Ms H was a sexually provocative little girl and that whatever happened she had brought upon herself.

Both daughters developed severe difficulties in adolescence. The patient, who is bright, began to fail at school, left at 16 to become a waitress and began to follow her mother's pattern of drug-taking and sexual promiscuity. After two years, she tried to change her life by going to live with her father who was more stable. Her sister had a major psychotic breakdown and was found an analyst by her father. She too moved in with their father, attending analysis, with spells in hospital when necessary. Her sister's delusional system involved Ms H, who was confused by her with their "perverse" mother. By the time she was 19, Ms H decided that living in her father's house was unbearable and she moved in with a friend, an older divorced woman with young children. For some years, she had a more stable life. Her friend recognised that she was intelligent and encouraged her to take "A" levels and to go to university, which she did.

Referral for treatment

Ms H decided eventually to leave her friend's home, wanting to "reclaim" her own life, and she returned home to live with her father and sister. After this move, however, she developed serious problems. Her mother was now living with a man who was a drug addict. Ms H embarked on a campaign to try to get her to take some responsibility for causing the family's problems. She struggled constantly with her sister's delusions about Ms H being "a pervert" and the cause of her illness, a projection into Ms H of their mother's illness. At the same time, she had confrontations with her mother which would sometimes lead to Ms H physically attacking her. Ms H was also very frustrated with her father, who was well intentioned, but struggling. Overwhelmed by what was going on Ms H had a breakdown. She attempted suicide and spent a short time in hospital. Her father arranged a consultation with a psychoanalyst whose opinion was that though Ms H had been in a serious (borderline) psychotic state, she was insightful and might be able to use analytic therapy.

First phase of the analysis – who's doing what to whom? The intrusive object located extra-transference – in the family

In the early work with me, Ms H alternated between moving expressions of gratitude that for the first time in her life she had someone who listened to her and extreme distrust, expressed as sneering contempt for me as the latest in a long line of intrusive objects, or as she called us, "abusers". I was experienced as labelling her as sexually provocative and psychotic. As a result of repeated interpretation of this situation in the transference, Ms H began to trust me more. She then embarked on a sustained effort to get across to me her experience of a lifetime spent in an ill family and how this was still continuing in her current life. As I listened to repeated material about confusing and disturbing family events, I began to feel that taking up Ms H's internal states and the transference, though essential, was not enough. I felt she needed a "mapping of her landscape" (Roth, 2001) that took in both her current life and her history – experiences in her external as well as her internal family.

I will now describe part of a session at this time as an example of the material that led me to adopt this perspective.

Clinical vignette illustrating Ms H's experience of and reaction to her sister's illness

One day Ms H reported that her sister had railed at her in ways echoing, yet again, her descriptions of their mother's perverse behaviour. She was "a tart, perverse and sexually provocative". Her sister was in a mad, angry, deluded state, demanding she agree with her. Though Ms H's father was present, he could not restrain her sister. Frightened by the intensity of her sister's hatred and fearing that she would physically attack her, Ms H resorted to what she felt was the only solution that seemed possible at the time – she stripped naked. This had the effect of silencing the accusations and her sister recovered temporarily from her psychotic state. Ms H, however, felt confused, shamed, humiliated and worried that by stripping she had confirmed her sister's distorted view of her. She told me of other occasions when she had tried to withstand such attributions and had been beaten up by her sister.

She went on immediately to tell me for the first time a recurrent dream she had had since she went to live with her mother and sister after the divorce. *She was trapped on a ship, occupied by dead and half-dead creatures, whose entrails exuded from their bodies, touching and dirtying her.*

The transference meaning of this dream was clear for me, capturing a terrifying version of the relationship with her analyst, and this was what I interpreted first. Ms H said angrily that I was not listening to her, she needed me to connect with what was happening to her in her family. I felt, at that moment, that Ms H was right. She was not just being defensive. It seemed to me, on reflection, that "the point of urgency", as Klein describes it, was at that moment extra-transference. I felt she needed me to be an effective father, a "third object", with eyes to help her see for herself who was who and what was going on in the disturbed interaction with her sister. We came to see this incident and her dream as paradigmatic, representing her experience of a family in which she was exposed to the world of illness and madness, and in particular of objects against whose invasive projections she felt helpless.

Listening to many repetitions of such material in her current life with her mother and sister, I developed the hypothesis that my patient's exposure to her mother and sister's illness in the present was also a recreation of their mother's ill projections into both children in the past. I thought it likely that Ms H's solution in adolescence, as in this current incident, was to accept and introject the "alien" projections; to become a version of the sexually provocative object, probably allowing her mother to preserve a self-image of herself as sane, in the way she had described her sister regaining her mental equilibrium when Ms H accepted her mad attributions, but at the cost of identifying with an "alien" internal object. Ms H and I now began to see this process as the source of her rage with her family and at the root of the violent outbursts. This view of her difficulties also helped deepen our understanding of her fear of my potential intrusiveness in the analysis. From the time these issues were clarified, Ms H became determined to develop her mind, her capacity to see for herself and to make sense of her relationships – to undo the passive responses to her sister's and mother's illness.

IDENTITY AND THE STRUGGLE TO "BE"

Over the next two years, Ms H began to make significant moves in this direction, successfully taking "A" levels, qualifying in a caring profession and moving into a house of her own.

Second phase of the analysis: who's doing what to whom? – The "intrusive" object in the analysis, "here and now"

After several years of treatment, Ms H's problems emerged fully in the transference. Though she had been very angry with me at times the violence was only so far expressed toward her mother and very occasionally toward her father. Her father was diagnosed with a terminal illness amplifying, perhaps, the need to find a robust father in the analysis. Explosive issues began to surface in the sessions around two familiar areas; first, the labelling of Ms H as sexually provocative, and second, the diagnosis of her as psychotic, like her sister. I suggest that these two issues, linked to her mother's and sister's problems, formed the core of the "alien" projections with which Ms H had to struggle.

Who is the perverse one? The patient's experience of being perceived as perverse by a perverse analyst

I will describe first how the issue of perverse sexuality erupted in our sessions. As noted, Ms H had always been seen by her family as sexual and provocative and she was blamed for the sexual abuse she experienced at the age of 12. Ms H, in turn, believed, with increasing conviction, that she had actually been innocent sexually at the age of 12 but had been drawn into her mother's perverse world. She had tried repeatedly to get her mother to accept this, and now, this battle erupted in the sessions. Ms H read critiques of the way psychoanalysis treated sexual abuse and became angry that analysts contribute to the confusion by blaming children for sexual abuse. Freud, she claimed, had initiated the lie that little girls were "begging for sex", a lie she, therefore, believed was adopted by me. She was furious at any attribution of sexual feelings to children. She began to scrutinise every word that I used and to find me guilty of slips of the tongue and forms of words that revealed my own unconscious "abusive" thinking. She pounced, for example, on the word "seduced" which I used once in a session. She was enraged. What had happened to her was not seduction, which suggests a sexual act. What happened was an act of violence, of rape, perpetrated by an adult. She became increasingly certain and vehement about this. She began also to be furious about my suggestion that she had identified with her mother as a defence against facing painfully mixed feelings stirred by seeing her mother and her illness clearly. This interpretation had, up until now, been seen as helpful. She now felt it implied that she had had enough mind to choose to be sexual, like mother. What she increasingly wanted me to understand was that she felt that until recently she had had no mind. It was not enough for me to interpret that she felt her mind had been shattered; I had to agree with her that her mind certainly had been shattered. At these moments in the sessions, I was under pressure to agree that I was abusing her by not understanding this.

It was extremely difficult to hold on to my analytic identity faced with this onslaught. Ms H used her growing intellectual powers to sow seeds of doubt in me about my unconscious attitudes to her as a woman and as a patient. I realised she needed me to take her views seriously, to accept that she was raising issues that might well be problematic for me personally and may well be a continuing problem for all analysts. Sometimes, I succeeded in being able to accept her experience of me as unconsciously abusive, to allow even that my profession might indeed be fallible and to describe her resulting predicament with me. At other times, inevitably, I would become defensive, or even found myself arguing back, which only made things worse, and she would shout at me. After one such episode, Ms H, whilst very angry, overturned a table and threw a lamp at me. Over the next period of treatment, there was a series of violent incidents in which objects were thrown at me or pictures in the consulting room. Occasionally, I was attacked physically and had to restrain Ms H and protect myself. For a period of about two years, more stable work alternated with times when the threat of this sort of violence hung over the sessions.

A step towards understanding what was happening between us was linked to my discovery that I could nearly always contain the threat of violence by accepting entirely Ms H's version of events. I experienced a pressure to repeat, in a mantra like way, "I understand that you have been a victim of violence, from your mother, your mother's friend who abused you, your sister, and now from me". Saying these words always calmed her. If I deviated one inch from this formulation, for example, suggesting "you *feel* you have been abused", Ms H would threaten violence, clearly feeling her version of reality was being questioned. The pressure was to agree, without thinking, without analysis, that I was an abuser, that responsibility for every aspect of the violent incidents was mine. At times like this it felt I was at risk of being intimidated into not having a mind of my own. It came to me gradually that I was experiencing the pressure to enact Ms H's own "porous" solution to dealing with her mother and sister's invasive projections, to internalise and agree with them. If I switched off my mind and shut my eyes, there would be no quarrels. I began to interpret to her that she needed me to really know what it felt like to be intruded into, to be on the receiving end of violence, which was why she did what she did. These interpretations began to alleviate the situation as Ms H conveyed gradually that she felt understood.

My early attempts to preserve my freedom to think about and to describe this situation invariably went wrong. For example, in one session, I thought I noticed a sequence of events that lead to a violent incident. The first event happened inside Ms H's mind, a memory of being called "seductive". Through some kind of "pressure into enactment", I found myself using the loaded word "provocative" in describing her behaviour. As this kind of thing happened many times in retrospect, I suspect I was being nudged unconsciously into the position of the bad object, but at the time it felt as though the word just slipped out – I was being crass and insensitive. The word "provocative" set off an assault on me. Now the internal persecutor was external, in me, and I was accused and attacked. The experience reminded me of Segal's (1993) description of living out her patients' "predictive dreams" – I felt utterly powerless, like a puppet. My attempt to track such sequences was experienced by Ms H as me taking back my initial understanding of my own culpability and reverting to blaming her. As time went on, Ms H became more used to my dogged attempts to follow such sequences. She began to tolerate these explorations and eventually to participate herself in the process of disentangling.

A session in which the analyst was experienced as misperceiving Ms H as "mad" like her sister

The second issue that stirred Ms H to assault me was any suggestion that she was psychotic, like her sister. I will now describe a session in which this happened. The session was preceded by a phone call from the patient after a family event during which Ms H had lost her temper with her father and hit him. During the telephone call, she was distraught, alternating between remorse and blaming me and my "useless therapy" for not helping her to control herself. I was anxious about the state Ms H was in, wondering if I should phone her GP, but encouraged her to come to the session the next day which she did.

Session material

As Ms H came in, a piece of the couch cover was trapped in the door. She said, "I feel sorry for that piece of cloth, don't you?" She released the cover and smiled. She said she had seen the patient who precedes her. She hates this woman who looks like a mental patient. Coming to sessions is like being with her family, it makes her ill. She burst out, "Why do I need therapy when I'm normal?"

I said she felt trapped by me into being a patient; she feels coming here for treatment is undermining her normality; I am pushing illness into her.

IDENTITY AND THE STRUGGLE TO "BE"

Ms H agreed warmly. I needed to think carefully about whether she needed treatment at all. She had managed to survive in her ill family. She spoke about her father's birthday party and how ill her sister is. Her father has devoted his life to trying, unsuccessfully, to look after her sister, as he had done with their mother. Her sister is his only priority.

I said she felt I did not see her strengths, only as mentally ill like her sister. She wanted me to recognise how hard it was to deal with her fears of losing her father and of her fury with her ill sister. She had badly needed to speak to me about these feelings last night but seemed worried this meant she was mentally ill. I referred to this predicament as a trap.

Ms H said then that just before the parents' separation, she saw one of her mother's lovers going into the family house. When she confronted her mother, she denied it and accused her of having a dirty mind. She had felt utterly alone and wondered if she should tell her father. She decided not even to remember what she had seen with her own eyes because it would only cause more quarrels. She said she had remembered the incident, right now, for the first time. There was a vivid sense of Ms H recovering her capacity to see, of her memory coming alive.

I said you are remembering having to shut down your own mind and to deny what you saw with your own eyes but are now feeling you can see what was going on.

She smiled and said she was pleased she had remembered that. It was a sign that she was increasingly able to cope. She began to elaborate on this. She went on at some length talking about her growing mental prowess, with mounting excitement. I found myself worrying that Ms H, after a moment of better contact, was getting manic and might need extra support between the sessions. My next intervention was, I think, prompted by these anxieties.

I said she needed me both to recognise, that she has eyes and a good mind, but also that she needs my help with her disturbing feelings, particularly as she gets stronger and connects with her anger, as had come out last night at the party.

Here, Ms H's mood changed. I think it likely that she picked up my anxiety about her mental state. She replied, angrily, "You assume I need more and more therapy, which suits you, just fine. It's just endless money for you!" She went into a rant that I was familiar with about the greed and self-serving motivation of analysts.

I described the change in atmosphere. When I talked about her needing my help, she felt I had lost touch with her; I was now just self-serving, pushing illness into her, taking away her pleasure in her ability to see things clearly.

She said, crossly, that what she needs is normality and kindness, not therapy. She relented a bit and appealed to me, less angrily, "With a family like mine I've done alright, haven't I?"

I said she wanted me to recognise her ability to see and to deal with the serious illness in her family and her feelings about it. At the same time, she is worried about managing between sessions, needing me to register how upset she was at the party and how difficult the next month will be as she has to deal with her father's cancer. I referred again to the trap, the difficulty in feeling that allowing her need for our sessions was tolerable.

This interpretation calmed Ms H. She described feeling scared and alone. She felt angry and isolated. She became reflective and sad. She regretted hitting her ill father. She wondered if she should go to her GP and ask for some Valium. Ms H then stopped short and grimaced. It was as though having heard herself give voice to this thought she rebuked herself. Her mood changed to anger. She shouted at me, "But Valium is for sick people, people with 'mental illness' who need hospital"!

It is here, at this point, I think that I lost touch with Ms H. I took her remarks about Valium as a sensible recognition that she might need extra support from her GP, not seeing that she had moved into feeling persecuted by the "alien" intrusive thought that she was psychotic like her sister. I think she may have needed me at this point to interpret simply that she was worried that the therapy was not enough to help her upset states, particularly her grief and anger. As it was, I think she experienced what I actually said as a projection into her of my own real anxiety that she was in danger of a psychotic breakdown and that I could not cope with her.

I said to her that she was worried that the therapy is not enough. I went on to suggest that she was feeling as a result of the outburst at the party, perhaps sensibly, that a discussion with her GP about options if she felt in crisis – medication, or even the respite of hospital, might help.

At this point, Ms H screamed at me. "What did you say? Hospital? You want me to go to hospital? Do you? Options, you say, well I must consider the option that you are mad, mustn't I? You call yourself a psychoanalyst, but you're mad"!

I said she felt I had misunderstood her; that I myself was over-anxious about her, had lost touch with her strengths and was now pushing my own anxieties into her.

This interpretation came too late. She shouted, "Do you know what a mental hospital is like"? She picked up a wooden bowl and threw it at me, then the telephone. I moved to restrain her, but she walked away. She shouted, "Are you going to work with me, can you take it"? I found myself saying that I would continue to try.

She shouted, "Try! You've got to do better than that! I'm certainly not coming back here"! She then walked out of the consulting room, tipped over a chair in the waiting area and left the house slamming the door.

I felt shattered; anxious for Ms H but also upset that I had failed her at a crucial moment. In supervision, I understood that she needed me to hold on to the belief in the containment provided by the analysis. I reached a feeling of some confidence that she would get back to me – we had survived several such incidents. The next evening Ms H did indeed telephone. She was, during the phone call, alternately remorseful and raging. She was furious with me for saying I would "try". She accused me of being the cause of the outburst. I had, by going on about hospital, undermined her confidence. She shouted that she has a good mind and is successful at work. She screamed at full pitch, "Endorse my sanity"!

I said she wanted me to endorse her sanity by encouraging her to come to our next session to look at what had happened, as I thought the understanding of these events was central to her difficulties.

Ms H was on time for her next session, calm and reflective. A friend who has witnessed her angry outbursts suggested she attend a religious retreat, but she thinks our sessions are what she needs. She confirmed that she felt I had given up on her when she heard me speak of hospital. She talked of being alone with her fear and grief about her father's illness, and her sister deteriorating. We went over the session, establishing that what had provoked her was me losing touch with her particular problems, seeing her as ill like her sister rather than in her own way.

Comment on session

In several sessions, as here, I believe that I found myself projecting into Ms H my own anxieties and misperceptions, provoking violence and the worry that the treatment might collapse. In an amalgam of my own difficulties being triggered – here, my anxiety about whether I was equipped to deal with a patient in a disturbed state without looking to a doctor – and Ms H's need actively to recreate and to re-enact a living experience of dealing with her "alien" internal object, I believe I became at times an actually intrusive object, which she let me know was a frightening, mind destroying and violent experience. The only way she could get this experience across to me was to put me through a similar experience; through her own violent assaults, she frightened me and all but destroyed my capacity to think. I was encouraged to enact a version of the ill object but also to be the child whose identity was being threatened. Ms H was herself struggling with confused fears of perverse sexuality and of psychosis, fears many times forcibly projected into her, which she needed to get across to me as a step toward defining the "foreign body" in her mind. She needed my help in disentangling the ideas that she was perverse like her mother and as mad as her sister from a clearer sense of her own disturbance.

As this view of the violent episodes in the sessions became more established, Ms H. would often say, moved and appreciative, "Now you understand". She began to be able to threaten violence rather than actually be violent. Discussion of these tense experiences became very important for her. For the first time in her life, she could understand the violent attacks on her mother, father and sister and how, up until now, these had always rebounded on her, inviting her family to say, "You see, you are crazy"! Her ability to hold on to the experience of this understanding was fragile, however, and she needed to repeat the experience on several occasions, until, over time, the violence between us, real and threatened, faded away. I think she needed our relationship to survive, not just once, but regularly enough to experience and to internalise a mind able to think when being projected into in a violent way.

Subsequent developments

The turbulent period of the analysis described in this chapter turned out to be crucial for the work with Ms H. I think it led her to get a firmer hold of her identity in a new way. She came to feel she had at last been able to confront the intensity of her rage toward her ill mother and sister and she was grateful that together we had survived the experience. She dealt with the subsequent death of her father, including sorting out arrangements for the ongoing care of her sister, which fell to her, in a mature way. She grew in confidence in her professional work. She managed to find a *modus vivendi* with her mother, accepting that she would never be the mother she dreamed might exist, or a mother who could admit her difficulties and the impact these had had on her children.

The analysis continued for several more years. Very slowly, Ms H was able to allow curiosity about and exploration of her sexuality, and even to think about this as part of her childhood experience, without feeling that she or I or the analysis were perverse. I think she re-connected with herself as an ordinary, sensual child, able to disentangle herself from a distorting, "foreign body" view of herself as perverse whenever she allowed herself to experience sexual feelings. Something of this, a more ordinary Oedipal experience, was worked through in the transference. She eventually met a man with whom she developed an important relationship, the first relationship of any depth she had had. Her partner got a job overseas and she decided to move abroad with him, and to finish the treatment. She was happy about this decision, feeling that as well as separating from her analyst, she could now let go of the entanglement with her mother and sister and that her own life was beginning again. Since the end of treatment, I have heard occasionally from her. She sought my advice about an analyst in the country where she now lives, but overall I hear she is doing well.

Summary of themes

As I have suggested above, the central work of the analysis was for Ms H and I to try to disentangle what was self and what is object in her experience of intrusion, in order for Ms H to find her identity and have this "endorsed" by her object. The sorting out process that took place between us involved Ms H re-projecting the "foreign body" into me in as violent a way as it was projected into her as a child. This is what, in essence, happened in the turbulent period of the analysis I have described. Once again, I would like to emphasise that Ms H's violence, though it had disturbing resonances, was not primarily an expression of negativity, or illness, but it served a vital self-preservative and communicative function. The violence was, I believe, primarily about establishing her own identity. As a child, Ms H adopted the "porous" solution of agreeing with her object's version of her. She dealt, initially, with her mother and sister's ill projections by internalising and identifying as part of herself what had been attributed to her, with devastating consequences for her identity and for the development of her mind. Though angry confrontations with her family were avoided for many years, this was at the cost of being driven to become what she eventually saw her mother was and required her to be – a perverse, "low-life" figure. As she developed no-entry defences and began to identify with the aggressor, the intrusive object, she became uncontrollably angry and violent in ways that her family linked with her sister's psychotic illness, amplifying her confusion. I had to struggle to see that Ms H's violence was not simply a symptom of illness, and to reach a different, more containing view than she had experienced before in her family of origin. I think that in her earlier life, Ms H's emerging identity was eclipsed by the introjection of a "foreign body" version of perverse sexuality forced into her by her mother and later reinforced by her sister. She was unable to manage this experience except through explosions of violence alternating with remorse.

Until the analysis, Ms H was unable to grasp the nature of her own problems, confused as they were with her mother and sister's difficulties. During the analytic encounter with me, she was able to re-live the experience of being intruded into, and her violent response to this, gradually enabling us to see what was going on. She not only began to effectively keep out projections from me, that is she developed no-entry defences, but she began to re-project violently back into me, to identify with the aggressor, standing up for herself and giving me a direct experience of what she had been through. I had slowly to understand what was going on and to help her to find a language to deal with what was happening between us. She gradually was able to experience her own identity, as a relatively healthy person in an extremely ill family. This recognition led not only to her rage about being misperceived but also, eventually, to the pain and sadness of belonging to an ill family for whom she cared deeply. Only when Ms H could distinguish herself from her ill objects could she develop a firmer sense of her own identity and get on with her life. Once the problem of the "alien" internal object had been worked through the atmosphere of the analysis changed. After the crucial stage described in this paper, our work settled and developed into a more ordinary analytic experience in which Ms H's sexuality and her anger, her love and her hate could be experienced more safely. Her sense of herself became clearer and she felt confident also that I was now seeing her more clearly.

References

Bateson, G., Jackson, D. Haley, J., and Weakland, J. (1956) 'Towards a theory of schizophrenia'. *Behavioural Science*, 1 (4): 251–64.

Britton, R. (1998) 'Subjectivity, objectivity, triangular space'. In *Belief and imagination*, Ed. E. Bott Spillius, pp. 41–58. Routledge: London.

Freud, A. (1936) *The ego and mechanisms of defence*. The Hogarth Press: London.

Freud, S. (1917) 'Mourning and melancholia'. In *SE* 14, Ed. J. Strachey, pp. 117–40. The Hogarth Press: London.

Freud, S (1920) 'Beyond the pleasure principle'. In *SE* 18, Ed. J. Strachey, pp. 7–64. The Hogarth Press: London.

Fraiberg, S., et al. (1975) 'Ghosts in the nursery; a psychoanalytic approach to the problem of impaired infant-mother relationships'. *Journal of the American Academy of Child and Adolescent Psychiatry*, 14 (3): 387–421.

Grinberg, L. (1962) 'On a specific type of countertransference due to the patient's projective identification'. *The International Journal of Psychoanalysis*, 43: 436–40.

Klein, M. (1946). 'Notes on schizoid mechanisms'. *The International Journal of Psychoanalysis*, 27: 99–110.

Laing, R.D., and Esterson, A. (1965) *Sanity, madness and the family, Vol 1, Families of schizophrenics*. Tavistock: London [Basic Books: New York (1965)]!28.

Rosenfeld, H. (1983) 'Primitive object relations and mechanisms'. *The International Journal of Psychoanalysis*, 64: 261–67.

Roth, P. (2001) 'Mapping the landscape; levels of transference interpretation'. *The International Journal of Psychoanalysis*, 82 (3): 533–43.

Searles, H.F. (1959) 'The effort to drive the other person crazy – an element in the aetiology and psychotherapy of schizophrenia'. *British Journal of Medical Psychology*, 32 (1): 1–18.

Segal, H. (1993) 'The function of dreams'. In *The dream discourse today*. Ed. S. Flanders, pp. 100–7. Routledge: London.

Simpson, D. (2014). "Some Consequences of Being the Wrong Child: Effects of the Intergenerational Transmission of an Ideal-Ego." *British Journal of Psychotherapy* 30: 181–196.

Skogstad, W. (2013) "Impervious and intrusive: the impenetrable object in transference and countertransference." *The International Journal of Psychoanalysis*, 94 (2): 221–38.

Tustin, F. (1973) *Autism and childhood psychosis*. Jason Aronson: Hogarth/New York.

Williams, G. (1997). 'The "no-entry" system of defences: reflections on the assessment of adolescents suffering from eating disorders'. In *Internal landscapes and foreign bodies; eating disorders and other pathologies*. Ed. G. Williams, pp. 115–22. Duckworth: London.

Williams, G. (1998) 'Reflections on some particular dynamics of eating disorders'. In *Facing it out: clinical perspectives on adolescent disturbance*. Eds. R. Anderson and A. Dartington, pp. 79–97. Duckworth: London.

Williams, P. (2004) Incorporation of an invasive object. *The International Journal of Psychoanalysis*, 85 (6) 1333–48.

8

A LOST CHILD

The failure to develop an identity

Judith Jackson

Introduction

In this chapter, I explore aspects of an analysis of a man, who, although already middle-aged, a husband and father, experienced himself as a lost child, without an identity. In particular, I focus on the way not having space in another's mind, impacts on the development of one's identity. I take as my starting point Wollheim's (1980) contention that 'somewhere at the core of personal identity… is a…property called mental connectedness' (p. 303). This is 'not simply indicative of personal identity, it is creative of it' (p. 305). Linked to this is Bion's (1962a,b) concept of an alpha functioning mother who can offer the child an experience of a mother capable of processing her infant's most primitive undigested projections, i.e. a containing carer who fosters mental connectedness and the potential for the growth of a personal identity (p. 2). The internalisation of this repeated experience of having a space in somebody's mind and of being understood enables the child develop his own capacity to think and eventually to develop a space in his own mind. Implicit in such an idea is that this space, based on the internalisation of a containing object, is essential to the development of a core sense of self – of a separate identity.

Throughout Mr A's analysis, two features emerged which drew my attention to a specific problem in relation to Mr A's lack of a formed or even coherent identity. First, I noticed that my countertransference experience was affected in an interesting way: I became aware of a disturbance in the sense of my own analytic 'identity'. Mr A's way of talking in sessions was evacuative, a 'pouring out'; his contact with his internal world felt diffuse and confused. I found myself frequently feeling like the 'lost child' with no proper structure to my thinking. This is connected to the second point I hope to illustrate – that of the link between identity and continuity, one could say the 'temporality' which defines and limits the self. It seemed that through his development, Mr A had been unable to locate himself in space and time and continued to feel lost as to who and where he was in life. One recurring memory of his childhood, which illustrates this, was of waiting and waiting to be picked up – after school, in the park, or wherever – by a mother who failed to arrive on time if at all. Being 'picked up' – that is, held and contained – is, as noted earlier, important if the individual is to form a coherent identity, and there appeared to be an absence of a containing object who could provide a sense of his *continuous* experience that was held securely in the object's mind. (As Sharon Numa suggests in her Introduction, this can be linked to Winnicott's notion of a 'continuity of being'.) There were times when my countertransference experience was of being mind-less. Throughout his analysis, Mr A struggled with time, and I became aware that I, too, became unaccountably muddled about some times and dates, perhaps caught in a projective identification with his internal objects. Mr A's patterns of sleep and wakefulness were also disrupted without him being able to make a natural transition from one state to the other.

Mr A sought analysis at a time when his marriage was crumbling and his carapace (described by Esther Bick, 1968, as a 'second skin') of an adult identity was no longer concealing his difficulties in holding his world together. I attempt to show how an understanding of the deficits in Mr A's internal parental objects, probably linked with problems in his early relationships with his actual parents, unfolded through powerful projective identification into the analyst which, in turn, impacted on the analyst's initial loss of identity in her work with this patient. The analyst's disentanglement from these projections, and recovery of her own capacity to think, seemed important in enabling Mr A to internalise a sense of being understood and held in mind. This impacted on his sense of himself and led to his capacity to take more responsibility for himself as an authentic adult.

Michael Feldman (2009) writes that 'it seems to be intrinsic to the nature of our work that we try to build up a coherent picture of the patient's history'. He argues that 'the patient's history is embodied in his internal object relationships and is manifested and expressed in the transference-countertransference relationship. It is primarily through the experience and understanding of these relationships that we can hope to bring about internal changes' (p. 72).

The patient's history

At the centre of Mr A's childhood was a mother who had been abandoned by both her parents as a young toddler, a mother with a fundamental lack of roots. I was only ever given a sketchy impression of my patient's mother, but the trans-generational impact of the experience of being 'lost' and disoriented is striking. According to Mr A, she seemed to be there and not there. He conveyed that she said very little about her early experiences although always trying to convince others, and probably herself, that she felt looked after. She was a very light sleeper, needing total silence and darkness when she went to bed, which impinged on everyone around. As noted, Mr A, himself, had considerable difficulties in falling asleep as though somewhere identified with his mother's unconscious dark, terrifying internal world. This was a relentless persecution for him. He also told me that his mother would 'give all her stuff away, as she didn't need much', suggestive of her limited attachment to her possessions and sense of belonging, which left me with the impression that she may have believed herself to be a possession of no value.

Mr A's father was described as a somewhat passive and depressed man, who could never reach out to my patient. My patient recognised, with some shame and sadness, that he secretly denigrated his father when he became an adolescent. He described his sense of him as a man who was looked down on by his own family and seen as a failure. His father suffered a depressive breakdown during Mr A's adolescence, which seemed to be linked to being made redundant from work he had enjoyed. Thus, as well as a mother with her own experience of being a lost child, Mr A did not feel able to turn to his father as a substantive, alternative parental figure. This left my patient with a rather limited sense of his roots. Childhood seemed to offer little meaningful contact, and there was a pervasive depression that unconsciously infiltrated his world. Mr A depicted a picture of himself as a child who floated through these early years without ever being properly noticed or registered. He did not feel unwanted or unloved, but there was very little physical contact, and he was always longing to be hugged. I came to understand that one crucial aspect for seeking analysis was to try to find in his analyst an object who could 'know' him.

Mr A had few friends and struggled academically and, although good at sports, managed badly whenever he lost. After scraping through school, he went into a training program which offered security and a steady income. Disruption in an experience of continuity was re-enacted in his many changes of location as Mr A frequently moved from job to job, town to town, often gambling his earnings and eventually coming to London in his 30s. There he met his future wife and lived in a small, friendly enclave, which seemed to offer him a sense of belonging and of being sheltered. At the time of his referral, some ten years later, he was already a father of young children. His marriage, however, was in a bad state where he constantly felt attacked by his wife, and he experienced severe anxieties.

The initial meeting

When I met Mr A for the first time, I was struck by how lost he appeared. My initial impression was of a tall, gangly, awkward, deprived child, with his ill-fitting clothes and an uncomfortable presence. He seemed to have very little conviction about himself, and, therefore, about what could be offered in an analysis. He told me that previous attempts at seeking help had failed him. He spoke at length about his difficulties with his wife. I had the impression that, on the one hand, he had found someone who was lively and confident, potentially able to offer him a different quality of relating from that of his parents, involving, perhaps, a clearer recognition of his identity. On the other hand, he felt attacked and undermined by his wife, who continually voiced a never-ending catalogue of complaints. When he spoke about his childhood, he conveyed a sense of his profound experience of being neglected, of living alongside, rather than being in the minds of his parents. It looked as though his unconscious resentment of this parental experience was being lived out in his fractious relationship with his wife.

First phase of the analysis: the recreation of the experience of a parent who does not register the infant

In the early months of the analysis, sessions were filled with endless accounts of the fights and ongoing dissatisfactions between him and his wife, him and his children as well as in his social life. Furthermore, there were also considerable problems at his workplace. Soon after starting the analysis, he was made redundant by the large company where he had been working. Although he was fearful of not being able to make a living, it was, however, also an opportunity to re-evaluate his career, and after the first year of analysis, he embarked on a training programme in a community setting, which, he hoped, could offer him a new direction and the potential to work and provide for his family. In spite of the early difficulties in his analysis, it looked as though he was beginning to feel he might have a place in my mind and he appeared to identify with his analyst as a caring figure in his choice of a new profession.

The outpourings in the early sessions, in particular, seemed chaotic and empty, an evacuation with limited reflection, a formless outpouring of all that was going on in his life. He was taken over by obsessional ruminations about what a bad person he was, under the dominance of a punishing superego-ish voice inside him, which bullied and denigrated him. I soon became aware that the absence of conviction and emotional resonance was repeated in the analysis as though we both inhabited a home where there could not be any meaningful contact. He was, in a sense, continually waiting to be 'picked up' and I could not locate him. I also could not locate myself in the transference and appeared to occupy several positions at the same time. Sometimes, I felt like a kind of a lonely child, helplessly observing his parents' problems and their difficulties in communicating. Similarly, I frequently felt as if I was being pulled into being a marital therapist invited to give him advice, or strategies, or like a parent, who continually needed to check her child's homework, only to find, as it were, that he had yet again mislaid his schoolbag.

For much of the time, my overall experience was of having to watch over a clumsy toddler who was always bumping into things because he did not know where he was going or the boundaries of his 'self'. Throughout such moments, I felt that I was being nudged into being actively engaged with all his difficulties in quite a concrete way. I was also aware that I was starting to feel like a wife, who complains about a husband who is not the kind of man she wants him to be. I felt that contact with him was limited to a surface containment. There was a repetitive feel to all his ruminations. He seemed to have little sense of boundaries and a limited awareness of my consulting room or my real presence, and mindless in relation to time. Mr A had very little capacity to process his experiences, feeling easily attacked and humiliated. There were endless accounts of how enraged he felt because his wife always set herself up as the one who was right and he was made to feel at fault in any and every situation. In the analysis, he therefore felt great relief when I could take account of my making a muddle about dates and took responsibility for this instead of blaming him in the way he had expected me to. I could acknowledge that he may have experienced me as not looking after things properly in my mind and I think it was important to him that I was not defensive about my shortcomings.

In this early phase of the analysis, although it often felt as though I was losing my way, I think that he was, in fact, communicating vividly through projective identification into me his confusion about where his problems lay – inside himself or inside his object or both. This confusion seemed to be what I was repeatedly having to process in my countertransference, easily losing a sense of conviction about my interventions and questioning my analytic identity.

A vignette from this period following Mr A's not attending a previous session without phoning me to cancel

Tuesday session

He looks a bit dishevelled and walks to the couch quickly.

P. It's been a rough few days – several things happened – I don't have a phone anymore – sorry I didn't phone yesterday to tell you what's going on but didn't have your phone number.
A. You seem stressed.
P. Yes – I don't have all these numbers – realize I need to get another car – it used to be OK – but its deteriorated – when I turn a corner it goes very slow – My wife's uncle is coming next week and I'm going to go with him – he'll help me find a car – Its dangerous to drive this car – I have to make sure … Then last thing – my glasses broke – they are a very old pair – he laughs.
A. You don't actually feel like laughing – you feel as though everything in your world is breaking down.
P. Yes, I don't – I feel quite stressed – there's a lot going on – and there's this project for the training I have to complete – and I'm not managing to pull it together very well.

A. When you tell me you lose everything, you also lose me and I seem to become like a broken down pair of glasses, who has poor insight into your difficulties and you feel you have nobody and nothing to turn to, to help you, especially over the weekend, but instead you feel stuck and at risk.
P. It's not you, it's me – I can't manage anything at the moment.

He then goes on for the rest of the session with many details about his failures in his work setting and a fear of being compared to others in the group who are doing better than him.

By the end of the session, Mr A had, indeed, lost me as a helpful figure. He was by then both projectively and introjectively identified with his analyst as an internal mother, an object who fails him, who does not see him and who is felt to be preoccupied with her own insecurities and anxieties. (And his not coming to his session was already inviting me to be the forgotten, unnoticed child who is waiting and waiting.) All this, just when he needed, both as my patient, and most likely as a child, a figure who felt intact and contained enough to listen and pay attention to and help him with his worries. Freud's (1917) insight in his paper 'On Mourning and Melancholia' where he describes the 'shadow of the object falling upon the ego' was thus enacted in this session.

At moments like this, Mr A had lost his individual identity which was eclipsed by his identification with his failing parents, which I was representing in the transference. I noticed another aspect to this experience of failing. The affect was one of the passive resignation to his predicament and there was an unconscious invitation to me to join him in resignation of my own capacities. As his analyst, I needed to challenge him about his acceptance of his carelessness, in all aspects of his life, including his carelessness over the missed session. I also needed to notice how readily I fell into seeing myself as the broken pair of glasses rather than the helpful uncle analyst he could return to after the weekend. An unconscious osmotic entanglement was being enacted in which I was nudged (Sandler, 1976) into becoming the failing object in his internal world. I slowly became aware of the parallel between my experience of failing to reach him, and his communications about himself. At times, I became a 'dutiful' mother, functioning on automatic pilot, without being able to trust my experience of Mr A to find an effective way to reach him. At other times, I was more able to describe the recreation of the loss of identity he experienced at moments when he felt that, like his parents, I could not see him clearly.

Bion (1961, p. 149) described the way projected states of mind can produce in the analyst a 'numbing feeling of reality' about themselves. Robert Caper suggests that this is a fairly well-recognised occupational hazard of doing analysis, where there is an experience of 'an acute loss of intelligence on the part of the analyst' (Caper, 1998, p. 267). He goes on to say that

> Under favourable conditions, however, the analyst is able to carry the analysis further by bringing into play…his ability to establish enough distance from the patient's projections to permit him to recognize that they are projections, and that the state of mind he is experiencing has arisen from outside himself. To summarise this process, the analyst tends to fall spontaneously into a counter-transference illness as part of his receptivity to the patient's projections, and he must cure himself of it if the analysis is to progress.
>
> (ibid.)

It took some time for my awareness of what was happening between us to develop and take shape for me. Though it often did not feel like it at the time, I think that my efforts to connect with, and to articulate his experience, enabled Mr H both to feel his own identity was being noticed, and to identify with a caring figure, who took him into her mind.

A similar dynamic was present in Mr A's conscious and unconscious feelings about his father. The absence of an effective and helpful father with whom to identify was present from the start of the analysis. This was expressed repeatedly when bringing up recollections from his childhood as well as when he appeared openly worried about his capacities to be a safe father to his children. Whilst he attempted to be dutiful, he was often absent-minded, careless or even cruel. He brought many enactments based on an identification with his memory of a failing father in which he revealed that he did not know how to be a responsible father. If he was playing with the children, he would forget how tall and powerful he was in relation to them and any 'rough and tumble' would often end up with one of them getting hurt, and any irritable or excitable gesture, meant that the play would end up in tears. When he communicated all of this, he felt intense guilt and anxiety, even bewilderment that it could happen, just in a flash. At such moments, his wife would then accuse him of being aggressive and violent. There is also something here about his struggles to gauge temperature and distance. This left him feeling blamed by both his wife and his children as well as blaming himself for being a neglectful parent, albeit longing to be a fun loving father, who could be available to his children.

He spoke about his father's love of gambling which he realised that he had taken on to some degree. He started observing that he could spend hours surfing the internet for bargains, which was reminiscent of his earlier years of gambling and clearly linked with an identification with his father. The bargains were usually unrealistic, and like an adolescent, he would get lost in the excitement of his potential win. He would often be seduced into buying some cheap second-hand object instead of an appropriate replacement or repair. Invariably, this would not fit properly and in the end and cost him more money than paying for a new one in the first place. He was very forgetful, parking his car and not buying a ticket, or would always be losing things, his keys, his wallet, his phone, leaving them in odd places and then having to go to considerable lengths to retrieve the forgotten item. It felt like another enactment of a parental relationship in which he was not kept in mind and was easily lost and forgotten. And, it reflected how lost Mr H continually felt, not knowing who he was, what he really wanted, and where he was going. His identity, incoherent in both its spatial and temporal aspects, seemed unformed and muddled up with in-attentive objects.

He often came late to his analysis giving an endless variety of so-called valid reasons, but it was clear that he seemed to suffer from a basic deficit in a capacity to manage time and routine. In the sessions, although I tried to find a connection with him, I frequently experienced myself as empty and lost; feeling as though some essential ingredient was absent – without knowing exactly what that was. He would often say, in response to an interpretation, 'I'm sure that's right – it makes sense – but it makes no difference'. I seemed to step into the role of a single parent, without a husband or father, with whom to have a dialogue, having to find an alternative third position (Britton, 1989) all by myself, in which I could begin to see and to describe what was happening.

Gradually, however, I began to recognise the oscillation between the different projective identifications into me leading me to feel as though I became either a lost child or an inadequate parental figure. I realised our sessions were inhabited by 'ghosts in the nursery' (Fraiberg et al., 1975) – the ghosts of an inadequate mother and of an unsafe, weak and ineffective father.

Second phase of the analysis: the emerging of Mr H's identity as distinct from that of his internalised parents

The first dream Mr A was able to bring to a session opened up the potential for exploring his separating out further from his parents and the development of his own identity.

Mr A's first dream

> I was driving my car. There was a car next to me with a couple in front with naked babies on their laps. They were having sex with them – gyrating – I felt disgusted.
> I don't want to have such a dream.

A LOST CHILD

He first associated with a rock star who is a paedophile and asks – how do people degrade themselves like that? He thought about three boys who were kidnapped and could be abused. He worried about his own children growing up and told his wife he was worried about them. He thought his mother was possibly worried about him – but added that he mainly worried about the 'fact of not being able to protect your kids all the time'. I noticed this was a protective thought to have and also a realistic awareness of the pain of parenting.

He told me he had had the dream on a Friday night when he had been asked to go next door to look after a young boy because the mother had to go to hospital as she was about to have another baby – and the father had to take her. He had felt uncomfortable having to stay with the boy and sleep in the same room. I was aware of feeling suddenly quite shocked by what he described – totally taken by surprise, alert to the atmosphere of anxiety and paranoia about child sexual abuse. I thought about his difficulties in sleeping and his fears about a 'dangerous intruder' and how he, sometimes, kept a screwdriver under his pillow.

I said that he was telling me how much the dream horrified him – and that he might worry that if he did manage to sleep, then he might have more of such disturbing dreams. I added that perhaps the dream itself felt like a dangerous intruder, coming into his sleep, and attacking his mind, and suggested that he must have felt anxious about telling me the dream, too, perhaps afraid of shocking me.

He agreed that it did feel like that and that he was shocked too.

I wondered about his being an onlooker in the dream – like a parent who stands passively by, unable to help the children – like he worried about the kidnapped boys who could be abused – even beginning to worry that his own children could be in that position too and that he would not be able to protect them.

He replied that he notices his own carelessness in his care of his children; he hugs them too hard, their trampoline play is not monitored properly, they hit each other and cry, sometimes one gets hurt or slips, and he turns a blind eye to it all. He quickly defended himself, adding that it is not black or white but also acknowledging that his wife does take care all the time. He wondered if he envies his children for having parents who could notice and take proper care and then says that one cannot be kind all the time. He thinks about his sense of being powerful, behaving towards his sons in a contradictory way, similar to how he treated his dog a long time ago, smacking and then hugging, getting impatient and then rewarding them, setting them up to be frightened of him. When he gives the children sweets, he feels he is their hero. Sometimes, he does not let his son win at a game but then notices how important it is, and then he lets him, which pleases his son. He refers to his father as having given him the belt only once, which he believed was because his father did not pay attention or was probably much too accepting of whatever he did.

I responded by suggesting that he brought the dream to show me a sort of parallel world he lives in – he is in the car alongside the car in the dream – needing me to see this part of him, not turning a blind eye to a cruel, perverse, sadistic world he also inhabits. This world is disturbing and alarming, he cannot sleep in case it appears with greater intensity making him feel quite mad. I added that through the dream he conveys a sense of a world where children are at the mercy of very unsafe adults. He is beginning to be able to see this world more clearly and to bring it for us to explore. As well as worrying about himself as a father, he is also unsure whether he is at risk, as he might have felt as a child, with parents who did not properly notice what he was up to – and now, as a parent himself. I pointed out that the dream seemed to have been sparked off by having to babysit the boy next door and sleep in the same room, creating a scenario which he seemed to fear could put both the boy and himself at risk, being left on their own, unsupervised.

'Yes', he said, 'maybe I am quite mad, and maybe that's why I can't sleep'.

I suggested that he was frightened that I, too, could be a mad, unsafe figure, messing with his mind in some perverse and dangerous way in the analysis, getting excited by my ideas instead of somebody who was able to take care of him properly.

In bringing in the dream he was, perhaps, in projective identification with me, beginning to look at the relationship between parents and a baby. Although the content of the dream is sexual and perverse, it may be the nearest he could get to formulating the experience of his mother and father's anxieties and limitations being projected into him. His associations are about his worry, that, as a father, he could act with violence to his children; he is acutely aware now of the past being repeated. This is in contrast with the couple in the dream who seem indifferent to being witnessed.

The dream both depicts an experience of being a victim and at the same time, the splitting off of the experience – becoming a passive bystander – an onlooker. My patient's associations would suggest that he had become acutely aware of his potential to becoming a neglectful parent, having been more actively able to notice his behaviour and, as a result, making attempts to act in a different in the way. The idea of a 'naked baby' also suggests the infant's lack of resources, feeling completely helpless. This raised the question about Mr A's difficulty in being the driver, taking charge. In the transference, I had been, until, now continually faced by his propensity to be the impotent bystander in the relationship. In this sense, the dream could be considered as a turning point where he could become more connected, imagining not being cut off from himself and his objects, looking at relationships from a third position (see Britton, 1989) which, until this point, had not been possible. It seemed an achievement to have a dream in which the problem of the child with an ill parent/s was so clearly depicted.

The dream and subsequent sessions opened a door into Mr A's unconscious. From then on, he began to remember more dreams as well as becoming more open about his night terrors. He exposed how tormented he continually felt, by a cruel, bullying voice in his head telling him he is rubbish, 'you are so useless'. These taunts could be whirling around in his head in the middle of the night, and as he tried to find an anchor, something to hold on to, the hateful, sneering voice 'wouldn't shut up'. His experiences reminded him of the biblical Jacob struggling with the angels, battling all night. He also saw another part of himself trying desperately to keep himself on track, to give himself a sense of normal balance.

He later told me that he had 'this vision of somebody standing over me, urinating over me, whacking me, subjecting me to all sorts of things, doing something violent'. He feared that someone could come into the house, roughing him over, perpetrating some violence, physical or sexual. He said 'when I fall asleep, it's like going into the lion's den'. These fears and phantasies seem to express his confusion between his own violence, which he believed could not be contained or acknowledged, and his fears of the violent intrusions of his parents' unconscious projections linked with his experience of being treated callously as a child. They also revealed how Mr A oscillated between becoming a bullying figure towards his children and, on the other hand, desperately wanting to rescue them and struggling to give them a different kind of loving experience. With time, he had become more open about these terrifying phantasies, experiencing the importance of coming to the analysis to talk about these things. 'If I had to tell my wife, she'd stick me in a psychiatric ward'. He struggled, I think, with the conflict between his identifications with callous and intrusive parents and a fierce attempt to dis-identify from them, as he tried to embrace a new, more benign identity.

What was remarkable was Mr A's capacity for continuing love and forgiveness towards his parents despite his increasing awareness of their limitations and his rage about this, which he was now more able to face. He told me he felt that his parents had no malice; they never intentionally hurt him but, sometimes, did neglect him. He told me, 'They did not know, they lacked education and understanding'. And further:

> Funny, I always said to myself, there two things I wanted – that my parents be more loving and show it. I longed to be given a hug – they never did. I did not realize at the time,

I thought their behaviour was normal? I wished my father could have rescued me when mother and I had rows; sometimes we both became too emotional.

It seemed that I was observing the beginning of his experience of me as a containing object, able to stand and understand the intensity of his love and hatred, his violent feelings, which he felt were mad and out of control. At the same time, he could see what had happened between himself and his parents more clearly. As he was able to see and to separate himself from with his parents, he progressively revealed how difficult he found being on his own. When his wife went out with the children, instead of enjoying the peace, he could not bear being left behind: 'what will I do by myself?' His feelings of emptiness became apparent and he also realised that he experienced analytic holidays or any breaks, excessively, not understanding the reasons. It felt as if his whole identity was under threat when his objects, who provided meaning and structure to his life, were physically or emotionally absent. He invariably muddled up dates and times after a holiday, leaving messages which then he would become fearful I had not received.

At the same time, whilst the analysis and also his wife and his children now offered him a sense of security, this new experience also stirred up his envy. Though it was clear that he valued my capacity to hold him in mind, his envy of this capacity led him also to maintain me either as an impotent father or as an inadequate mother, unable to have 'a mind of my own'. If he too became a better parent, he would envy his children for having better parents than he had. The development of insight into these feelings was very important to him as it seemed to have opened up the possibility for him to become less of a passive bystander in his life. He could monitor himself, his actions, more aware of his experiences, both external and unconscious. His identity as an inadequate adult or a lost child seemed to be clearly shifting, and I was able to gather more of a sense of him as a husband, parent and person capable of working, both at work and in the analysis.

JUDITH JACKSON

Final phase of the analysis: the strengthening of Mr A's emerging identity

We spent a great deal of time in the final phase of the analysis working on these themes and slowly there was an emerging sense in Mr A of a growing capacity to think and to be more aware of himself, as though he was discovering who he was. Nonetheless, he continued to be haunted by the question of how he would be remembered by his children after he died. He was worried that all they would remember were his outbursts and roughness and not his care and love for them. This anxiety may also have been a projection of his fear about what sort of parents he carried in his mind – absent, not really there and his uncertainty as to how he would hold on to them – and also, how I would hold on to him. He often spoke about death, as though it was just round the corner.

Mr A's fears and anxieties were, however, now being brought more openly into our sessions and he seemed more engaged in the analytic process. This development was highlighted by the following dream, reported in a session some two years on from the 'Car' dream, which also gave some indication of the important psychic changes that seemed to be taking place.

A Monday session

The session began with Mr H paying his bill. He then spoke about a car accident in which he had dented a woman driver's bumper. This led on to accounts of more car accidents and stories of the exploitative nature of his insurance company. It happened that my car, parked in front of my house, had a damaged bumper which Mr H claimed not to have noticed. I interpreted his mixed feelings about the analytic fee, his anxiety that I was exploiting him as well as his unconscious worry about his damaging feelings toward his analyst whom he valued. He then brought the following dream.

A LOST CHILD

Mr H's dream

> I was in a huge boat – a massive QE2 type – we were all on top. He added he had a funny thing about heights. We seemed to be going at quite a speed. I was watching the water below – exhilarating – usually filled with panic – but I was not. Strange. But I had to go into the bowels of the ship – felt confusing going downstairs – dark and damp.

He continued with another dream or a part of the same dream:

> I was trapped in a room, or a warehouse – I don't know if I was by myself or with other people, perhaps with my older son. We were all there and the water was building up – getting to my stomach. I worried what were we going to do… why was I not doing something? I noticed the door. I tried to use it. If I could break the glass on top of the door, the water could then pour out. I first tried to bounce up against the window, which seemed strange, but instead of giving up, I found something else – a huge steel pylon, and smashed through this window. It was a great relief.

He commented on the dream. He said

> what was interesting about both these dreams was that previously I would have been scared – trapped – I could not get out – but instead I broke through the window and felt a huge relief – it was safer – we were in the bowels of the ship and that had made me feel very anxious.

I interpreted various aspects of this rich and complicated dream, noting, in particular, his new ability to think and to do something effective to escape and to save himself, his son and his internal parents, the 'royal' family symbolised by the QE2, from a life-threatening threat. I then focussed on what I felt was most important, namely, his worry about damaging his loved objects through his hatred – his analyst in the transference and his parents and children and also whether he felt he could repair this damage. I wondered whether he was clarifying his fear that he could have been too much for his parents and that he could have damaged them irreparably. I reminded him that when talking about the car accidents he had told me he could not see the car behind him, which I had suggested could stand for his reproachful mother in the past, but who was also a figure who became hateful because she had failed to see him in the past. I took up as well his turning a blind eye to my damaged car, and to my presence sitting behind him, an elderly analyst who often, particularly in the winter, coughed a great deal, highlighting his anxiety about damaging me.

Mr A denied knowing or thinking about how old I was. At that moment, his anxiety could not be looked at, just as he had denied noticing my car. Nonetheless, he agreed that he was afraid of becoming like his parents and being seen by his children as a parent in the same way as he saw his parents. I wondered aloud if he believed they would see him as a failing, damaged parent. Yes, he said, I think you could add that. I think that in this interchange Mr A was beginning to be able to see how much his own identity had been confused with that of his parents. The analysis opened up his repressed hatred of them, his wish to sink, to kill the 'royal' couple and their internal babies, wishes which had emerged in the dream of the sinking QE2.

Unlike his earlier 'Car' dream, when he had felt unable to initiate any action to rescue the vulnerable, abused babies, and the threatened internal parents, in this dream, Mr A takes action to save his son, himself and others in the trapped space. He is no longer impotent and detached but decisive. He has a sense of power, of having a potent penis, symbolised by the steel pylon, which he uses effectively for the rescue of his loved objects (cf. Birksted-Breen, 1996). The dream demonstrates that with the help of the analysis, Mr A had been able to face his previously unbearable anxiety that he had irreparably damaged his internal parents, an anxiety that had led to a compulsive identification with them, and thus to little sense of his own, distinct identity.

A LOST CHILD

I suggest that Mr A was now attempting to free himself and future generations in his family from the 'ghosts in the nursery', the failing parents, as described above, or, from another point of view, from his internal 'identificates', the term used by Leslie Sohn (1985) to describe a fixed and concrete identification with an object, often perverse, which engulfs the self. I think the dream was significant and revealed that my patient was capable of and wanted to be connected to life. He came across as being more of an adult, attempting to conquer the fears which dominated his child self, and was able to recover his sense of agency as well as the capacity to experience unbridled joy – something 'exhilarating'. The material also suggests that he has a sense of a developing identity as a father, as an adult and as an effective man and is no longer so trapped in projective identification, drowning together with his depressed internal parents. He was neither passive nor manic, able to think about what means he had at his disposal, to protect himself and his children in a more ordinary way. It seemed that Mr H had also found in me some paternal strength and structure the more I was able to emerge from the diffuse amorphous contents of his inner world and speak to him about it from a third position.

The car damage incident could also be seen as evidence of a different view he had developed of me – as someone who could withstand the bumps of life and just get on with it. When I took up his fear of my being old and dying before the analysis was completed, he told me that he never thought of me as old, that he saw me as robust and really enjoying my work and I could continue working even though I might be old. He may well have been needing to reassure me, but at the same time seems to have internalised something of my robustness, my resilience in the face of his attacks, and with it, developed a different experience of himself and of his masculine identity. I felt that being able to address and begin to work through the implicit issues of loss, time and (indirectly) mortality contributed to Mr H being able to make contact with his wish for life.

JUDITH JACKSON

Some concluding thoughts

In her lectures on technique, Klein (1936) suggests that

> We should always keep in mind that analysis of the transference situation is not merely bringing out repressed feelings of the past in connection with early objects, that it is not simply a repetition of past relationships, but it is also a means to develop feelings that could not develop in the past..... This means that the patient's object relations are changed. A more rational attitude towards the analyst develops and this implies a changed relation to the object world in general.
> (Steiner, 2017, p. 84)

Here, Klein is emphasising the developmental aspect of the analytic relationship and the internalisation of the analyst as a real and new object.

I think that the experience of analysis enabled Mr A to have an experience of 'mental connectedness' (Wollheim op. cit.), which enabled him to develop the core of a personal identity. My patient discovered that there was an object, akin to Bion's (op. cit.) concept of an 'alpha functioning mother' who could 'use her own mental equipment for giving a meaning to the meaningless' (p. 2), take him in, 'know' him as he was, not just exist alongside him as a passive bystander to his confusion and potential violence, or sit in judgement over him, as his inner voices did. He could then begin to know himself, recognising his own propensity to lose himself and gradually acquire the ability to be in the driving seat of his life.

Harris and Bick (1987) have written about those mothers whose capacity to be close to the baby with **all of herself** – to allow herself to be deeply receptive to the baby's needs – is interfered with by anxiety and depression. Perhaps such a situation was the case with Mr A, where his mother's compromised capacity for reverie and containment made it impossible for Mr A to develop a proper experience of himself over time and in space, including within the psychic space of his mother's mind. The containment of the analysis allowed the patient to confront and explore both his hatred and his love making it possible for Mr A to repudiate his continued identification with the drowning depressed object and break free using his phallic potency.

In the very last session of his analysis, Mr A suddenly became aware of not having a watch. He was astounded that he had never properly thought about this before and determined to acquire one. I interpreted that he was aware of his experience of being watched over, in the analysis, of time passing, of my having an eye on both his inner and external world and that he felt not only more able to watch over his own life, but that he recognised it was essential to do so; my patient was clearly wishing to develop a capacity to manage time and space, a 'sense of past, present, future; of order and sequence; of development; and of causality' (Canham, 1999, p. 160). It was also an awareness of the ending, of the time we had worked together, being now over.

This interesting and moving final material of the analysis suggested to me that having an internal 'watch' is akin to having an identity, having a sense of knowing who you are and what is going on inside you. My gradual ability to find Mr A, first through finding my own sense of self, and then being able to 'pick him up', so to speak, together with his developing capacity to make use of the analytic experience, forged the potential for psychic change and for the creation of an identity.

References

Bick, E. (1968) The experience of skin in early object relations. *Int. J. Psychoanal.*, 49: 484–486.

Bion, W. R. (1961) *Experiences in groups and other papers*. London: Tavistock.

Bion. W.R. (1962a) *Learning from experience*. London: Heinemann.

Bion, W.R. (1962b) The psychoanalytic study of thinking. *Int. J. Psychoanal.*, 43: 306–310.

Birksted-Breen, D. (1996) Phallus, Penis and Mental Space. *Int. J. Psychoanal.*, 77: 649–657.

Britton, R.S. (1989) The missing link: parental sexuality in the Oedipus complex. In *The Oedipus complex today: clinical implications*. Ed. J. Steiner (pp. 83–101). London: Karnac.

Canham, H. (1999) The development of the concept of time in fostered and adopted children. *Psychoanal Inq.*, 19: 160–171.

Caper, R. (1998) *A mind of one's own: a Kleinian view of self and object*. London: Routledge.

Feldman, M. (2009) *Doubt, conviction and the analytic process*. Selected papers of Michael Feldman. Ed. B. Joseph. London: Routledge.

Fraiberg, S. Adelson, E, and Shapiro, V. (1975) Ghosts in the nursery: a psychoanalytic approach to the problems of impaired infant-mother relationships. *J. Am. Acad. Child Psychiatry*, 14 (3): 387–421.

Freud, S. (1917) Mourning and melancholia. S.E., 14: 243–260.

Harris, M. and Bick, E. (1987) *Collected papers of Martha Harris and Esther Bick*. London: Clunie Press.

Klein, M. (1936) The Analysis of Grievances. In *Lectures on Technique by Melanie Klein* (2017) ed. J. Steiner. Routledge, London and New York

Sandler, J. (1976) Countertransference and role-responsiveness. *Int. Rev. Psychoanal.*, 3: 43–47.

Steiner, J. ed. (2017) *Lectures on technique by Melanie Klein*. London and New York: Routledge.

Sohn, L. (1985) Narcissistic organisation, projective identification, and the formation of the identificate. *Int. J. Psychoanal.*, 66: 201–213.

Wollheim (1980) "On persons and their lives" pg 303–305. In "Explaining emotions" Ed. A.O.Rorty. University of California Press. 1980.

9

FORMING AN IDENTITY

From somatisation and hypochondriasis to hysteria and beyond

Anne Amos

An identity is a sense of one's self together with a feeling that one has agency in the external world and it relies on having an inner world composed of a matrix of identifications, some conscious but others much deeper and more primitive. The patient I discuss in this chapter presented for help when all her sense of personal agency had broken down: she was confused, anxious, frightened, lost and unable to make a decision. Slowly, with time, I was able to understand her underlying primary identifications, as these emerged in the transference, which enabled her to develop some capacity to see herself and think symbolically. She thus gained some inner strength and her own identity began to emerge.

From the initial fragmentation and confusion, which I will describe in the first half of this chapter, identifications emerged which are more typical of hysteria and these are subject of the second half of the chapter. For my patient C, the particular constellation of internal object relationships that are the hallmark of hysteria can perhaps be seen as a developmental step from the fragmented anxiety state that characterised the somatisation and hypochondriasis of the early phase of her analysis. Dividing my patient's analysis into a first phase and a second phase does not reflect the to and fro of the actual clinical situation but attempts to capture the real transition and development that occurred in C's analysis over some years of analytic work. I will end with detailed clinical material

DOI: 10.4324/9781003266624-10

that captures C's conflicts over facing the pain and loss surrounding separation from her primary objects, using her own mental capacities through identification with a maternal object and moving away from a hysterical solution to her own identity.

First phase

Anxiety and a fragmentation

In contrast to her athletic body, C did not seem to have a mind that could hold onto, nor process, thoughts and experiences when she presented for psychoanalytic help in her fifties. C's well-functioning, attractive, trained, athletic body had held her together throughout her life but this defensive structure had failed her and she felt overcome with anxiety, much of this was focused on illness and fear of illness. In my countertransference, I, too, felt overwhelmed with confusion and anxiety and my experience of C's sessions was in complete contrast to the pretty, perfect body that I looked at, as for many months at the beginning of her analysis C did not lie on the couch. The sessions were chaotic, confused and fragmented with C talking a great deal, doting from one subject to the next as if terrified of leaving a gap or giving me, or her, the tiniest moment to think: she seemed on the run from allowing me to make any contact with her. She was like a little rabbit caught in the glare of my psychoanalytic headlights. C's analysis was a scene of endless verbal activity, and she reported copious dreams that poured out of her, like liquid, running one into the other. There were dreams of drowning, dying, moving all over the world, terrifying dreams of tunnels that never ended. To distinguish dreams from other material or catch form or meaning, that I was in any way convinced of, seemed almost impossible. I struggled to write up the sessions, nor could I satisfactorily present my work to colleagues. Both she and I felt to me to be merged in anxiety and confusion.

C was acutely sensitive; in a raw skinless way, she seemed to observe and feel but could not mentally process nor give meaning or significance to her feelings and observations. This was often extremely painful to listen to especially when she 'believed' or implemented the latest instruction or opinion that she had been told, which seemed a kind of stupidity, in a person who turned out to be far from stupid.

The body as a carapace

When C talked endlessly about her body with her numerous physical complaints, she would talk as if very sensitive to all aspects of her body, knowing with apparent certainty when she is going to 'get a bug'. Any illness, the smallest cold, really seemed like a catastrophic blow, and when, in fact, ill, she really suffered, consumed with her physical complaints and tormented with a conviction that she was going to die. Simultaneously, she spoke with much authority about her body and seemed to feel things in her body in great detail seeming hyper-alert and hypersensitive to any physical sensation.

As is discussed in the introduction to this volume, Ester Bick, using Wilfrid Bion's ideas of the container/contained, describes the development of a second skin as a defence against the experience of the earliest unintegrated states, where the baby is unbounded unless contained by a mother's 'nipple in the mouth, together with the holding and talking of the familiar smelling mother' (1968, Page 485). Bick goes on to suggest that the earliest containing object is experienced physically, like a skin, so that the baby can then develop a boundary between their inside and their outside which gives an opportunity for an internal space for mental capacities and symbolic functioning to develop. If the baby does not experience this containing mother and cannot develop a sense of inside and outside, she suggests he develops a pseudo-independence, a second skin or a carapace, using certain mental functions or innate talents. For C, her well-functioning body, perhaps her musculature when she was a small baby, functioned like a second skin. The development of her body and its athleticism seemed to have been in complete contrast to the development of her mind. She seemed to have little internal space where she could think symbolically and consequently she had little sense of self.

For many years, C's body had also been more than a carapace as it was also the scene of action, admired, potent and successful. Her identity seemed to have been entirely a 'body-identity', divorced from any sense of internal mental space. There was, until she reached her fifties, nothing wrong with it; in fact, it was almost phallic like in its independence and effectiveness. It just needed to be trained well. Perhaps, it was no surprise that her husband too was a beautiful, admired athlete with whom she could identify.

A serious cost for C of her successful body carapace was that it did not seem to contain an adult feminine self nor her fecundity. She seemed more like a sweet, pleasing, prepubescent girl. At the beginning of her analysis, C could not accept that her marriage of some twenty years to an internationally successful and admired sportsman was over. It seemed too painful for C to face the cruelty and neglect which had long been evident in this relationship, which repeated an earlier experience of marriage to a physically abusive man. This seemed to be a repetition of her father's neglect and lack of concern for his family. When C entered her adolescence, her father left the family 'on business' but, in fact, had a clandestine relationship for many years while a pretence was perpetuated that her parents were together and they were an intact and happy family. C had been pregnant twice, the first pregnancy was terminated in her mid-twenties, encouraged by her husband and mother, and the second, some years later, ended in a miscarriage. When her infertility was investigated in her late thirties, she had already reached menopause. C conveyed her mother as someone who was full of anxiety too with whom she tried to fit in with but actually felt very resentful towards.

A dream

A painful and exposing dream from some time towards the end of the early first phase of C's analysis captures some of the flavours of the fragmented mental state that I have been describing.

FORMING AN IDENTITY

C was beginning to be more able to symbolise by actually having a dream of an experience of evacuation of mess and chaos, rather than actually enacting it in the sessions.

A middle-eastern man and she were walking together, but she had to go to the toilet. She left him and went into the toilet and there was diarrhoea everywhere. She spent a long time cleaning herself up and there was not enough toilet paper. She rejoined the man who complained she had been too long but she explained she had to go. Then she needed to 'wee' and there was a door into another toilet but there were many people in it and to get to the actual toilet it was necessary to climb down a slippery steep slope. She did this and then she realised all these people were leering at her.

Much could be said of this dream, but I want to emphasise the mess and the dark and impatient male/father figure, and the container is a toilet that is hard to reach, down a slippery slope. It was as if C felt full of bad stuff, shit and wee that she struggled to clean up and without her beautiful, athletic body to cover it all up, was there for all to see and leer at. There was no maternal containment, only a toilet to hold the contents of her body and her mind, which was full of all the messy, angry shitty feelings she had inside her.

The analysis as a container

Containment is not only the capacity of the analyst to hold the structure of the analysis, which mattered a great deal in this analysis, and certainly supported me when I felt mired in confusion and chaos, but also to provide meaning to the patient's experience. The importance of containment in the development of identity and the enduring stability of that identity has been elaborated more fully in the introduction (this volume).

For C, the safely bounded space of the concrete structure and regularity of the consulting room functioned as an elemental, external container for her, rather like a toilet. Quite often, she would arrive for her session saying, 'I feel so full up', as if the need to evacuate mental experience was urgent. I was very aware of her need to evacuate and her dependency on the regularity of her sessions and the consulting room. However, because of all the confusion and chaos that was projected into me by her endless talking she was frightened of me, needed to observe me (by not lying on the couch) and certainly depending on me and experiencing me as a person felt almost impossible. I was a frightening figure for her as she experienced me as full of her unprocessed and unwanted bits that had been projected into me. She would often listen politely to what I had to say but then move on as if she couldn't take in anything from me, couldn't understand what I said or hold a thought in her own mind. Alongside this, she very much felt she needed her analysis – often becoming physically ill in the breaks and on one occasion, very seriously so, with septicaemia.

As I described her fears and her fear of me, slowly over the first few years of her five times a week analysis C became less incontinent, less overwhelmed with anxiety and more able to take something in. Externally, C's marriage had come to an end, she had set up home on her own and was seriously engaged in her own professional and academic development. In her analysis, C talked much less about her body and seemed much less prone to illness. She had started to lay on the couch and her internal world seemed to be taking some shape as she started to use her mental capacities and become more tuned into the world around her. Internally, she seemed much less fragmented, as if she was now relating to whole objects and she began to accept me as a maternal caring object. However, I began to notice that this brought into focus a particular constellation of unyielding identifications that has been observed and discussed in hysterical patients.

Second phase

Identifications in hysteria

Hysterical patients are caught up in unconscious identifications which they powerfully enact with those around them, as was the case for C in this second phase of her analysis. She acquired a static caravan, parked in a muddy field next to a large forest that she visited at the weekends, again an external structure that held her together. Here, she met X with whom she became completely preoccupied. All her day dreams, hopes and desires were centred on him.

Freud (1908) described a particular enactment in a patient who in a 'hysterical seizure' takes off her clothes with one hand whilst making an effort to keep them on with the other hand. Freud considered she was simultaneously unconsciously identifying herself with a man raping a woman and with the woman being attacked. Ron Britton (1999) develops this particular aspect of the character of the identifications in the hysteric in his re-analysis of the case of Anna O in the light of more historical information and with more contemporary understanding. He shows that the central defining feature of the hysteric is the use of 'projective identification to become, in phantasy, one or other or both members of the primal couple'. Following Klein's observation that theatre and performances of all kinds symbolise parental intercourse, Britton suggests that the hysteric 'gets in on the act, mounts the stage and takes on one or other of the parental parts' (1999, page 5). The erotic transference, usually in a female patient to a male analyst, is a powerful defence against the bleakness of the primary maternal situation or as Britton succinctly puts it 'the formation of the sexual couple becomes the death of the nursing couple' (ibid.). Britton makes clear the bleakness of the maternal transference and the tendency to return again and again to romantic or sado-masochistic phantasies that function as exciting alternatives that merely ape life and liveliness. All of these characterised an aspect of this second phase of C's analysis.

When C first developed a relationship with X, I thought perhaps this was a developmental step for her as she moved on and accepted her marriage was over. Maybe it was a real opportunity for her to have a loving sexual relationship with somebody who shared some of her interests. When I found myself feeling doubtful about this relationship, I thought I was being nudged into being her over-anxious and intrusive mother, even the envious mother who had encouraged C to terminate her pregnancy. She could persuade me that all she needed was this person called 'X' to do this thing called 'love her' and all would be well. She was kind, generous and sweet to 'X' in the hope of securing his 'love'. In contrast to this, I felt unsure and undermined, doubtful of what I could offer and very questioning of myself. But slowly, I came to learn that this relationship had no qualities of mutuality or concern, but put C in to a state of excited hope and desire and then great persecution and utter devastation when the real X did not respond in the expected way but was cold, dismissive and rejecting. It was as if my job was to clean her up and make her sweet, so she could understand 'X' even better, to be a kind of servant mother/analyst with whom she discussed X. She would then take interpretations meant for her and apply them to X. The idea that she needed her analysis to help her understand herself was absent. When I could see more clearly the nature of her identification with a sexual parental couple, the analysis could move on, but as Britton describes I had to tolerate and live through the nursing couple – C and I – being wiped out by the sexual couple – C and X.

Clinical material

The session I will describe some five years into C's analysis when there was more movement as she tries to connect with a maternal object in me and that side of herself that can retain and contain thoughts and feelings. The excited sexual couple – C and X – were less dominant but continued to exert a powerful exciting pull for C even though C was more in touch with her feelings of dependency on her analyst. Both elements of somatisation and also the manic activity which have destroyed so much thought and connection for C earlier in her analysis can still be observed, albeit with less intensity.

It is a Friday session, about two years after X appeared in her analysis and not too long before the summer break. Unusually for her, C had missed the previous day's session to go to a work-related event. Some weeks earlier, she had been invited to a party on the forthcoming weekend of a disabled child, the daughter of her friend, where she would have been more on the periphery. She had rejected this invitation as she wanted to go to the caravan as she hoped X would be there. This I had understood with her as representing a rejection of a mother, or analyst's, pride and pleasure in her daughter's development and turning with excitement and anticipation to X, who was likely to reject her or be cruel in some way. We had also talked about her painful feelings that, at the party, she would neither be the special birthday girl nor be the mother celebrating her daughter's development, instead, she would have more of an assistant's role. In a sense, connecting with Britton's ideas, she was invited as an audience, rather than be part of the 'act' on the stage. By not going to her caravan to be with X, she would also risk experiencing an analyst who was going off for her weekend and all the feelings that go with being excluded, feeling vulnerable and separate.

Session

C arrived a little early for her session and hobbles in without her shoes on. (She had been complaining of a sore foot for some days.) She tells me she is tired and has decided not to go to her caravan this weekend instead she will go to the party on Saturday. She spoke with the girl's mother who was very pleased C was going to come but she says, in a quieter voice, the problem is Sunday evening when she will feel lonely and sad. She has no plans for Sunday although maybe she will do her work and get it finished before the summer holiday. I say to her that she seems to be trying to bear the feelings of sadness and loneliness when there are no sessions and yet stay connected to me and I thought the atmosphere between us was of tentative contact. She told me about the work event which had caused her to miss the previous day's session and her surprise that her colleagues were pleased to see her and she travelled by underground, without giving it a second thought, something she had not done for years. She had also met someone she used to know, somebody who, she says 'had got on with her life' and it made C feels years behind. This friend had children and was quite successful in her work. I interpreted to C her difficulties in staying in touch with me and with her friends when she has to cope with competitive feelings and her worries as to whether she has anything to contribute.

In a way that was quite familiar to me, she didn't respond to my trying to engage with her but goes further away, becoming upbeat, fearful I thought, of too much closeness with me and being dragged further into feelings of anxiety and competitiveness. She said: 'I like London; I shouldn't go off to the caravan all the time. I had a message from someone I know there, telling me about a tribute band playing nearby this weekend which I would have really loved'.

She continues in this cheerful way saying that a theatre leaflet came through her door and there are really good productions with discounted seats, so she said that she booked for three performances for herself, 'what I would have paid for one ticket'. I found myself wondering why doesn't she book more seats and go with a friend.

Eventually, I respond to this by saying it's as if she now doesn't think she has friends and she seems to have gone off all on her own in an excited state.

This comment seems to bring her back and she becomes more thoughtful again, saying that she doesn't know why that happens to her. She re-read some entries in her diary last night and she can see she has always had doubts about X. She then says emphatically that she doesn't want a relationship with him, he doesn't treat her well and she's not putting up with it and yet she says that she keeps going back. In fact, she thinks she couldn't resist him if she saw him. She continues saying that somebody she spoke to said that she once had a relationship like that and the only thing was not to see him. Still talking in a reflective manner, C says that she can't understand why sex is so good with him but nothing else is and wonders if this is what draws her back: it's never been like this before she says. With her ex-husband, it was over fast and was never enjoyable but with X it just goes on and on. It is good for him too she told me but then with bitterness added he used to say, 'you're gorgeous' but now, he just says 'it's gorgeous'.

When I said to her that she seemed to be facing her need for emotional and mental connections not just bodily ones that go on and on, she seemed thoughtful and then remembered a dream.

She was on a bike and it was dark and she had arrived at a city and this old woman was there. She was lost and she asked the old woman the way to a town near where she has her caravan and the old woman replied '30 miles'. She was feeling very tired and it was raining. The landscape then seemed like India with tall trees and creepers hanging down. The road came to an end and a bridge of creepers went over a ravine, again still like India. She then watched herself fall into the ravine as if she had divided into two parts, one that was watching and the other who was now at the bottom of the ravine and calling for help. The part of her that was at the bottom of the ravine was unable to move and despite shouting could not get the help of the two men who came along on bikes. The men did not seem to know one another but one had some food he shared with the other. They both ignored her.

She comments bitterly, but not without some irony, that the men ignoring her 'is the story of my life' and tells me that 30 miles is the correct distance from London to her caravan. I suggest that I seem to her to be this old woman who lets her go off up the hill in the rain to this creepy place where she falls into danger when I leave her at the weekend.

She then tells me that what comes straight into her mind is what X had said about his mother which is that she never feeds him enough and she doesn't buy proper food but the cheapest as she doesn't realise that there is a difference between what an old lady eats and a man who is fit and active. It was very common for her to reply to my interpretations by going straight to X in her thoughts, as if I hadn't spoken. But, this time, I did not comment on her doing this but replied that she must feel that I, too, don't give her enough to manage. She says that although it is what suits her as she can then go the caravan for a longer weekend, she wishes her session wasn't so late in the day on Monday and that although she has plans for this weekend she doesn't know if she will be able to resist going off to X in two or three weekend's time. We were then able to make a link with the men who ignore her at the bottom of the ravine who she 'falls' for and she talks of her fear of depression and getting ill, especially during breaks. I thought we were in touch and she smiles at me as she leaves, not hobbling, but still carrying her shoes.

Discussion of the clinical material – introjections and identifications

There is a sense in this session that C is feeling her life is developing; she has been to a work event where she felt recognised, she chooses to go to the little girl's party and even allowed herself to stay closer to her analysis and her developing life by planning to get ahead with her work, so she could have a summer holiday. But, she is tired with a sore foot and seems vulnerable in an ordinary way, quite unlike the devastating illnesses and overwhelming anxiety of the first phase of her analysis. She faces the pain of loss and not being central at the party for the little girl and in realising her friends/colleagues have got on with their lives, leaving her feeling left behind and jealous. She is concerned how she will be with the approaching summer break and even on Sunday when she does her work. She is tentatively relating to me as if she feels I can understand her loneliness and depression and know about the mess she can get into. When she feels more in touch with a containing maternal figure in her analyst, she seems less driven to rush off in an excited and manic way to the caravan with X. The difficulty, however, is the conflict between having a reflective internal space where she faces difficult feelings and a wish for the excitement of having a wonderfully admired body, a hard, external carapace or having the powerful father all to herself and being part of an eroticised primal scene. Part of her wants to restore her familiar defences and be a fit, active man rather than have to exist on what she claims to be the meagre diet from her old lady analyst.

The dream captures some of the landscape of C's underlying primitive identifications: she is lost and there is an old woman, who signposts her off into a creepy place where she falls into a ravine and needs help, but there are only neglectful men, who feed each other but not her. This reflected her sense that I am with someone else at the weekend and have a life that sustains me from which she is excluded. This maternal object excludes C by sending her off in the direction where she falls into an abyss with figures who neither see her nor feed her. An excluding old woman, though, is a person which is in stark contrast to the earlier toilet dream of C's analysis where containment is a receptacle for the mess of faeces and urine. No help is available from any paternal figure. The bleak internal object relationships revealed in the dream can be transformed by eroticisation and excitement, the hallmarks of hysteria, but the dream highlights their essentially bleak and utterly desolate nature with its dark, frightening, menacing atmosphere.

Developing her own identity

In this session, C has the capacity to have thoughts of her own – she knows, for example, that there is something damaging for her with X as she read it in her diary, even making a painful, ironic 'joke' about the story of her life being neglected by men. She questions the quality of the contact with X, realising her body is not her whole self, as it used to be, and she wants more from a relationship than body contact. I think she also feels and understands how she is in danger of her mind getting into a mess again, falling into a ravine, without contact that recognises her emotional needs. But she is also frightened of feelings of dependency on and rivalry with her analyst as they make her feel 'not nice'.

Over the time of C's analysis, there has been a slow but vital transformation of the analysis and her analyst in C's mind. Initially, the containing function of the analysis was a receptacle needed to capture her confused, messy feelings and her fragmented mind. Then, as her excitement with X took over, the role of the maternal object in the analyst was a downgraded figure but a person, nevertheless, rather than a receptacle. However, she is a person with a lowly undervalued function, cleaning C up and making her sweet for the highly desired and exciting father. Finally, in the session discussed, C related to an analyst providing understanding, someone who has the capacity to think about her experience; there was a quite different quality of care and containment.

This transformation in C's experience of her analyst reflects the development of her own mind equipping her to face and mourn so much of what she has lost in her life, including her manic and hysterical defences. She began the session by saying that she was tired and was staying away from the excitement of being with X, but she was also aware that this might not last when the long summer break from the analysis comes around again. Her identification with the observing and containing analyst has, over the course of her analysis, entered the constellation of her identifications with neglectful and sexualised internal objects and altered her internal landscape. This has also enabled her to differentiate herself from her primary objects, so she is no longer so caught up in the excited pull of entering the primal scene and more able to face the painful exclusion from the parental couple. Thus, C gained a surer, more secure sense of herself and a personal identity, no longer so dependent on an external carapace, a second skin, her well-tuned athletic body, nor did she need to turn, with excitement and without insight, to a hysterical solution to real development.

Summary

Throughout her life, C's 'body – identity' had held her together until anxiety broke through and her body could no longer function as an effective carapace. Initially, in her analysis, C related by projection, evacuating her confusion and anxiety into her analyst. With the containment provided by analysis, the patient's verbal activity and daydreaming began to reveal the extent of her hysterical identifications. Identification with a very downgraded maternal object and much excitement and involvement with a cruel and neglectful father. Like Freud's hysterical patient who both identifies with the person being raped and the attacker (1908), C's athletic body for many years contained both a phallic-like identification with the neglectful father and the anxious mother who could not contain and retain emotional experience. As somatisation and hypochondriasis are experiences in the body, or in the overlapping arena between body and mind, the primitive hysterical identifications may have been camouflaged by the morass of confusion that characterised the early phase of C's analysis. It may be, though, that identifications only emerge when the patient has been sufficiently contained to be able to relate to whole objects.

Through the containment provided in understanding and in living out these primitive identifications which she repeated in her analysis, C began to develop an internal space for mental capacities and symbolic functioning, a prerequisite for an identity of her own.

References

Bick, E. (1968) 'The experience of skin in early object-relations'. *The International Journal of Psychoanalysis*, 49: 484–486.

Britton, R. (1999) 'Getting in on the act: the hysterical solution'. *The International Journal of Psychoanalysis*, 80: 1–14.

Freud, S. (1908) 'Hysterical phantasies and their relation to bisexuality'. In *The Standard Edition of the Complete Psychological Works of Sigmund Freud*. Ed. J. Strachey (vol. 9, pp. 159–166). London: The Hogarth Press.

Klein, M. (1923) 'Early analysis'. In The Writings of Melanie Klein (vol. 1, pp. 77–105). London: Hogarth Press

10

'IF YOU ARE NOT MY MUM, WHO ARE YOU?'

A woman's analytic journey from a melancholic identification to an identity of her own

Orna Hadary

In this chapter, I describe the analytic work with a patient who was imprisoned in an internal, melancholic relationship with her maternal object. This internal state came to life in the transference which was intense and marked by the patient's omnipotent and concrete phantasy that the analyst was her mother, the ideal mother she had always longed for. The analytic experience and understanding, combined with the patient's determination to overcome her difficulties, enabled her to mourn her lost object and to separate, gaining freedom and capacity to become herself.

In his original and far-reaching paper 'Mourning and Melancholia', Freud (1917) describes the melancholic's solution to the loss of a love object. The melancholic incorporates the object into himself, thereby getting rid of the reality of the loss. Another part of the ego, 'the special agency', which was later named by Freud as the superego, becomes extremely self-critical and self-accusing. By attacking himself, the melancholic expresses his unconscious hatred to the object that had left him. Freud shows us how in this way the melancholic tries to hold on to his love object and at the same time to express his hate towards the object that has caused him such suffering. This is a brilliant, detailed description of pathological identification.

Ignes Sodre (2005) makes a profound and enriching contribution to our understanding of Freud's paper and the conundrum of melancholia. She describes how the loss of an object turns into the total possession of the object in the internal world. Complex and hostile relationships take place in unconscious phantasy between the self and the object. She shows the duality of the melancholic condition: rage towards the deserting object as well as deep sorrow at being unloved and deserted. The attack on the love object evokes persecutory and unbearable guilt which may bring a new wave of sadism and attack. The attack is also towards the self which inflicts pain on the loved object and feels unlovable.

John Steiner (1992) writes about the normal process of mourning which he divides into two stages. In the early stage, the mourner fights the reality of the loss and tries to possess and preserve the lost object by identifying with him. The mourner faces a paradox: he has to accept the death of his object even though he is convinced that he cannot survive the loss. It is only gradually and with a lot of pain that the mourner is able to face the fact that he cannot protect his object and has to allow him to die. This is the second stage of mourning. When the mourner can give up his identification with his object, he can move on to accept the fact of his death. He then can reach a differentiation between himself and the object. This usually brings a sense of relief at being alive and separate. The relief creates a fresh wave of guilt that has to be dealt with.

The capacity to mourn and to accept the reality of separateness between self and the object is a crucial part of development. Concrete and omnipotent phantasies turn into symbolic ones and the reality can be differentiated from phantasy. These processes are at the heart of the depressive position. They allow one's identity to develop and to grow.

Sodre writes:

> The sense of identity stems simultaneously from the differentiation of the self from its objects and from various identifications with different aspects of the objects. All object

> relations depend on the capacity to remain oneself while being able to shift temporarily into the other's point of view.
>
> (Sodre, 2004, p. 54)

Working through the Oedipus complex is a central part of the depressive position. Ron Britton (1989, 1998) describes how the capacity of the child to recognise and to accept the parental couple creates a triangular space which allows the child to observe himself and to observe others, thus getting a perspective on his objects and on himself. This is the basis for forming an identity.

The process of developing a personal identity is explored by Richard Wollheim (1984). His ideas and their relevance and contribution to psychoanalysis are discussed by Edna O'Shaughnessy (2015). She elaborates on his concept of mental connectedness, the capacity to continue to feel oneself over time and through changes, which forms continuity and unity in the experience of the self. The process of forming a personal identity is an active and a creative process.

Clinical presentation

Mia was an attractive and intelligent woman in her twenties who was pursuing an academic career. She felt distressed and frozen following the sudden death of her mother in a car crash. Feeling unable to overcome her loss, she decided to seek therapeutic help, a year after her mother had died.

Mia grew up in America. Her mother used to work outside the home for long hours, which meant that Mia used to come home from school to an empty house and had to manage on her own. She remembered feeling lonely and constantly missing her mother. During her childhood, Mia felt close to her father and needed by him. He used to share his feelings with her and she was pleased to be her father's confidant.

Her mother's sudden death shook Mia deeply and she suffered from panic attacks and depressive moods.

A WOMAN'S ANALYTIC JOURNEY

The analysis

Mia was keen to tell me what was on her mind. She talked about the details of her daily life, her memories and phantasies. She brought vivid dreams and her associations were rich and imaginative. After a short time of working with her, her symptoms lifted and she felt able to work and to engage with her friends. She was appreciative and became intensely attached to me. She evoked maternal feelings in me and I felt protective towards her.

This 'honeymoon' period between us was shaken when I had to ask her to slightly change the time of one of her four weekly sessions. Mia reacted angrily, blaming me for being unreliable. She became suspicious and hostile, wondering if she could ever trust me again. She reacted in a similar way when she happened to see another patient arriving when she was leaving. She felt that a 'proper' analyst would have protected her from seeing other patients or any other person approaching the house. I was taken by surprise, feeling told off and under pressure to fit with her picture of me and her expectations; otherwise, her world would be shattered.

These incidents helped me to understand that my patient's capacity to recover from her loss and to re-engage with life was dependent on a particular transference that she had developed. She saw me as an ideal mother who was attentive, loving and always present for her daughter/patient. This mother had a complete understanding of her daughter's needs and wishes, even without words. In her mind, it was a perfect dyad, existing in parallel with her ordinary life and relationships.

In one of her sessions, Mia talked about the Pieta, Michelangelo's famous sculpture of the Virgin Mary holding Jesus. While the sculpture is of the Virgin Mary holding the body of the dead Jesus after he was taken down from the cross, in my patient's perception it was a sculpture of a mother holding her alive child in her arms, both mother and child absorbed in looking lovingly at each other. My patient described a real-life incident, in which a man attacked the Pieta with a hammer, causing severe damage to the Renaissance masterpiece. Later on, the sculpture was restored and put behind a panel of bulletproof glass. For Mia, this attack had to do with terrible envy and hate of a man who could not bear to see the ideal love of the mother and child. 'The gaze' that united mother and child became in my patient's phantasy an expression of perfect maternal love and devotion which she had always longed for and believed she had found in her analysis.

In my patient's mind, the bereaved mother holding the body of her dead son became a mother holding her live child, both mother and child engaged in a loving gaze. This reversal of perception captures her main defence: the terrible loss and pain turned into a happy and a loving union. I thought that the bulletproof glass had become, in my patient's phantasy, a barrier against the reality of loss, protecting the patient from her unbearable pain, but also imprisoning her together with her idealised object, myself in the transference, with no possibility of movement and development.

For my patient, the ideal relationship with me was not to be confronted by reality. She thought that it was my duty to ensure that nothing would challenge her view of the analytic relationship. When she faced the reality of boundaries, rules and limits, she turned from being the 'loving child' to feeling abandoned and furious. I came to think about the man who attacked the Pieta as a version of the analyst, who wanted to penetrate the glass barrier, to introduce reality and to help the patient to break free from her frozen and stuck state of mind.

Mia's insistence on seeing me as her mother was an omnipotent and delusional phantasy, which had a tremendous grip on her. The intense, love relationship with the lost maternal object was enacted in the transference. I became the ideal mother she had always longed for, rather than the actual mother she had lost. This protected her from the painful need to mourn her real mother. I thought that the actual death of her mother revived earlier feelings of a little girl who wished for an exclusive relationship with her mother and felt the reality of separateness from her mother as a terrible loss. It evoked her rage and unconscious phantasies of taking revenge on the mother who had caused her such pain. Holding on to a perfect union of mother and daughter in the transference helped my patient to feel better and to function well in the outside world.

A loss of a passport

During the analysis, my patient talked a few times about losing her passport, either as a concrete event that had happened to her or as an image which appeared in her dreams. I thought that this was a poignant representation of her wish to lose a sense of herself and to merge with the maternal object.

I would like to give an account of a dream and the communication in the session between patient and analyst following the dream, to demonstrate the significance of this image:

In her dream, England was under a threat, maybe from a possible invasion. She decided to leave. She was queuing at the airport. She realised that she had forgotten to take her passport. She was alarmed that she would have to go back to London to collect it, this felt dangerous. Then, the scene changed, and she was with her mother at a train station. They were going down a staircase and the ceiling was collapsing. They got on a train and Mia became agitated, realising that she had forgotten her suitcase. She should not have cared so much, as the main thing was to be with her mother, but still she felt worried. She tried to ask other passengers for help, but they were young and carefree and did not respond. Gradually, her mother became weaker, stopped talking and seemed like a puppet. Her mother's seat turned into a bed and her mother had to lie down.

The dream reminded her of the time she had to go back home after her mother had had the car accident, as at the airport she realised that she had forgotten her passport. Later on, she understood this incident as linked to her dread of seeing her mother in hospital. She also felt guilty about her reluctance to go.

I said to her that I wondered whether she felt guilty now, as she was beginning to feel better and was having more of a life of her own.

She said that she did not know how to be now. She felt as if she was in a void.

I said that engaging with her own life felt like leaving her mother and me behind.

She agreed with that. She felt that moving forward meant losing me and that was an unbearable thought. She added that in the dream when she was going down the stairs to the train platform, she knew something was wrong and the ceiling was falling down.

I said that staying with her mother felt disastrous. It was difficult for her to imagine that she could live her life and, at the same time, keep a link with me and with her memories about her mother.

She said she was not sure she could do that.

The dream expressed the internal battle between the need to hold on to an all-consuming relationship between mother and daughter, and the patient's need to have a sense of herself (her passport, her own suitcase). Identification with the mother led her to a deadly place (down the staircase, the ceiling was collapsing). She struggled with an awful dilemma, as getting better meant losing her analyst. This made her feel stuck and unable to move.

The role of the father

I became aware of the contrast between Mia's perception of me as the ideal mother and her disappointment and hostility towards her father. She often had complained about him, seeing him as intrusive and boundary-less. She needed her boyfriend to be with her whenever she met her father. She imagined that if she engaged with her father, she would lose her independent life and would be imprisoned by his needs and demands from her. While I knew that her father had his own difficulties, I thought that she projected into him her need to possess and control the object. Her relationship with her father had struck me as expressing a complex set of identifications: my patient becoming the analyst, having to manage a figure who was craving an exclusive relationship with no boundaries, like her.

Her hostility towards her father can be understood in the context of the oedipal situation. As a child, Mia used to have a very close relationship with her father and he used to share with her his feelings and difficulties. This was a satisfying link which excluded the mother and freed her from her intense need of her mother. This was also a way to avoid recognition of the parental couple and the hostility of feeling outside the couple. Later on, the hostility was directed towards the surviving parent, the father, while the lost mother turned in her mind into an idealised object. Mia's oedipal phantasies and struggles were expressed through the analysis in dreams in which she triumphantly attracted a paternal figure and became a part of the parental couple.

Vampires

Vampires often appeared in Mia's dreams. They were dangerous and frightening intruders who got into her home and threatened her. She tried to fight against them and to get rid of them, but she felt also like their victim.

In stories and folklore, vampires are usually described as creatures that are neither dead nor alive and exist by feeding off the living, generally in the form of sucking their blood. I thought that the dream image of vampires captured the tormenting relationship of my patient with her object: on a pre-conscious level, the vampires represented an intrusive and incestuous paternal object who got into her private space, threatening to break boundaries. However, fundamentally, in the unconscious, the vampires represented a dead mother who was envious of the living and able to live only through her daughter. In identification with this mother, the patient longed to live through me, as if we could share the same blood system. The vampires represented the aggressive and cruel side of the melancholic relationship with the internal maternal object, the wish to take hold and to possess the object through sucking their blood.

Detailed clinical material

I would now like to present in detail two consecutive sessions from the fourth year of Mia's analysis, a short while before a Christmas break. I think that at that point in the analysis, the picture of a perfect union of mother and daughter was starting to crack and she was beginning to be in touch with a more realistic view of me. However, this was in a constant conflict with her desperate need to hold on to an idealised relationship with me.

Session 1: Thursday

Mia was ten minutes late for her evening session. She said she did not want to come today, she went with friends for a drink and wanted to stay with them, to have fun. She wanted to spread her wings. She did not know what stopped her. She noticed that the books on my bookcase were rearranged.

I said that if I touched the books, she felt that I spread my wings and that was frightening.

She said that she imagined that all my books were about her and for her.

She then said she was looking forward to the Christmas party at work. She would arrange to sit between her two bosses. They would all enjoy spending the evening together. She thought they were like a couple of good parents. She had to write down the dates of my Christmas break, she had already forgotten them.

I said that I wondered whether she felt as if she did not need to remember the dates of my break, she could pretend she was just moving from one parent to another and she would be fine.

She said that if I was a good mum, I would be waiting at home for her and she could go out to have a good time and would not have to worry that I would disappear. She still imagined that I would agree to meet her father and that I would cure him. We could have Christmas together and I could be a part of the family. After a pause she added, 'If you are not my mum, who are you? I am afraid I cannot do this last bit of work we need to do; to understand who you are. I feel stuck.' She began to cry and said, 'I can't lose you again. I know I did not lose you in the past.'

She talked about arriving to most of her sessions ten minutes late. In those ten minutes, she was in a dream. In the dream, I was her mother waiting for her and it was OK to come whenever she wanted to.

I said that, for a long time, she had been making a deal with me in her mind that I would allow her to be together with me in that boundary-less way for ten minutes, and she could be my patient accepting my boundaries in the rest of the session.

Session 2: Friday

She was again ten minutes late. She said she did not want to come, particularly as it was Friday. She felt an urge to cancel the session. She thought that I would understand. She was worried that we would have a revelation here today and she would be left with it on her own at the weekend. She had an image in her mind of a picture underneath a picture. She became tearful. She did not want to reveal the picture underneath. Not today. She knew we were in a process of looking at it, but she wanted a mum. She was walking in the street saying again and again, 'I wish my mum was here.' She did not want anything else.

I said that in her mind there were only two options, either I was the beloved mother she always dreamt about, who would fit perfectly with her needs, or I turned into a harsh analyst who completely wiped her out of her mind during the weekend.

She had in mind the sentence she said to me yesterday, 'I don't want you to leave me again.'

I said that the change in her perception of me felt like a death sentence to the ideal mother she was trying to hold on to. This felt unbearable.

She said that she felt embarrassed to cry so much when actually her life has become so much better. She mentioned a book she was reading about a woman who lived in her dreams, while vampires were about to attack her.

I said that the ideal mother of her dreams could easily become a dangerous vampire who could attack her and hurt her.

Commentary

Mia tried desperately to hold on to a relationship of an ideal mother attending to a perfect daughter in a timeless universe in which the relationship was fixed and immune to change. When she had to be in touch with the reality of the analytic relationship, she felt a tremendous sense of loss and she did not know whether she would survive.

Her question 'If you are not my mum, who are you?' may imply another important question, 'If you are not my mum, who am I?' Giving up her idealised relationship with me as her mother made her feel lost and disoriented. However, in a paradoxical way, separating from the maternal object was crucial to her growing capacity to develop an identity of her own. The vampires who came to attack 'the woman in her dreams' were indicating a realisation that her split-off phantasy world was impossible to sustain.

Shifts in the analysis

Gradually, a significant change began to take place. While my patient felt a longing for a mother, the insistence to see me as her mother diminished and finally disappeared. The delusion turned into a symbolic connection and she developed a more realistic understanding of my role. There was a sense of freedom in our discussions as a result of recognition of my separate life and her joy to live her own life. She became engaged in new projects and professional initiatives and had plenty of creative ideas and plans.

Childhood memories came up about her mother and their connection, in which I could see her love for her mother and her sadness of her loss. She could connect better to her past and, at the same time, be enthusiastic about her future plans.

I would like to end this chapter by describing a dream from her last year in analysis and a condensed brief description of the dialogue between us that followed. In her dream, she was hiding in a tiny box. She was desperately trying to stand up but did not manage to; she could only lie down there like an embryo.

She said, 'It was like, I forgot the word I am looking for, like being in a coffin.'

I said that, for a long time, she wished to be safe and protected in her relationship with me, like in a womb. But she realised that if she had not been able to grow and to stand on her own feet, the womb would turn into a coffin.

She said that she felt relieved to find words for her dual need to be close to me and to be herself. She was now reminded of another dream she had in which she gave birth, had the baby in her arms and was breastfeeding. It was like a miracle.

I thought that my patient by now had a sense of herself with her thoughts and feelings, with her history and her plans for the future. The dream's image of giving birth captured her sense of becoming herself, having an identity of her own.

Discussion

At the beginning of her analysis, my patient developed a concrete and omnipotent phantasy that her analyst was her mother, the ideal mother. This phantasy brought a relief from her pain and suffering, enabling her to recover her good functioning in the outside world. I understood this phantasy as a manic defence against the unbearable pain of loss. I think that the actual loss of her mother evoked in my patient a much earlier difficulty of accepting the reality of separateness between herself and the maternal object. The wish to possess the mother and to be united with her turned into a delusional belief that she has found an ideal mother in her analyst and an ideal home in her analysis. When my patient had to confront the reality of the analytical relationship, for instance, when I asked her to change the time of a session, her world was shaken and the admiration and love she felt turned temporarily into hostility and suspicion.

Melanie Klein (1952) saw idealisation as an omnipotent phantasy of a perfect object with whom one can have an exclusive and ideal relationship. The prototype for this relationship is the blissful state of the baby sucking the breast. Any aggressive feelings towards the object are denied and split off. Denial and splitting help the infant to protect his love for the breast and to create an order and coherence in his early internal world, where love and connectedness are differentiated and separated from hate and aggression.

John Steiner (2020) calls the idealised omnipotent phantasy 'The Garden of Eden Illusion' and comments how painful and, at times, unbearable it may feel to face reality. The analyst needs to be able to sympathetically support the need for illusion and at the same time to be aware of the need to relinquish it and to help the patient through the process of disillusionment.

In her paper 'Who's who', Ignes Sodre (2004) describes how delusional phantasies shape the relationship with the object. They are at the basis of excessive use of projective identification that leads to a loss of a sense of self and, paradoxically, at the same time, to a rigidity in character based on new boundaries created in phantasy between self and object. In this situation, object and self become locked in fixed ways of relating to each other, rigid and brittle, with little scope for movement.

This rigidity was typical of the first phase of the analysis, in which Mia insisted on seeing me as her ever-present mother while she took the role of the loving daughter. She felt that her well-being depended on the two of us strictly keeping to these roles. The reality of boundaries and limits in the analytical setting was threatening and had to be ignored or distorted in ways that would keep the phantasy intact.

In a later stage of the analysis, Mia's capacity to differentiate between phantasy and reality had grown and developed. Frustrations in the analytic situation no longer felt so catastrophic. She began to realise that holding on to her phantasy locked her in a deadly dyad. We could see it in her dream in which the protective womb turned into a coffin. I could see her healthy determination to move on and to develop. However, she still felt very frightened to tackle the question of who I really was for her. She had to face a tremendous sense of loss, which she was not sure she could survive. This process was slow and painful, with steps of development followed by temporary regression and doubt. Gradually, the concrete phantasy turned into a symbolic connection with the analyst and with the mother that she had lost.

Mourning the ideal object and accepting the reality of the separateness of the object are necessary for development of a personal identity. They create a space to know oneself as a separate human being with one's own wishes, desires, memories and plans for the future. These processes are not only necessary in order to adapt to reality, but are also motivated by an internal need to become independent, with a mind of one's own.

Towards the end of her analysis, my patient could indeed 'spread her wings', gaining freedom to live her life and to develop her independent personal identity.

Note

In the introduction and discussion, I have used the masculine pronoun throughout, while aware that it relates to any sex.

References

Britton, R. (1989) 'The missing link: parental sexuality in the Oedipus complex'. In *The Oedipus Complex Today*, J. Steiner (ed.) (pp. 83–101). London: Karnac Books.

Britton, R. (1998) 'Subjectivity, objectivity and triangular space'. In *Belief and Imagination*, E. Bott Spillius (ed.) (pp. 41–58). London and New York: Routledge.

Freud, S. (1917) 'Mourning and melancholia', *SE* 14.

Klein, M. (1952) 'On observing the behaviour of young infants.' In *Envy and Gratitude and Other Works* (pp. 94–121). Reprinted by Karnac (Books) Ltd., London (1993).

O'Shaughnessy, E. (2015) 'Mental connectedness.' In R. Rusbridger (ed) *Inquiries in Psychoanalysis* (pp. 223–231). East Sussex and New York: Routledge.

Sodre, I. (2004) 'Who's who?. Notes on Pathological Identification.' In *Pursuit of Psychic Change*, The Betty Joseph Workshop, E. Hargreaves and A. Varchevker (eds.) (pp. 53–65). East Sussex and New York: Brunner-Routledge.

Sodre, I. (2005) 'The wound, the bow and the shadow of the object'. In *Freud: A Modern Reader*, R. J. Perelberg (ed.) (pp. 124–141). London and Philadelphia, PA: Whurr Publishers. Also in Sodre, I. (2015) *Imaginary Existences* (pp. 161–182). London: Routledge.

Wollheim, R. (1984) *The Thread of Life*. London: Cambridge University Press.

Steiner, J. (1992) 'The equilibrium between the paranoid-schizoid and the depressive positions'. In *Clinical Lectures on Klein and Bion*, R Anderson (ed.) (pp. 46–58). London and New York: Routledge.

Steiner, J. (2020) *Illusion Disillusion and Irony in Psychoanalysis*. London and New York: Routledge.

11

LIQUID FEAR

A Dissolving Identity

Sharon Numa

I have borrowed the term 'liquid fear' from the Polish sociologist and philosopher Zygmunt Bauman (2006) as it resonates with what I believed to be my patient's internal state. Bauman used the term in a sociological context to describe a social ill within contemporary Western life, and one with significant psychological consequences that has an interesting link to the kind of internal object relations described by Ron Britton (2003) in his elaboration of Bion's (1959) concept of the ego-destructive superego. The use of the term 'liquid fear' caught my interest because my patient Mrs A, who was dominated by a crushing autocratic superego, was subject to the experience of a melting visceral type of fear, beneath her more brittle hard-edged external carapace. This constantly shifting fear invaded her psychic life leaving her with a feeling that she had no form or solidity. She frequently borrowed her mother's phrase with which to describe herself – 'a scrap of nothing'. The sense of lacking identity was not well served by the defences she used to manage her fear and give herself form, which I will describe further on. Bauman points to uncertainty – such as one feels in the dark – as prompting what he calls 'derivative fear', that is:

> …a feeling of insecurity (the world is full of dangers that may strike at any time with little or no warning) and vulnerability (in the event of the danger striking, there will be little if any chance of escape or successful defence…)

> A person who has interiorized such a vision of the world that includes insecurity and vulnerability will routinely, in the absence of a genuine threat, resort to the responses proper to a point-blank meeting with danger; 'derivative fear' acquires a self-propelling capacity.
>
> (2006, p. 3)

These aspects of vulnerability, insecurity and a sense of danger were indeed inner states of my patient that fed and propelled each other. I also recognised the author's argument that this state leads to a degree of withdrawal from a world felt to be full of unspoken dangers, and the loss of confidence in the ability to cope with such threats, particularly as the fear has become separated from its original source. In Mrs A's case, there had been in reality a murderous, cruel and oppressive 'state' which gave unconscious support to her internal organisation. There was a family history of the holocaust: her mother's much loved father and both of his parents had perished in the concentration camps when her mother was nine years old.

Bauman looks to explain the way *obedience* is demanded by the State of their citizens in return for supposed protection from fear, without which there is a threat to their very existence (Melanie Klein argued that the primitive ego's most fundamental fear was that of annihilation). Although Mrs A did have a sane and dependent part of the self which could be recognised, it was also mocked and ridiculed by the more hidden narcissistic superior part of her, a cruel superego. The split-off aggressive part of the self, unconsciously identified with an internal object she believed did not want her to thrive, to grow up, to develop and have a separate identity and life of her own, also allowed her to be infantilised by her husband and bullied by siblings.

Britton's elucidation of a type of relationship between the ego and an envious superego helped me to understand Mrs A's plight, and I would suggest that Bauman's concept of the relation between the state, obedience and liquid fear can be linked to Britton's idea that even in an autocracy, we can sometimes make changes by altering the constitutional relationship between leader/autocrat and subject or citizens. In terms of analytic work, even where the adverse nature of the superego remains in place, we can help the patient by changing the relationship between ego and superego. Britton argues that self-observation is an ego function, not a superego function. The ego may judge in a realistic light, whereas the superego draws on moral judgement to judge and restrict the ego. Instead of seeking a balance, the superego may seek 'to subordinate the ego and demand subservience' (p. 73). This is the 'authority' that patients may need to overthrow. He explains: 'In particular it can help to wrest from the superego the function of judging both internal and external reality. This I think of as the ego's emancipation' (p. 104).

Such a shift is implicitly part of a move from the paranoid schizoid to the depressive position. Britton says that in the case of an ego destructive superego, one may have to actually 'depose the autocrat' since this type of superego is not merely harsh, it is destructive to the ego (which I believe inevitably means an attack on personality structure and personal identity). In my view, this is so because compliance and appeasement of the tyrannical superego create a psychic split, as substantial areas of emotional life have to be silenced and split off, dividing the self, attacking its creativity and development. As has been suggested by a number of authors referred to in the Introduction and in Chapter 1 (Numa), the reality orienting functions of the ego and the exercise of competence and mastery are central to a healthy sense of identity. Britton notes that in cases where the superego usurps the reality-orienting function and the use of judgement that rightly lie within the province of the ego, raising itself up in the internal world as judge and jury, the ego comes under threat from an *internal* 'police and judiciary' (op. cit., p. 118).

Freud (1933) describes a certain moralistic severity of the superego in the melancholic patient which leaves the ego feeling helpless and at its mercy. He speaks of the way in which the overly severe superego ill-treats, humiliates and abuses the 'poor ego' and links this to the question of guilt, the tension between ego and superego.

I felt that Mrs A suffered at the hands of a harsh superego whose activity drove her to aspire to 'inhuman' standards of perfection, while usurping the reality-orienting functions of the ego.

Klein has made the important point that the ego can only survive the hostile internal object by the internalisation of and identification with the good object.

Mrs A's complex and difficult internal relationship with the primary maternal object, as well as between parts of the self (ego and superego) sets the stage for significant problems of identity. In describing the ego-destructive superego residing in the psychotic part of the personality, Bion (ibid.) makes a statement that I feel can be applied to Mrs A in that it illuminates the intensity of the threat under which she laboured.

> The internal object which in its origin was an external breast that refused to introject, harbour, and so modify the baneful force of emotion, is felt, paradoxically, to intensify, relative to the strength of the ego, the emotions against which it initiates the attacks. These attacks on the linking function of emotion lead to an over-prominence in the psychotic part of the personality of links which appear to be logical, almost mathematical, but never emotionally reasonable. Consequently the links surviving are perverse, cruel, and sterile.
>
> (p. 315)

The cruelty of Mrs A's harsh superego was most clearly manifested in her submission to abuse (I'm stupid, useless, I'll never be anything, I'm a scrap of nothing) and the ever present persecutory guilt that sanctioned this as well-deserved. This cut the patient off from any contact with the possibility of a 'good' creative self. At the same time, there were not only unconscious but conscious reasons for guilt which showed her just how 'bad' she was: the patient could show a startling degree of aggression in an underhand way, as was demonstrated on a particular occasion when she rushed to purchase an item she was fond of that her husband had broken, knowing that he had set about doing just that. She admitted she would savour the moment she would say it was 'too late, already done'. This suggested that the patient could not allow her objects to make reparation but held on to grievance in a mood of triumph. Within the analytic relationship, the attack on a good creative link was more subtle and reflected her inability to make use of the potential space between us that Winnicott (1971) refers to as the location of 'play'. Instead, interpretations and observations were met with a kind of inverted logic in which things were 'explained' to prove (unfailingly) that the patient had been wrong or useless on the distressing occasion under discussion. These chess moves, in which she countered whatever I said with a closed kind of 'knowing' seemed to me to give her some unconscious masochistic and sadistic gratification. Her 'arguments' against herself were indeed presented as Bion describes, as 'logical, almost mathematical, but never emotionally reasonable'. Things were thought about in a concrete way: they were either right or wrong, black or white. I was reminded of her telling me that she never played as a child. Concretising her experiences and thinking in this way — which soon showed itself to be despotic and tyrannical (in a manner that we associate with paranoid-schizoid functioning) — I think allowed Mrs A to cling to apparent solidity in the face of 'liquid fear'. Fixed beliefs, 'knowing' about her guilt, and exactly in what way she was guilty, meant that the real question of what the balance of guilt and responsibility might be could not be considered. Hence, in the analysis during the early years, there was little room for movement, little room for 'play'. This cruel 'attack on linking' had a deadening effect on the analytic work though it gradually and very slowly shifted over time.

The absence of a 'third', a helpful resourceful paternal object with whom to identify, a father that might have provided form or structure, some solidity, did little to mitigate Mrs A's internal structural and emotional deficits. She saw her father as passive and weak.

It seemed to me that Mrs A's difficulties were due to the faulty or failed introjection of a good object (at the earliest stages, the mother's breast). The precarious position of the good object meant that it had to be fiercely protected from the aggressive, murderous and destructive parts of the self which were therefore split-off, leading to an internal situation where integration was at some level experienced as catastrophic. Thus, her sense of identity had remained under-developed and unstable. A melancholic identification with the maternal object clearly felt safer than recognising her aggression towards an ambivalently loved mother whom she defensively idealised. The usual 'reproaches' to the self which Freud showed us are in fact reproaches to the object of identification were particularly severe and cruel in Mrs A's case and it is the impact of this on her sense of identity that I chiefly want to explore here since I think this patient demonstrates how the severity of the internal object/superego intensified the need for splitting, creating a deep division within her personality structure.

Bion (ibid.) suggests that a pathological superego arises as a result of serious failures in communication between mother and child, which are experienced as attacking the link between mother and child. The mother, in such a case, does not allow the child's communications 'in', the child feels shut out and instead of a normal superego, a 'super' ego (in a position of superiority) is set up above the ego rendering it unsafe. Both elements, the refusal of ingress and the superior quality of the superego, emerged in Mrs A's analysis.

The Patient

Background

Early in the analysis, Mrs A brought this dream:

> She and her sisters were young, and in the family home. They were standing outside of the parental bedroom – all of them crying and hammering on the bedroom door begging to be let in. The parents did not come out or open the door.

A DISSOLVING IDENTITY

This gave me an early insight into her experience of being refused ingress, of being unable to project into an overburdened, unhappy maternal object, but it also suggested the presence of a couple in a hostile alliance against her. In the analysis, weekend and holiday breaks, when she was shut out of my room, were also particularly difficult in the early years of the analysis. Mrs A would feel terribly alone, hopeless and depressed but would occasionally contact me in the hope of some relief.

There was one area in which Mrs A had managed to feel pleasure and that was in raising her son. For years, she had dreaded and feared the thought of having children and she felt that it was only through (a previous) therapy which she had embarked on several years earlier that she had managed to become pregnant. Her fear had been that she could only produce a deformed baby. It seemed that this was an identification with a mother who had tragically had a stillborn infant boy with various defects. She was, I think, identified both with the non-viable baby and with the mother of a damaged child. In addition, Mrs A was a 'replacement baby' for this dead child, and this impacted on her weak sense of identity since she believed her mother really wanted a replacement *boy* (the baby boy I speculated was linked in her mother's mind with the lost father). Though the baby was given a name, he was never to be mentioned again, joining mother's father and his parents behind the wall of silence. Mrs A's own son was in some sense felt to be a reparative gift to her mother.

Mrs A's mother was full of unassimilated losses that could not be spoken about. There were certain house rules in which anything that came from the world – news, television programmes, people – that had the potential for upsetting her was forbidden. Long periods of 'radio silence' were imposed. On one occasion, when the family GP visited the house to express his concern about the children, her mother became distressed and he was summarily ejected. The silence of un-verbalised psychic pain is a situation familiar in holocaust survivors and their offspring, impacting on later generations. I imagine that 'radio silence' unconsciously conveyed a number of things such as fear of knowledge, fear of facing any painful reality, but perhaps also the wish that the children should be silent about their emotional needs. Despite this, Mrs A tried to find her voice in therapy. In her first therapy with Dr X, she had spent months in silence feeling she did not know what to say, what was inside her or why she sought therapy. She only knew she felt somehow desperate.

Although initially very defensive and protective of a good image of her mother, the patient eventually spoke of her sense of great loneliness as a child. She said that if one of the children was distressed or needed help, her father would shield her mother while offering nothing of himself: 'don't bother your mother' being a familiar refrain. She remembers one of her sisters crying for nights in her bed; no direct comfort was offered. The children all struggled with depression into adulthood.

Over time, I learned of the more frightening mother: angry, harsh, and scary to other children, who would not come to the house. She frequently lost her temper or humiliated my patient for being 'useless' in a particular area of schoolwork, an area of skill that Mrs A masochistically found a place for in her current life trying over and over again to master the subject she most hated and felt most defeated by. This I assumed kept mother close internally but also kept Mrs A enslaved, further illustrating that there was to be no 'emancipation of the ego'. She brought a dream in which she was a school prefect, standing at the top of the school stairs (the superior superego) waiting to reprimand the other girls as they came up the stairs. There was no doubt some relief to be gained by this identification with the aggressor. However, she was clearly also the 'told off' schoolchild. This role of superior prefect perhaps expressed an expectation of my analytic position.

Mrs A attended twice weekly before moving to a full analysis, which lasted seven years. She described feelings of anxiety and helplessness, feeling depressed about reaching her stage of life having 'achieved nothing'. I was struck by the fact that the patient constantly anticipated catastrophe, opprobrium, punishment or cruel humiliation from her interactions with the world (which were therefore reduced). Fear and anxiety were clearly ego restrictive and she seemed to feel, referring back to Bauman, that in the event of danger striking there would be 'little chance of escape or successful defence' (op. cit.). It was as if the patient's ego functioning was paralysed, in a state of terror. Nothing could be ventured, curiosity and exploration were felt to be either impossible or dangerous, and learning therefore problematic. Even as a child, Mrs A apparently had little curiosity and interest in anything, and despite being initially considered quite bright, she did not fare as well as she should have at school. Throughout her adult life, she continued to feel 'stupid', without a proper mind and with no opinions of her own. Yet, she was the one family member who pursued psychological help, the other members relying on anti-depressants.

In part, Mrs A identified with a harsh maternal object (who perhaps also self-protectively 'identified with the aggressor'). Mrs A initially kept the 'bad' hostile object in relation to the angry therefore 'bad' self out of awareness; to the fore was her identification with the mother that had sustained painful losses, was withdrawn and depressed and fearful of the world. Mrs A was jumpy, easily alarmed, vigilant; sometimes, feeling a sickly feeling in the stomach, the object of her fears often formless but fear awaiting her as she woke.

Her inner world felt bleak and unforgiving. During the analysis, Mrs A received a letter from a nanny who had abruptly left the family so many years earlier. The letter was an apology for the way she had left which, the nanny explained, was because she could not endure 'Bleak House' a moment longer.

The defining inter-generational trauma of the holocaust hung over the home and played a significant role in the transmission of terror and anxiety. Other significant losses were to follow. Not only did Mrs A's mother lose a baby but also one of her adult children to a terminal illness. Mrs A was in identification with a mother in perpetual unresolved mourning, sitting by the grave and inhabited by ghosts.

SHARON NUMA

The Analysis

A DREAM

The very first dream that Mrs A brought to analysis was as follows:

> She is with her mother in a (dark?) room. She is anxious, she goes over to the mother to sit on her lap. As she sits, her mother dissolves 'like mercury'.

The dream of a dissolving object that cannot 'hold' her, a maternal object who lacks solidity, vividly frames the central problem for this patient. As if in opposition to the dissolving liquidity of her object, Mrs A herself had become superficially quite hard-edged, holding herself in a distant rigid way, aloof, while internally experiencing profound anxiety (an early infantile anxiety) about the 'dissolution' of the incipient, fragile self; she was therefore forever in a state of 'liquid fear'.

The rigid carapace and cold defensive narcissistic withdrawal interestingly gave the impression to others that Mrs A could be very fearsome, and indeed there was a well of unexpressed anger and bitterness beneath her fragility. Klein has illuminated the process by which the phantasied projection of destructive hatred into the object creates a terror of the potential aggressive attack, represented in phantasy as coming from 'outside' of the self.

In contrast to her striking appearance, a tall erect and elegant woman, Mrs A sought to 'dissolve' into an object felt to have clearly defined lines, who might supply her with an identity. She also felt small and wanted protection 'under the wing', as she put it, of a big object. She borrowed the backbone of the object, using this as a refuge from the experience of feeling vulnerable, a shameful, unformed self. It soon became clear in the analysis, however, that the phantasy of introjecting a strong rescuing object was easily transformed into enlisting the help of the powerful object to join with her primitive superego in order to strike fear more effectively and attack any attempts at freedom. In projecting her aggression, the patient had lost contact with any capacity for assertiveness. She had, in her view, 'no backbone'. Mrs A's confusion between harshness and strength led her to depend on firm judgements emanating from the hostile alliance between aggressive individuals and the cruel part of herself. There were many highly critical, angry family members who could be recruited for this role. She could then orient herself around their inner conviction and righteousness. In the analysis, Mrs A attempted to enlist me to join her in attacking herself and felt frustrated and upset when instead I interpreted her activity, as this felt to her as if I just didn't understand 'how stupid she was' and was offering false reassurance or appeasement. I would be experienced like the (maternal) grandmother who had run after her saying anxiously 'Your mother does love you *really*'. On the other hand, it was possible that the defence of borrowing the backbone of her objects unconsciously included a hope of finding an object able to stand up to the intimidating pathological organisation.

Henri Rey (1994), though discussing borderline patients, gives an interesting description of patients not unlike Mrs A where the normal process of projection is replaced by excessive splitting and fragmentation under the sway of persecutory and elemental anxieties, thus fragmenting the ego and impoverishing the self. He argues that good and bad parts of the self may both be projected – with the good aspects often being split-off and 'housed' in the analyst for safekeeping because of the fear of their destruction. The patient may fear the loss or theft of important parts of the self. It was striking that during Mrs A's analysis, there were many dreams in which her valuables (which were secreted away in apparently 'safe' places that never felt safe) were stolen or lost. Only towards the end of the analysis did this dream with its many iterations have a different outcome, as she chased the robber and retrieved her jewels. Rey notes that there is constant vigilance and anxiety; identity is unstable and prone to diffusion. He suggests that such patients have an external shell or carapace but no 'vertebral column', without which he suggests aspects of identity are borrowed, stolen or imitated, which further creates a sense of insecurity. (Again, this links with Bauman's notion of derivative fear being fostered by vulnerability and insecurity.) Rey further argues that, in these cases, identity depends on the moment by moment evaluations of their objects; hence, there is constant fear of identity *dissolution*. Rey would seem to agree that this picture arises where there is faulty introjective identification, identifications imbued with fear and persecutory anxieties, resulting in enormous difficulties in stabilising the ego. The implications for identity development and security are clear. Freud, in the case of melancholia, went so far as to suggest that a certain type of extraordinarily harsh and severe superego is committed to the death of the ego (1923).

My clearest sense of Mrs A early in the analysis was of someone who felt she was a 'nobody'; I felt she was left adrift by a mother lost in her grief and rage, but that in addition, the 'identities' of both her dead sister and the dead baby cast a shadow on her own so that she was unable to struggle out of the shadows and discover who she was. (How could she compete with the idealised dead?) Unconscious awareness of her mother's inner world as one populated by cruelly murdered and dead objects, I think left Mrs A as a child filled with uncontained terror, in the belief that emotional experiences could not be survived, or that hatred and cruelty would always 'win'.

When Mrs A first came to her analysis, there was a striking absence of *overt* complaint either on her own behalf or that of her siblings: no protest and no defiance. The belief in her own 'fatal flaw' underwrote every account of how she found herself in this sterile situation. She spoke with some interest, however, of the way in which her mother's 'badge of disability' was idealised within the family. This disability referred to the fact that her mother's legs, and therefore walking, was seriously impaired for some years following an accident while she was in fact pregnant with Mrs A. There was no doubt a link in her mind between mother's ill fortune and her own conception and birth. After a time, Mrs A could see that she too proudly wore the 'badge of disability'. Her idealisation of her mother as a damaged heroine who had indeed sustained many traumatic losses, including the loss of her youthful healthy body, also meant that my patient could not directly express any aggression or hostility towards her. How could she attack a damaged object?

I speculate that survivor guilt was deeply embedded in Mrs A's mother which, in turn, was added to my patient's own survival shame and guilt. Her maternal grandfather had rescued the patient's mother and maternal grandmother, bringing them to England, fleeing the Nazis, then returned to rescue his own parents, but failed in that attempt: all three were caught. Mrs A herself harboured an unconscious belief that she too had survived 'at the expense of' the dead baby and of the sister R who died prematurely in her late 30s. This called into question my patient's entitlement to life, unconsciously based on feelings of guilt, and responsibility for harm. Mrs A saw herself as the 'wrong survivor' and the 'the wrong baby' who could not enliven or restore mother.

Faced with the extent of horror, of death and damage, Mrs A unconsciously felt hopeless and inadequate in the face of the enormous reparative task. This feeling was further compounded by the fact that she had projected good aspects of her self – all the potential for achievement – into R, another idealised internal object. R had been clever, a professional, which she believed drew her parents' approval, a very scarce resource. Despite R having been deeply unhappy and on anti-depressants for years, Mrs A saw her sister as successful: she had done work of merit. This she attributed to an enviable quality: R's *defiance*, while *she* was fearful and condemned to shame. *Defiance* suggests an important link to Britton's notion that the ego has to 'overthrow' the autocracy to gain independence. There was an occasion in the analysis when Mrs A spoke of her admiration for an adolescent girl who had travelled across the country to see her son, without telling her parents what she was doing or where she was. I was interested that Mrs A did not see this as reprehensible or worrying, she simply admired the girl's 'chutzpah'.

In fact, the ability to use her own judgement *was* impaired by the projection of her critical thinking into the object who became the 'brains' (thus weakening the integrity of her ego). This I believe is what her first therapist had meant when, she reported, he said 'you make yourself stupid'. I soon discovered that Mrs A unconsciously required me to be a type of auxiliary ego, someone who 'knew' and could tell her what to do, an 'R'.

Sitting by the Grave

I frequently felt that the analysis was the scene of a 'life and death' struggle. In the first few years, the atmosphere was often one of gloom in which very little that felt creative or fruitful was allowed to develop between us. It seemed that this analysis was also to be a 'stillbirth'. I was simply invited to join my patient, with her mother, to sit at the graveside, and in the worst moments, to watch the internment of the child, with all its potential. In this sense, there was a profound attack on linking, as described by Bion (above). However, Mrs A attended regularly and faithfully. Her mood oscillated between expressions of her many fears (of poverty, of jewellery theft, of her husband D losing the business and fear of his frequent ill-tempered accusations and rages) and ruminations that her 'lack', her 'fatal flaw', would be discovered and deservedly condemned. Occasional shifts in her state of fearful anxiety and low self-esteem did not last. There seemed to be no end to the variations in dispiriting and cruel attacks she could make on herself, while being absolutely resistant at this point to seeing her accusations as being levelled at me/the maternal object for being 'useless' to her although I suggested on many occasions that she was not only talking about a 'useless' her but of the two of us as a useless mother/baby couple.

The countertransference was complex since I either felt dispirited by this, or wished to 'shake' her out of her masochism (and then would have enacted the role of her autocratic superego) or was prompted to feel outraged on her behalf at the way she was being treated, perhaps being pulled into an alliance against another – usually her husband. If I questioned her view of herself and her extremely punitive approach to her ordinary human errors, Mrs A would suggest that her errors were not 'ordinary', they were particularly 'stupid'. Beneath this, outside of her awareness, was a phantasy of narcissistic perfection, a perfect her that should – perhaps *could* – exist.

It was difficult for Mrs A to feel at all convinced that there was an element of gratification and excitement in her masochistic activity, but I felt certain that in taking up this position she could defeat and triumph over her maternal object/analyst while simultaneously triumphing over – and sacrificing – the part of her that was in need of care and attention. Mrs A tended to use any insight gained through my comments – such as her deep sense of grievance – with which she agreed, as a stick with which to beat herself rather than to expand understanding in the service of development. In fact, my attempts to introduce 'understanding' as opposed to judgement were generally met with arguments based on the concrete, curiously inverted logic that I described earlier, which would return us both to a position of hopelessness. If as a result of our work together in a session Mrs A felt able to venture beyond her internal prison, she would come alive and feel hopeful, but this would soon be ruthlessly quenched by further anxieties and caveats, aborting her embryonic attempts. When such moments did occur, she reminded me of Freud's (1938) description of the amoeba quickly withdrawing its pseudopodia at the slightest obstacle. Later, in the analysis, Mrs A rather poignantly referred to this as a tiny flame of a candle that would suddenly and rapidly be extinguished.

It took me some time to realise that Mrs A unconsciously needed me to carry hope on her behalf. However, I had to be careful not to harbour any *specific* hopes since that would be struck down. I knew that this degree of hopelessness and destructiveness was also a form of resistance to the analytic work. Mrs A later described how she could only feel 'safe' if she did not move, if *nothing changed* – despite the evidence that this defence did not guarantee any degree of real internal security, only such safety as compliance with autocracy can offer.

There seemed to be a crucial conflict: if one mourns and tries to move on, there is the threat of guilt followed by retaliation for forgetting and betraying the dead. Being caught in an identification with a mother inhabited by dead victims meant that she could never fully come alive since *living itself was an act of disloyalty*. Mrs A's did not feel able to aggressively assert a right to liberty and a separate identity when loyalty was defined as 'sitting by the grave' in identification with the dead, with the damaged maternal object. This however meant the psychic 'death' of the self.

The Court Room

As time went on, the tone of our sessions did change. Mrs A became more curious and brought her own understanding a little more actively (allowing links to be made, curiosity and learning to expand), but I also gained deeper insight into the frightening courtroom in which she lived, where the more she dared to strive for autonomy, the more the malignant superego attempted to exercise its full authority. Britton describes patients who are 'internally menaced, particularly when they show signs of independent personal development, sexual maturity, or creativity' (p. 120). He notes that the *fear* of envy is prominent, and this was apparent in Mrs A's anxiety that if she had anything good, it would be stolen.

Now, however, there seemed to be a battle developing: the more Mrs A was able to have a mind of her own, the more malignant the internal organisation became. During this period, I felt she very much needed me as a firm object to help her stand up to the terrifying object and internal threats.

A clearer view of the 'court room' as it was played out in our sessions, however, gave us the opportunity to address this envious tyrannical part of herself. I will try to give a flavour of this from a week's analysis, through brief vignettes and a session.

A DISSOLVING IDENTITY

Monday

Mrs A had managed to recognise certain hostile spiteful feelings she had towards another woman Y. She had been able to think about this with a bit of understanding and some 'ordinary' rather than persecutory guilt, and she felt sorry for her role in the dispute. She had been able to tolerate the idea of her envy and jealousy towards Y and allowed the possibility of some envy towards me.

Tuesday

On Tuesday, she reported that following yesterday's session, she had been able to have a genuinely helpful conversation with Y, and both had felt closer and better. There was a sense of relief and surprise that she had been able to be 'straight'.

Wednesday Session

MRS A: I woke up feeling afraid, wishing I needn't ever have to move. A horrible feeling in my stomach. (pause) I don't know what I dreamt – ... I just realise that it's safer for me if there is no change in my life or in my routine. I just get frightened. And now I'm supposed to reconcile the figures for the business. But I know I'll get it wrong. (She continued for some time about the task, her fear, her husband's anticipated fury and so on).

ANALYST: Perhaps what you've just said is a clue to your feeling of fear and anxiety. The internal shift in how you were able to think about Y, and talk with her about it, though it was important and felt relieving, now feels a source of anxiety. It frightens you to even think you might 'reconcile' your very conflicted and opposing, sometimes envious, feelings about her (Y) and about me.

MRS A: Well, it looked for a moment as if I could have a better relationship with Y...but I don't know.
(pause) Then in a more animated tone of voice:

I wanted to tell you…Beryl (an acquaintance) had her event, it was a nice celebration. I suddenly had the idea to bake her a cake and take it for the event. So I did! And it came out OK! It didn't collapse…even if it wasn't perfect.

(I felt that she was quietly pleased; it was known between us that she had always been afraid of trying to bake, and also of spontaneous acts, so this was a significant step. I also noted that she could tolerate the 'imperfect' cake).

SHE CONTINUED: That was a cake my mother used to bake for T (her son). But I'm no good at baking. …So it felt good to even try the recipe… She was good at those cakes. Anyway, Beryl was pleased… so I was pleased. Later on when I heard that no one else had done that sort of thing for the occasion… I was even more pleased! So you see, it was all selfish, it wasn't real kindness. (Now sounding harsh) It wasn't generous really. It was all about me… "I was the only one who did that", pleased with myself. How do I know I was being sincere? You've said I don't trust my love. Well perhaps I shouldn't.

(The mood of the session had begun with anxiety, then shifted to something more hopeful as she told me about the cake, but now she seemed both deflated and 'satisfied' with her analysis of the situation).

ANALYST: You remembered something good from your mother and felt that I also offered you something helpful on Monday, which you were able to use. These memories of your mother doing something for your own child, as maybe you felt with me, helps you to reconcile a bit with her – and things felt better. You talked to Y. You felt on impulse that you would bake a cake for Beryl to celebrate her achievement, you could be generous. But then something in you gets very active and is ready to spoil and deflate, to bring about an *internal* collapse –. You had a spontaneous wish to do something special for a friend, but you've managed to store up and use what I said to join in the attack on yourself – destructively attacking the 'good' connection between you and me in your mind as well as between you and Beryl. Maybe you also suspect my motives, perhaps what I offer is based entirely on my own self-importance – not genuine.

Thursday

The following session begins with Mrs A agitated and anxious. She says apropos of the forthcoming weekend away with her husband:

> I'm worried about my usual thing... a burglary. And just as I was saying that to you the other day, guess what, J (her husband's colleague) has been burgled! I know you'll say I shouldn't worry, but these things do happen. And I asked D to put in additional security locks and he waves it away – "it'll be alright; we've got locks" ... Yes, we do, but we need more ...There are all sorts of robberies going on. J's robbery took place around 2 am. It all makes me afraid. I almost don't want to go away...

Analyst: You seem to hear what I say as perversely denying the reality of burglaries. But what you conveyed to me yesterday was that for you 'security' means being 'locked in', not moving, not going away from your usual mental home which is surrounded by fears of theft and intrusion. Immobility is your 'security lock'. I think this is what we witnessed in yesterday's session over the cake where you robbed yourself of a good feeling with Beryl and a good contact with me, and you feel stuck in this cycle, which ends in fear and defeat.

Mrs A then went into a detailed account of the various robberies she had heard about over time, as if the only thing she could now contemplate was a concrete burglary. I began to feel worn out and misunderstood, contradicted at every turn whenever I spoke, as the patient sought to justify and reinforce her fears.

After a time, possibly in the hope of shifting to more symbolic territory, I raised the question as to whether the patient believed I would punish her for her act of freedom, for leaving in the hope of enjoying a weekend as a couple (even though she would not in fact be missing any sessions).

The session ended with her saying suddenly that actually her impulse to make the cake had felt spontaneous, at the time, she likes Beryl and it seemed a nice thing to do.

I thought in the vignettes, we see some progress towards ordinary rather than persecutory guilt in relation to Y who is important in her life, allowing a move towards reparation – but then this comes under threat; will her progress be stolen?

A way of understanding this material might be that Mrs A believes that if she takes and uses something from me, something of her 'mother's recipes', she has 'stolen' the good thing (cake/breast) and feels anxious.

Black and white thinking would frequently return after periods of progress. Mrs A persistently held herself to account for her failures, and often indirectly me for mine. She prosecuted her case forensically for someone who was 'stupid'. I was often to say, that in this terribly unrelenting internal situation, there was never a witness for the defence and no mitigation.

During this phase of the analysis, Mrs A could begin to disagree with things I said, though not often in a straightforward way since she wished to avoid open conflict, and her challenges were, of course, always framed in terms of guilt or innocence, blame or exculpation.

Between Life and Death, from Murderous Superego to Humanity and a Sense of Identity

Over time, Mrs A began to exercise more independence of thought and action as well as to own some aggression and defiance; she became more courageous and lively, less fearful. Interestingly, she kept an unusual pet animal that was in fact quite aggressive, presenting occasional danger to others. Naturally, this pet which was often kept 'locked up' had been the focus of a great deal of analytic attention. Mrs A finally made an attempt to tackle this 'pet' problem.

A DISSOLVING IDENTITY

Mrs A began to stand up for herself but suffered when there was a need to challenge any authority figure. On one such occasion which involved medical authority, she dreamt that there was a potential assault by dangerous men which she could avoid if she 'kept her eye on the good person', which she did in the dream, thus managing to avoid capture. This dream also had associations to a TV programme called 'The Designated Survivor'. Her guilt at being a 'survivor' which we had broached many times could be thought about again, in a way that felt bearable to her. Nevertheless, it was clear that threats and fears of extermination had been aroused by her attempt to robustly address the difficult external situation. Perhaps, this was made more vivid because it was her *body* that Mrs A had to entrust to the 'medical men' who were transformed into dangerous, threatening male figures. What she may have experienced as analytic 'surgery' I suspected was bound up in the dream but what felt most immediately available and significant was the shadow of tortured bodies – bodies tortured by Nazi men. It was as if her finding a backbone to protest about how she was being treated mobilised the internal state authority, which attempted to return her to captivity.

Some five years into analysis, Mrs A brought a dream which was to express a pivotal moment:

> I am a child, standing in front of my mother. There's a table. She is saying something, and I angrily jump up onto the table and shout defiantly "I am **not you. *I*** haven't damaged my legs. I **will** jump onto the table!" My mother looks furious and says "and if you do, see what will happen! I will cut off your legs."

This raised an important tansference issue. We could see how Mrs A feared the envious destructiveness of an internal mother who threatened retaliation in kind (given that her mother's legs were damaged) if she were to stand up to her, separate and claim her own identity. This view of the maternal object helped explain the fear Mrs A had most of her life in relation to having children: she came to recognise that in phantasy her mother was felt to be vengeful, envious and retaliatory and could not allow her any creativity – either normal babies or a normal life of her own. Could I, her analyst, allow her to develop her own identity and her own life?

The forces which operated to rob Mrs A of freedom were considerable, and there were movements towards freedom, followed by retreat. In a positive development, at the time, she began to consider leaving the office in which she worked, imprisoned with a task she hated which reminded her of ancient humiliations. Perhaps, she could do something that she might actually enjoy in a different area of work. She began to make investigations (daring to envisage an 'emancipation' of the ego) and was excited and invigorated.

Mrs A then had the following dream, which shows something of the life and death struggle between a superior superego and another a part of the self that makes a bid for freedom but is deemed to be greedy.

> I am leaving the office, which is like a small hut... I want to go out. It's sunny outside... I open the door and walk out; I'm holding two ice cream cones, one in each hand which I was enjoying. Then I looked up and saw my parents sitting together on a balcony looking down at me, accusing me silently of being greedy. They are very angry and disapproving. I run back into the hut... I wonder if I can get out through a small window.

There are various interesting aspects and symbols in this dream (such as the cones, presumably representing the wished-for good breasts), but here, I want to highlight the battle with the imprisoning, humiliating and accusing force of a hostile parental couple who drive her back, away from emancipation. It is interesting that the parents are on a balcony which as E. O'Shaughnessy has pointed out is the location of a pathological superego which watches the ego from a 'higher' place but is 'dissociated from ego functions like attention, enquiry, remembering, understanding' (O'Shaughnessy, 1999).

Mrs A did take up the new line of work; she was good at it and was appreciated by her new colleagues, which she could acknowledge with pleasure. She understood that the 'hovel' she had believed to be her future reality and destiny had always been the state of mind she inhabited.

Some months later, the mood of the sessions again shifted. Mrs A confronted difficult feelings of sadness and regret, particularly for the loss of time and opportunity, now that she had a sense of life's possibilities. It was a painful time for me as well as for my patient who faced depressive anxieties, which meant relinquishing the phantasy of complete restoration that would undo the damage of the past in a total way. The dream of 'actually' recovering what was lost or 'stolen' from her gave way to a sorrowful acceptance of reality. In the process of mourning, both regret and remorse had to be confronted as well as her envy of those who had built up 'a life' over time which was a theme taken up in the transference. While expressing both anger and sadness, Mrs A, nevertheless, retained some hope that now life could be different.

Despite feeling bereft at her son leaving home, Mrs A could say in a spirited way, 'Well, *he* isn't sitting by the grave is he? He's saying 'I'm off Mum'! She was deeply relieved that the cycle of entrapment and paralysis had been broken.

In the summer, the patient has a dream of wearing a colourful dress which seemed partly to be associated with a dress I had worn, but particularly with an art exhibition Mrs A had visited that had paintings with vibrant colours. She also began to enjoy music (which as a younger woman she remembered she had felt moved by but again that flame had been 'extinguished'). Winnicott has argued that 'playing' (as I felt she could now do in the analysis) leads on naturally to cultural experience, to music and art. I interpreted that the patient now felt able to allow herself to come alive and allow some colour into her life. I felt hopeful that

Mrs A was perhaps able to internalise an 'alive' object who could also allow her her own colourful dress, her own identity.

Less controlled by a murderous superego, Mrs A no longer felt gripped by 'liquid fear'. An 'ideal' outcome had to be given up in favour of ordinary progress – not only was 'ordinary' aggression more accessible but so were her feelings of love and concern. With some sense of having a backbone, the patient could reclaim for the ego certain functions and abilities, reducing the projection of both good and bad aspects of the self, but she could also begin to reclaim from the internal object the right to freedom, and entitlement to her own separate life and identity.

References

Bauman, Z. (2006) *Liquid Fear.* Cambridge: Polity Press.

Bion, W. R. (1959) Attacks on Linking. *Int J Psychoanal.*, Vol. 40, pp. 308–315; also in *Second Thoughts* (pp. 93–100). London: Heinemann, 1967.

Britton, R. (2003) *Sex Death and the Superego.* London: Karnac (Books) Ltd.

Freud, S. (1923) The Ego and the Id. *S.E. 19.*

Freud, S. (1933) New Introductory Lectures on Psycho-Analysis. *S.E. XXII* (1932–1936). New Introductory Lectures on Psychoanalysis and Other Works.

Freud, S. (1938) An Outline of Psychoanalysis. *S.E. XXIII* (1937–1939). Part II.

O'Shaughnessy, E. (1999) Relating to the Superego. *Int. Journal Psychoanal.*, Vol. 80, pp. 861–871.

Rey, H. (1994) The Schizoid Mode of Being. Chapter 2, in *Universals of Psychoanalysis in the Treatment of Psychotic and Borderline States.* Ed Jeanne Magagna (pp. 8–30). London: Free Association Press.

Winnicott, D. W. (1971). *Playing and Reality.* London: Tavistock Publications.

12

IDENTITY AS THE THREADS OF MEANING THROUGH A PERSON'S LIFE

Denis Flynn

Introduction

This chapter describes a single case study of psychoanalysis in relation to a theory of personal identity. The man described was successful in outward terms, with a settled family life, secure profession and social stability, but he was deeply confused and in constant conflict within himself with a poor sense of his own value. This was beginning to alter when he entered a full analysis (five times a week lasting seven years) which started during his final years of work nearing retirement. The detailed clinical material presented here describes *a turning point in his emotional life*, occurring two and a half years into the analysis. There were signs at this point of the analysis of him moving out of the rigid positions he was hemmed in by and beginning to re-evaluate who he was, so opening up for himself the questions we would implicitly follow within the analysis: who am I? What is my identity? (Erikson, 1968, 1977). In effect the analysis would help him to recognise his inner disturbance, the resulting diffusion in his sense of identity and opened up the possibility to achieve real 'structural intrapsychic change', with an increased capacity for self-definition and a greater sense of his personal value (Erikson, 1966; Kernberg, 2006; Steiner, 1993, 2011).

A distinctive feature of this man, whom I will call Mr A, was a rigid character structure that I shall describe in terms of the role of omnipotent phantasy in his psychic life that was largely defensive but also destructive. Britton has described this type of narcissistic character structure as 'narcissistically detached', so Mr A was in effect in a 'psychic retreat' he was beginning to emerge from (Britton, 2003, pp. 145–178; Steiner, 1993, 2011). Underlying this structure were repeated traumatic failures to relate, from his early years which contained real experiences of chronic personal neglect, denigration and isolation, and in later development at different stages rigid patterns of relating to others. What also became apparent within analysis was that equally too there were repetitive attacks on linking at the earliest and deepest level aimed at wiping out or dissociating awareness and knowledge of his emotional states. In time, the process of redefining or rediscovering his personal identity went along with his painful recognition and courageous re-creation of links of further understanding. This was both to develop his mind and to have a more alive sense of his own bodily and mental states, to experience and know more fully who he was.

Before analysis, his omnipotent phantasy functioned to maintain an internal pattern of blocking links of emotional connection with others. Over time I realised that such patterns were not the total *fabric*, for he had significant emotional links as yet not fully realised in his main long-term partner relationship and family. Also, there were other fragmented threads seen in a cut-off split way to certain other dispossessed, discriminated against and disadvantaged characters, whom he supported often with frenetic care and considerable kindness. However, broadly, it was a chronic blocking of central aspects of his emotional experience and his connection to key primary figures and his family history and an inability to process his conscious and unconscious experience that underlay his omnipotent thinking.

Melanie Klein's work on primitive splitting and projective identification (Klein, 1946) describes this kind of abnormal or '*excessive* projective identification', which leads to splitting off of the bad that, in turn, weakens the ego, along with evacuative projection

IDENTITY AS THE THREADS OF MEANING

and loss of good parts of the self. The unconscious processes of denial and negation in Mr A's disturbed and psychotic states were aimed at *annihilation* of the object or awareness of the object. Capacity to make meaningful contact and awareness of his emotional states was therefore split and fragmented, dispersed or 'killed off'. This made sense within the analysis when we came up against more psychotic level of defences. In these moments, his personal history became unknowable full of doubt and deeply troubling, or conversely, it was defensively and falsely seen as 'already known'. His outlook then became rigid in a narcissistic defence.

This is characteristically an 'unbalanced situation' and prevents what Sharon Numa calls 'the dynamic equilibrium' between the paranoid-schizoid position (that is more fragmented and disturbing aspects) and the depressive position with more integrated aspects of the self and growth in self-awareness (Steiner, 1993). Movement away from more schizoid fragmented states associated with the paranoid schizoid position also cannot occur. It means being imprisoned in the present or in the past, blocking out what Loewald described as the 'ego's futurity' (see Introductory chapter of this volume). The original Oedipal objects, tied to libidinal aggressive relationships, cannot then be fully experienced and known, faced or given up in order to become in time properly internalised. A personality with a superego with a brittle rigidity cannot be given up.

To turn more now to the issue of personal identity, the possibility of change and the formation of a fuller sense of identity in a psychoanalytic way, I shall look at a philosophical underpinning of the concept of personal identity as it has been taken up by different authors. These include Richard Wollheim, Roger Money-Kyrle and following Wilfrid Bion's concept of 'thinking', Edna O'Shaughnessy, Giovanna Di Ceglie and others. Personal identity, for Wollheim, is known, *not* through *sameness* of traits, behaviour or mental states, nor simply in terms of either bodily or psychological theories alone. For any mental theory of identity involves some connection and awareness of integral aspects of bodily states and feelings; conversely, any bodily or corporeal theory of identity involves some recourse to mental intentions to adduce psychical states of mind (Wollheim, 1984, pp. 12–19).

Instead of sameness of either bodily or mental experiences, personal identity is to be approached by looking at *the unity relation that any life has to itself*, that is, as a relation that holds between any two parts of the same life. It is subjectively experienced and depends on imaginative creation of a sense of self, giving a unity to experience and a sense of identity in the process of a person leading their life over time (19). Wollheim describes this in his book's title as 'the thread of life'. In my view, in effect, there is not just one thread, but a series of threads, from different internal identifications, woven together to make one cloth in a particular fabric – an identity. In analytic terms, and following Bion, I think this identity involves a changing internal unconscious process with continuous transformations and new realisations about oneself and one's identity.

Wollheim describes how personal identity is developed from memories and phantasies. Memory represents the earlier event and 'conveys information' about it. Phantasy, although representing the past, does not convey information in the same way as memory, but it may convey feelings which elucidate and relate back to earlier memories and events. Hence, Klein's 'memories in feeling' in relation to primitive phantasies. The expansion of phantasy leads to the possibility of further awareness of detailed inner subjective states and to expanded states of mind. Bion's constructions of *models* allow abstracted elements of phantasy to be reconstructed over time to form an outline sketch of a link to the past. Over time, by comparison with and then letting go of other models formed, this link comes to correspond to the individual's own sense of *veridical memory*. Both memory and phantasy are in Wollheim's view dependent on earlier mental states in that they preserve and transmit a *causal* link between the earlier events and mental states and later events and mental states, and they further have *psychic force* because of that. The individual's ways of thinking and acting are therefore mediated through underlying persistent mental 'dispositions' (i.e. propensities to think or act) in a causal way with psychic force

IDENTITY AS THE THREADS OF MEANING

and 'a forward looking movement' – what Wollheim calls a 'diachronic expansion of the person'.

Wollheim's 'token iconic mental states' present and represent in a singularly vivid fashion earlier events in a person's life and their histories. These 'iconic mental states' 'are of individuals, but standardly they are of events, they may include parents…. historical figures, but they also can be things like (frightening figures)…. beasts of prey, or sweet smelling plants, or pieces of strange clothing' (1984, p. 62). For personal identity, transient states, memories and feelings, known analytically through states of free association (or in Bion's terms newly conceived realisations and 'dream states'), are as important as the continuing veridical memory of events that structure a life.

To look at the life of a person is, therefore, to look overall at *the whole cloth*, not just to trace a single thread or set of threads – but *to experience the feel, smell, touch and shape of the unique texture of the fabric, revealed in these 'iconic mental states' and their place within the whole of a person's life*. It gives attention to the *particular* fabric or *particular* shape of that person's experience at *critical times in a person's life*, that is known first in a non-cognitive or sensuous way then becomes more fully known when experienced more fully leading to growth of self-understanding, and this gives a unique shape to anyone's personal identity. I am reliant here on Bion's later thought that analysis at times can resemble more a process of 'psychomorphology' – experiencing and processing C category formulations of his Grid (the particular fabric of dream-thoughts, myths and models) – than a process of examining 'psychopathology', concerned with received ideas and memories derived from more cognitive E or F categories (conceptions and concepts) (Bion, 1970, p. 319). This especially occurs during periods of 'catastrophic change' that may begin to radically restructure a person's sense of their life, and this can be revealed in an analysis (Bion, 1966, Flynn, 2017). The sense of personal identity is, thus, not something that is proven, philosophically or, otherwise, but can only be experienced fully by a person within themselves. A personal identity makes sense when the individual relates together certain aspects of themselves and usually represents a coherence. Over time, this may be altered and partly changed so that, for some, there is a bringing together of these threads, and the subjective coherent experience, with a coalescing of coherent emotional states and memories 'into a fit' (Wollheim, 1984, 1999a,b).

Central in the construction of personal identity is the work of (the phantasy of) *introjection* – plus changes in *identification* and *projective identification* – and what Wollheim calls in similar but more broad philosophical terms, 'the continuity of experiential memory' and 'central imagining'. Relating this to Grinberg, it involves 'feeling oneself to be the same person over a succession of changes' (1999, pp. 162–163) when identity is developed from the successive assimilation of introjective identifications and the sorting out of projective processes. However, if original memories are lost, inaccessible, distorted or blocked, as they may be through powerful splitting and omnipotent phantasy (as we will see they were with Mr A), then normal assimilative introjection will be faulty or blocked. Other empirical and literature studies on identity also highlight that *the* central feature of identity is 'a sense of continuity over time' and 'an emotional commitment to a set of self-defining representations of self' (Wilkinson-Ryan and Weston, 2000, p. 529; Kernberg, 2006, p. 972).

Personal identity becomes known then through processes of change that occur via inner transformation at different stages of life, and during important developmental periods: infancy, childhood, adolescence, young adulthood, having a family and work, mid-life, older age and in movement towards death and the end of life. Importantly too, it is revealed within the transference relationship in the present within the work of analysis: 'a person leads his life at a crossroads…at the point where a past that has affected him and a future that lies open meet in the present' (Wollheim, 1984, pp. 30–31).

Bion from his text 'Attacks on Linking' onwards, and particularly in *Learning from Experience* (1962), describes in growing complexity how thinking is developed by connections that are made,

IDENTITY AS THE THREADS OF MEANING

or then broken apart or destroyed. Making and breaking links is a major continuing process in identity formation. A complete final sense of identity is never achieved by anyone, however, not just because of the ever-presence of splitting processes, but because '*mental connectedness* is *an ideal* achieved in different degrees, and never totally by anyone' (O'Shaughnessy, 2007). Wollheim acknowledges this, somewhat less clearly and definitively, when he noted there will be 'different measures of success that they have in making their lives of a piece' (1980, p. 299). Any construction and any sense of personal identity, linking past and present, is only achieved in a partial way and remains uncertain and incomplete but, importantly, can change and grow over time.

This tallies with Freud's view in *Moses and Monotheism*, 1938, that the identity relation of a people, in this case, the Jewish people, is an 'ideal unity'. The people came together and formed an identity as a people because of their shared experiences in the past and their shared belief in 'one God'. They also have in the present, and prescribed for the future, their shared rites and rituals in order to relate to God, and as such become his chosen people. Di Ceglie, following Money-Kyrle (1968), makes this point clearer. On an individual level, identity also involves not just orientation to an object, to make links, but a relation of 'mutual orientation'. It is not just the orientation of the child to the mother, nor the baby to the breast, nor just the mother's orientation to the child, but the dynamic positioning of the two parties involved and their relation to each other in a process of mutual orientation. In this model, the mother and child make links and growth occurs, and in so doing protect against splitting and the breaking of links (Di Ceglie, 2013). Identity as such is about a sense of development over time within a person and, importantly too, their orientation to their internal history and to other persons past, present and future. So a key area for identity is the orientation to home and culture, but also the orientation of a family, or home, or culture, to an individual, and whether this leads to the possibility of more connection, and ultimately more integration.

DENIS FLYNN

Clinical material

Mr A had a five times per week analysis which lasted seven years. He had a family and grandchildren, an early career in the forces in his native country and he was now head of a small high-precision engineering company in his adopted country. At the outset, he seemed tough-minded, omnipotent, rigidly rule-bound and emotionally distant, a bully obsessionally and remorselessly right, with others wrong and 'needing to be put right' by him. A chronic enmity and dissatisfaction characterised his relationships, especially with women, including his wife. Underneath, he was deeply confused and isolated, and I felt he was depressed with a hidden suicidality, which later I learnt had prompted his first turning for psychiatric and psychotherapeutic help.

In our first meeting, Mr A talked of his chronic sense of alienation from both his parents. He complained bitterly of his childhood, during which his mother constantly criticised and belittled him, mocking him, as an awkward child, with a cruel nickname – the 'animated pumpkin'. His father was away in his early years, so he was alone with his 'beautiful' mother, both drawn close yet repelled. He had little contact with his father on his return and dismissed him as weak and irrelevant, dominated by his wife.

He was interested in analysis but unsure and fearful of doing it himself. He had a kernel of hope when he found he could respond to a crisis in his daughter's adolescent life – he said simply almost incoherently 'something happened'. It sounded as if he was able to find something more alive in himself, to help her and then became closer to her again, and thereby not become trapped in (his usual) censoriousness and recrimination. In a quiet painful way, he whispered what he wanted of analysis, 'I want to be able to feel'. But at the end of this first meeting when agreeing to analysis, he said flippantly and ambivalently, 'I'm on for the ride'. This phrase suggested he was committing to analysis, but its sexualising ambiguity also shows this is mocked and made light of; it hints too at the

IDENTITY AS THE THREADS OF MEANING

uncertainty of what analysis could be and at his fear of confusing homosexual and sexual elements in his transference contact with his analyst.

However, as the analysis established itself, he became chronically emotionally stuck. He wanted assurances from me and protection from the 'black dog' of his depression. Emphatically, *he* did not want to be 'Shanghaied', deceived, by analysis. His dream in the third session was 'of the person behind him being a concrete post……… he was travelling and could not find his identity card'. It was the analyst he saw as cut off and insulated from him, like a concrete post behind him, even though he did not know who he was.

He was confused about men and women. He had had persisting idealised views of all women. They 'could do no wrong'… 'until one lied', then this switched to persistent denigration. Some men he saw in a romantically idealised way, mainly military and political figures, like Patton or Eisenhower, men who inspired in leadership like ideal father figures. He would break down in tears as he spoke of them. Other men he was drawn to were authoritarian figures like his headmaster, or homosexually motivated sadistic bullies. Quite soon, I became identified with such confusing figures in the transference.

Analytic progress was slow as he was rigidly defensive. Any personal insight was split off, denied or enacted in clashes between us. The atmosphere was often tense or fraught. At times, I wondered if he could take anything in, *whether he could introject*. He could dominate as his class or his money set him above others, including other members of his family, women or me. He feared coming and I could fear his dominating stances. But, I became aware too, in my countertransference, that I was keeping a wary distance from him, blanking out his wearied groans and sighs as he came into the room. I understood then that I too could become unconsciously enveloped by a malaise that *nothing could be achieved* in the analysis. I sensed then the terrifying fear of the emptiness that had led to his underlying depression and despair. However, his ways of obliterating awareness lessened over time in the analysis despite his and my feelings of frustration, fear and impasse. In time, I focussed interpretations on defensive aspects of his denial of having emotions, particularly in his transference to me. Repeatedly, and often when something had opened up a bit more, he said that gaps in our contact meant nothing to him, yet increasingly, I felt, he was emotionally affected. But, if I said this or suggested *he may feel* something, he vehemently denied it, saying I was deriding and humiliating him. This was like his mother had done, telling him he has a 'defect', 'having no feelings', now not just a defective child but a defective analysand. This led him to feel humiliation and depression and withdraw even more.

At times, something seemed to change: he made contact, took in and expressed his particular understanding, and something lightened. But often too there were flashpoints of misunderstanding when he seemed particularly enlivened by the contact between us. The transference relationship then felt less empty. No doubt he was, in part, excited by the sado-masochistic aspects of the conflict. But, he also seemed to take on that he was having a real emotional contact. It felt to me that something had changed. But typically, then all went quiet. I waited for more. Then sometime later (after a few sessions, or maybe couple of weeks), 'normal service was resumed' and silently his defensive stance was re-instated. Then he no longer accepted any link of understanding. Nor, he insisted, *could anything have happened.* For I was told bluntly, 'I have no feelings or curiosity about you'. He said this even though there were continuing indications in the analysis of his increasing curiosity about me and my life and development of an attachment to me.

An analytic session (Thursday)

First part of the session

About two and a half years into the analysis, a considerable shift occurred that affected his subsequent progress when he came to accept a meaningful link with me in the analysis. This was shortly

IDENTITY AS THE THREADS OF MEANING

before he was taking a week's holiday – the first unscheduled break that he had allowed himself to take. (I understood in this that something was more active in him.) He began the session in an unusually defensive position – being late and not caring. This in itself was very unusual, for he was never late nor would he allow himself to 'be in the wrong'. I thought that now he was more open to show or even enact something (Rosenfeld, 1964).

I interpreted, 'You feel guilty about being away for a week, and expect my criticism, so you are late and do something (unconsciously) to bring out my criticism'.

He listened and then perceptibly the mood changed. Unusually, he became clearly moved, reflective and depressed. He began speaking of death. In a quiet, serious tone, shaking with fear, he said in a strange monotone:

> I have had a lot of waking thoughts about dying. It is awful. I have a feeling of emptiness that the thought of dying gives me. I am afraid of dying…having to go to this emptiness…

But then, he paused for a long while and then I found him talking in a strange different voice – distracted and toneless (in what felt a *bizarre* moment).

> I was just now looking up to the ceiling where the grey green paint at the corner meets the white paint on the ceiling.

He paused for several moments…perhaps a minute or so.

He then added with slight but clearly painful feeling, 'As I look at this corner I feel a terrible feeling of emptiness'.

After a long pause I said, 'I think you fear death as a form of emptiness, a kind of oblivion'.

He seemed to acknowledge this with another fearful gulp.

After a long pause and silence, I now said, 'I think that in looking at the empty part of the change of the corner of the room, it's as if you put this disturbing feeling into that corner. It stays there … but then comes back into you'.

Another long pause, as he slowly even passively seemed to be taking something in.

I then said,

> I think your experience of an ending of the week today, and the ending coming up with the week away, brings to you a sense of something empty in the contact between us. This is painful, and you fear this coming back into you, and you wish to move away from it.

There was another, now long, more thoughtful pause.

Discussion of the first part of the session

I thought he was showing signs of his progress in the analysis, so unusually rather than being rigidly defended he opened up and overcame his resistances to contact. Then very quickly, with more emotional contact, he became more aware of his fear of death and the emptiness he was feeling. Then I understood and saw an attempt to wipe out his painful anxiety seeming to be evacuating it into the corner of the room. This seemed like an evacuative form of projective identification very like Bion's descriptions of a psychotic process, where emotional awareness is broken up and evacuated through a kind of temporary hallucination. But almost as quickly I thought that he was flooded with fear and anxiety: *the thought, now like a concrete thing*, also seemed to be coming back into him, like a thing re-entering him. My first interpretation described this as an *event* he experienced concretely. Then as I felt he understood this I spoke more symbolically about his transference experience that this break meant 'something empty was being experienced in the contact between us'. He was by then able to make sense of this (fragmented split-off) 'thing', then became calmer and moved back into emotional contact in the analysis. I think this movement was possible because he had begun to make contact with me and felt understood, particularly that he could feel that he was trapped in an isolated paranoid (schizoid) world (Bion, 1957, 1958; Sohn, 1985).

IDENTITY AS THE THREADS OF MEANING

The second part of the session

A shift had now occurred, I thought, recreating the link with the analyst. He now spoke deeply and with affect for the remainder of the session. He recounted, in an unusually painful and open way, how when he was about fourteen or fifteen years old, he had been staying with others in a convivial gathering hosted in his uncle's house and walked away in the early morning on a long distance trek without saying goodbye to his uncle. He realised with guilt that his (paternal) uncle, one figure whom he had felt shown love and support to him, had died without him saying goodbye. Now, in the present in the session, I also felt his longing for more emotional contact with me.

I said, 'You felt at that time that you had to avoid the experience of leaving your uncle before his death. You are struggling with putting aside your feelings about leaving me with the week you will be away'.

He paused, thinking, then spoke with chagrin of a time, a few years before, when he was a child about ten to twelve years old. When leaving this same house, his uncle had given the girls a kiss but not him. Instead his uncle turned to him and said, 'We don't do that now' – i.e. he was too old as a boy to be kissed by him. He said he was (deeply) 'hurt'. Then after a long pause, he near silently growled in acknowledgement… 'I wanted to get back at him' (to get back at his uncle, by not seeing him before he died).

I now said,

> You feel that your uncle left you to an empty feeling of being cast out and pushed away, by not showing affection and giving you a kiss as a child, so you may unconsciously have retaliated or got back at him by leaving the house without saying goodbye before he died.

'Yes I did feel that', he said calmly.

I linked now (and in later sessions) a number of strands. I said, 'I think you fear dying because it brings emptiness: like experiencing emptiness by being pushed aside'. On an Oedipal level, I added, 'you feel your father pushed you aside, repeating what your mother did, and what you feel your wife does'. I added, 'This is how you experience endings or absences here – the weekends and the week away you're about to take off from here: for while you plan to be away, you feel it is me, the analyst, who pushes you aside from contact with me in the analysis'. Very quietly he said, 'Yes'. He seemed shocked and stunned. It was just time and he left.

Discussion of the second part of the session

In the second half of the session, a transition had occurred after he had broken out of a more psychotic way of functioning that was rigid and limiting. This was a transformation that brought a freer flow of associative material on a more neurotic level, with insight into his relationship to men, his uncle, later his father and with his analyst. This opened up the arena of oedipal phantasies that had been blocked within him. The positive homosexual wishes made sense of the history, to have a father who could protect him from his mother, and now in the transference the analyst as father. He also gains access to emotions that, otherwise, are blocked out or diverted – his envy of the parental couple, and of the father and the mother, and his acute sense of personal isolation.

The work of this session as a whole, and others over time, led to an increased capacity in Mr A to reflect on his omnipotent projective identification, which he had used to kill off his awareness of his feelings and emotions. This omnipotence could kill off (parts of) his emotional life, his sexuality, his sense of his gender identity that had a particular upheaval after each of the deaths of his parents, and his capacity to have and to enjoy mutual and reciprocal relationships: all of which he had tried in his usual defensive 'narcissistically detached' position to keep totally within his control. I now understood more fully that his fear of death was so intense, amongst other things, because death would not only separate him from his good internal objects, but death would annihilate his

IDENTITY AS THE THREADS OF MEANING

ongoing significance for himself, so death would be experienced as a kind of psychic annihilation, like being trapped in an isolated paranoid-schizoid world.

The following week

Monday

He told me that at the weekend he deliberately delayed starting out to a family event ignoring his wife who wanted him to help her find the holiday cases, then furiously argued all the way in the car frightening her with his aggressive driving so his 'wife was demented'. He acted dumbfounded about his projections of his disturbance, anger and fury into others. Emotional connections once made could then be split off or flatly denied.

He then told a *dream*:

> We were in a hotel. There were two pubescent girls covering each other in shit, and mocking me. I went to report the situation to the hotel manager, but as I got to the desk my wife told me that I was not the first in the queue but was third. I said I was sorry and took third place in the queue. Eventually I got to tell the hotel manager about the situation.

At first, I thought the dream seemed to show his increasing internal awareness of breaking contact and a realisation of being the third. The 'couple' was here like an early version of an Oedipal couple, in angry conflict messing up or destroying the other, so like two pubescent girls covering each other in shit. When I interpreted this, he dismissed it saying he had 'no idea what the dream was about' – and I think implied too (not too thinly) …'nor do you'. I felt flat-footed myself in my response to him but also mocked.

He muttered something indistinctly about his 'envy of women' and 'the holiday cases' in the dream. I thought he was referring to a perplexing memory about this, which referred back to some material in a session a long time previously about a lithe young woman he saw skiing effortlessly that had first prompted his confusions about his gender; he had found my earlier interpretation of *his envy* to be meaningful; it had made a link for him to his deep underlying envy of his mother and his 'beautiful sister' who 'adored each other'. Also, the troubling memory about the holiday cases referred to hidden women's clothes and his confusions about who he was in terms of gender. He again now sounded anxious and excluded. Yet, it was he who had prevented his wife having a more enjoyable and productive time on the Saturday. One could see from his dream that meaningful events were 'covered in shit', anarchically and randomly like between the two 'pubescent girls'. He had dutifully 'owned up' to tell the manager – the analyst, and had agreed to wait his 'third place in the queue' to tell. But a fuller awareness was denied or covered over even though it left him feeling mocked – as I as analyst felt mocked, and he felt empty and impotent.

Tuesday

There was an unusually big shift, I thought, following his growing inner awareness in the dream he now spoke candidly about his chronic attacking behaviour towards his wife. He said quietly, 'I'm like a wild animal…. or people who keep wild animals', who 'despite all the care… is never satisfied and picks on something'. He was saying with guilty sadness that when he gets rid of or evacuates his feelings into her or into me, or annihilates them, when they are split off and projected, something of him is got rid of and he is left solitary. He thanked me carefully, 'with a steady eye' as he left this session, indicating I thought that his contact with me too was not now so insecure.

Wednesday

He began, 'I have never felt this before a session, but now I feel dread…fear…anger'. 'It's like I crossed a bridge (yesterday) and now I can go no further'. 'I feel "fraudulent"'.

IDENTITY AS THE THREADS OF MEANING

After a long pause I said, 'You feel if you go along with me, you cross a bridge and have to continue in contact with me'. 'Yes, exactly', he paused uncertainly.

He continued with a long painful memory of being at school doing gymnastics – which he 'hated' and

> I tripped and fell 'arse over tit'…and hurt my arm badly. The master was irritated with me and said (and here he spoke in a strange mocking tone of voice), 'You catching your tinsel?' "He paused in shame: he had been publicly mocked by the master in thinly-veiled derogatory sexual terms – his 'floppy penis'. But his mother's reaction was worse (than the master's) …." she rushed up to me and grasped me by the (hurt) arm….the sort of cruel thing she did all the time.

And, 'after that she laughed and kept taunting him calling his arm "your tinsel"'. He said he was 'always *in thrall* to women', to J his wife, and to his mother. He had felt his arm was hurt (bruised / swollen), but the master and his mother ignored this, dominated him and exploited his hurt with mockery and sadism.

A little later, he added that after this incident at school his father took him to the cinema, saying…'it was the first and only time he did that'. Painfully, he implied that only this one time could his father see his hurt and so could now care for him – he was aware of what he had sorely missed in his childhood.

After a pause, he went on to say that when he was a teenager his mother once asked him as a girl passed by in the street, 'Do you like breasts?' He told her he did. She then asked him if he thought the girl had a 'good uplift'.

As he paused there seemed a tension and a claustrophobic feel in the session with him. Both his mother's question 'do you like breasts?' and his answer 'Yes I do' are ambiguous, for the question could mean 'do you desire breasts?' or 'do you want breasts?' His answer, 'Yes I do', could also cover both possibilities, he 'desires breasts' as in ordinary heterosexual desire, or 'wants breasts' as in wishing to be a woman or dress/look like one. The 'good uplift' for the girl is her breasts that became desirable and enviable but then confused him. It was a complex communication from his mother that was too intrusive into his insecure private world and assuming a seductive closeness with her. I felt he seemed near, but too close, to something with his mother and with me in the analysis that could easily become intrusive and *confuse his thinking*. I thought the claustrophobic feeling that I felt in the session related to his fear, which would now be re-experienced with me in the analysis. He could be pushed back into chronic states of internal confusion – about care of his body, his gender, his masculinity and potency that could provoke internal attacks upon such links of understanding, breaking up his awareness.

Thursday

He talked of being distraught that when he was nine years old he could not play a card game the others were playing altogether at a family gathering. With huge relief, an aunt had consoled and taught him how to play, so he eventually felt included. He could feel part of the family or a group of others. He then continued for much of this whole session in something of *a dream state*, saying: 'When I was seven I found I could "pump up" bicycle tyres…I was so pleased with myself…it was such a real achievement…I felt after that if I could "pump up" bicycle tyres I could do anything'. He sighed with satisfaction, he could achieve or master things and be potent – have a potent penis. He then quietly reflected that his wife had always said that he was 'too sensitive'. He continued, '…how easily I become devastated', and '…if I feel shame, I react and attack'.

He had been speaking in effect of his claustrophobic fear of his mother's constant intrusions that had led to his chronic states of internal confusion, which his rigidity and need for absolute precision and certainty were supposed to combat. But, a newer more receptive aspect of mother, and perhaps analyst too, had now been found that allowed this rigid position to be relaxed and modified.

Conclusion: threads of identity

Mr A had experienced repeated failures in relating to other people, determined, in part, by disturbed, traumatic or empty contact with primary figures in infancy and middle childhood, but, in part, too by his unconscious processes of denial and negation that at times were part of a more psychotic level of defences. These were shown in his constant deep-seated aim to wipe out or dissociate awareness and knowledge of his underlying emotional states, so his central relationships were narrowed and prescribed and he avoided wider personal contact outside of certain rigidly set parameters. There was in effect a kind of *β-screen* against 'learning from experience' (Bion, 1962).

Initially, he demanded certainty in his thoughts, and his profession privileged high *precision* work and activity. However, the very *uncertainty* of analysis, including its procedures and structures, and his doubts about direct contact with the analyst tormented and troubled him. It brought out that something was missing from the father, so he would turn to other male figures that were either idealised or debasing, as evacuative identifications with an early confused self. He had felt narcissistically deprived of what he deserved and felt mocked, ridiculed and shamed by a mother who chronically could not be constant and more accepting of him.

An emotional turning point that I think helped him think things could be different, and got him to go into analysis, was when he felt he could become a father to his daughter, re-creating in his own life a sense of being part of a more successful Oedipal structure. His pride in her change and development reflected his satisfaction at finding hope for a more life-orientated direction within himself. In time as he could let go of aspects that blocked his sense of emotional and mutual contact, there was less breaking up of his experience, splitting of his objects and more integration. This opened up within the full body of the analysis other significant work on his repressions and defences that lead to the re-formation internally of other aspects of Oedipal structure that allowed a fuller development.

As these features were repeated in the analysis and we focussed on these central areas, progressively over time it led to an internal change in the formation of *an internal structure of thinking*. I find it useful to think in Bion's terms here that he was able to create a more flexible and mobile *contact-barrier* with increased capacity for *α-function* (Bion, 1962). He could then tolerate more and distinguish what he knew at an unconscious and internal level and develop his inner and outer awareness, his capacity for *α-function*. This put him in touch with new experience, able to have more alive emotional states in the present, leading to a greater flow of retrieved memories and phantasies from earlier parts of his life. So, he had an increased capacity to experience what was more emotionally and affectively real for him, his own *iconic mental states*, and look ahead to the future. He began to experience *a unity* in how he saw and lived his life as it changed *over time*, and a true 'diachronic expansion of the person' (in Wollheim's terms), and so, he developed more his sense of personal identity.

My focus on the detailed sessional material showed a turning point that he and I agreed had occurred within the analysis. The sessions immediately afterwards brought an unusual and unexpected rush of more thoughtful and connected Oedipal material allowing further relief and self-awareness. He experienced his fear of death, closely related to his way of totally disconnecting in a near-hallucinatory way and being alienated from a live good object. Re-experiencing his sense of loss here in his transference to the analyst brought out his intense feelings towards me, the analyst, related to longing, anger, guilt, regret and more. This moved his thinking back into the arena of his memories, conflicts and repressions, which became increasingly more accessible within the analytic process. In time this allowed him to open up and then address some of the Oedipal conflict he had experienced to then bring together more closely the threads of his identifications. Importantly, he was able to address more disturbed memories that permeated his life; about his mother, father, aunts and uncles, his sister, his wife and children.

IDENTITY AS THE THREADS OF MEANING

It was only very much later in the analysis with deepened contact that he got in touch with another aspect of his mother – as anxious, collapsed and chaotic. He related to the traumatic caesura of his mother giving birth to him alone on the living room floor. The scene he now recalled was one of isolation, chaos and despair, with his mother haemorrhaging blood all over the carpet when both mother and child nearly died. This *caesura* foreshadowed his real experience of hurt, isolation and emotional neglect as a child (Bion, 1975). Vulnerability was now part of him and his close relationships, not a split off feature of other 'disadvantaged characters' requiring pity or needing frenetic care.

Something much more differentiated in his thinking became possible with more acceptance of the power of his envy and jealousy about his mother, women and girls, in general, nieces and wife. Gender identifications became more constant again, less split off or relived through enactments. His sexual identifications incorporated his neediness and developmental shifts especially in early adolescence and also disentangled memories of when he was abused or misused. Domination through class and money were less important. The relaxation of total control, acceptance of difference and the shift to care and thoughtful consideration of his wife, especially through her illness, was perhaps the most remarkable noticeable outward shift in him. It brought a new sense of his own capacity, individuality and achievement.

Six months before the end of his analysis

When he was planning to finish analysis to coincide with his retirement, Mr A quoted a poem from Oscar Wilde about killing off his good emotional experience. He prefaced this by saying to me, 'I wish you could help me to see why I am such a cold fish'. Then he continued…. 'it's about "killing the thing one loves" ….and "the coward does it with a kiss"'. He could see his need to hold on to this important awareness. He quietly recited the last part of the poem:

> ...the Man had killed the thing he loved,
>   And so he had to die.
>   And all men kill the thing they love,
>   By all let this be heard,
>   Some do it with a bitter look,
>   Some with a flattering word,
>   The coward does it with a kiss,
>   The brave man with a sword!
>   (Oscar Wilde The Ballad of Reading Gaol,
>   1898, from section 6)

Formation of personal identity is always incomplete, and within the analysis, one could see Mr A bringing his experience together more meaningfully and then, in turn, having it be lost or unlinked and confused again. His own deep claustrophobic and hypochondriac anxieties recurred throughout the analysis whenever there was change. This repeated in severe form near the end of his analysis when his anxieties about his health and travelling in the dark became increasingly paranoid and appeared to trap him, sometimes preventing him from getting to analysis. At the same time, he was ready to retire and to finish the analytic work being done. The final poem he quoted near the end illustrated, to my mind, a new-found sense in him of knowing how 'all men kill the thing they love'. They obliterate good contact and meaning and set aside or avoid contact: he feared being the coward and movingly saw the need to be like 'the brave man with a sword' to re-establish contact in order to re-create new aspects of his experience and awareness.

References

Bion, W.R. (1957) 'The differentiation of the psychotic from the non-psychotic personalities'. In *Complete works*, Ed. C. Mawson, vol. 6, pp. 92–111. [2014]. Karnac: London and New York.

Bion, W.R. (1958) 'On hallucination'. In *Complete works*, Ed. C. Mawson, vol. 6, pp. 112–130. [2014]. Karnac: London and New York.

Bion, W.R. (1962) 'Learning from experience'. In *Complete works*. Ed. C. Mawson, vol. 4, pp. 259–365. [2014]. Karnac: London and New York.

Bion, W.R. (1966) 'Catastrophic change'. In *Complete works*. Ed. C. Mawson, vol. 6, pp. 19–43. [2014]. Karnac: London and New York.

Bion, W.R. (1970) 'Attention and Interpretation: A Scientific Approach to Insight in Psycho-Analysis and Groups'. In *Complete Works*. Ed. C. Mawson, vol. 6. [2014]. London and New York: Karnac.

Bion, W.R. (1975) 'The caesura'. In *Complete works*. Ed. C. Mawson, vol. 10, pp. 31–49. [2014]. Karnac: London and New York.

Britton, R. (2003) *Sex, death and the superego: experiences in psychoanalysis*. London and New York: Karnac.

Di Ceglie, G. (2013) 'Orientation, containment and the emergence of symbolic thinking'. *Int. J. Psychoanal.*, 94(6): 1077–1091.

Erikson, E.H. (1966) "The problem of ego identity". *J. Am. Psychoanal. Assn.*, 4: 56–121.

Erikson, E.H. (1968) *Identity, youth and crisis*. Faber and Faber: London.

Erikson, E.H. (1977) *Childhood and society*. Triad/Paladin: St Albans, Herts.

Flynn, D. (2017) 'Catastrophic change and the shape of what we Know'. Freud Memorial Lecture, University of Essex. https://vimeo.com/247112740.

Grinberg, L. and Grinberg, G. (1999) 'Psychoanalytic perspectives on migration'. In *Psychoanalysis and culture: a Kleinian perspective*. Ed. D. Bell, pp. 154–169. Duckworth: London.

Kernberg, O.F. (2006) "Identity: recent findings and clinical implications". *Psychoanalytic Q.*, 75(4): 969–1003.

Klein, M. (1946) 'Notes on some schizoid mechanisms'. In *Envy and Gratitude and Other Works*. Collected works, vol. 3, pp. 1-24. 1945–63 [1975]. Eds. Money-Kyrle, R., Joseph, B., O'Shaughnessy, E., Segal H. London: Hogarth Press.

Money-Kyrle, R. (1968) 'Cognitive development'. In *Collected papers of Roger Money-Kyrle*. Eds. D. Meltzer and E. O'Shaughnessy, pp. 416–433. Clunie: Perthshire.

O'Shaughnessy, E. (2007) 'On mental connectedness'. In *Inquiries in psychoanalysis*. Ed. E. O'Shaughnessy, pp. 222–231. [2015]. Routledge, New Library of Psychoanalysis Series: London and New York.

Rosenfeld, H.A. (1964) 'On the psychopathology of Narcissism'. In *Rosenfeld in retrospect: essays on his clinical influence*. Ed. J. Steiner, pp. 106–115. [2008]. Routledge: London and New York.

Sohn, L. (1985) 'Narcissistic organisation, projective identification and the formation of the identificate'. In *Melanie Klein today: developments in theory and practice, Vol 1 Mainly theory*. Ed. E. Bott Spillius, pp. 271–292. Routledge, New Library of Psychoanalysis Series: London and New York.

Steiner, J. (1993) *Psychic retreats: Pathological organisation in psychotic, neurotic and borderline patients*. Routledge, New Library of Psychoanalysis Series: London and New York.

Steiner, J. (2011) *Seeing and being seen: emerging from a psychic retreat*. Routledge, New Library of Psychoanalysis Series: London and New York.

Wilkinson-Ryan, T. and Weston, D. (1985) "Identity disturbance in borderline personality disorder: an empirical investigation". *Am. J. Psychiatry*, 157(4): 528–541.

Wollheim, R. (1980) 'On persons and their lives'. In *Explaining emotions*. Ed. A.O. Rorty, pp. 299–321, University of California Press: Berkeley, Los Angeles, CA and London.

Wollheim, R. (1984) *The thread of life*. Yale University Press: New Haven, CT and London.

Wollheim, R. (1999a) *On the emotions*. Yale University Press: New Haven, CT and London.

Wollheim R. (1999b) 'Emotion and the malformation of emotion'. In *Psychoanalysis and culture: A Kleinian perspective*. Ed. D. Bell, pp. 122–135. Duckworth: London.

INDEX

Note: Page numbers followed by "n" denote endnotes.

Akhtar, S. 154–155
alien internal object 174, 178, 186, 189
alien object 80–81
alien projections 41, 171, 174, 178–179
alpha function 42–43, 79, 96, 172, 192, 212; and meaning 26
Alvarez, A. 154
ambivalence 147, 157, 160; in relation to mourning 147
analyst's identity 19, 58, 75, 150
analytic attitude 12, 18
autobiographical self 31, 101

Bauman, Z. 245–246
belonging 15, 35, 44, 112, 166, 189, 194–195; and identity 48, 100, 102, 115
beta elements 42, 79, 94, 96
Bick, E. 100–101, 212, 217
Bion, W. R. 25–26, 42, 44, 51–53, 63, 78–79, 83–84, 97, 100, 139, 172, 192, 200, 212, 217, 245, 248–250, 258, 271–274, 288
body: carapace 217–218; image 29; in relation to mind 79–81, 84–86, 90–91

brain 70, 89, 91, 135–136, 139, 141–142, 258
breakdown 108, 123, 125–127, 133, 140, 164, 176, 185, 195
breast 25–26, 33, 37–39, 42, 53, 61, 93, 101–102, 108, 111–112, 115, 120, 128, 139, 143, 157, 162, 164, 242, 248, 250, 266, 275, 285–286
Brenman, E. 146–147
Britton, R. 7, 38, 46, 52, 79–80, 142, 150, 155, 174, 221, 232, 245–247, 260, 270

caesura 139, 289
Caper, R. 200
carapace 45, 193, 217–218, 227–229, 245, 254–255
central imagining 274
cerebral defence 92
cerebral mind 30, 81–84, 93
complacent 150
compliance 46, 247, 260
container/contained 25–26, 42, 44, 46, 100–101, 117, 141, 165, 217, 219–220
containment 15, 26–28, 30, 42–44, 46, 84, 90–94, 96, 100, 141, 167, 173, 185, 197, 212, 219, 227–229

INDEX

Contemporary Identity Politics and the Struggle for Recognition (Fukuyama) 14
continuity: of being 32, 44, 53, 102, 193; of experience 6, 53; and time 44, 53, 154, 274
countertransference 13, 19, 30, 50, 80, 93–94, 126, 149, 151, 159, 161, 168, 192–194, 198, 216, 258, 277; enactment 13, 19, 157, 201, 221, 289
couple 1, 7, 34, 46, 49, 68, 86, 92–93, 95, 124, 129–130, 143, 150, 154, 166, 202, 205, 210, 221–222, 228, 232, 237–238, 251, 258, 264, 266, 282–283
creativity and identity 102, 108, 120, 150, 247, 266
cruelty 41, 66, 68, 74, 110, 140, 218, 248, 256

Damasio, A. 101
Dante Alighieri 4, 31, 40, 99, 102–120, 121n2, 121n3
Davids, F. 64
"dead mother" 50, 163, 237
defences: against dependency 32, 34, 36–37, 50, 64, 67, 92, 150, 219, 222, 227; against depressive position 16–17, 36–37, 51, 111, 117–118, 140, 145, 167, 231–232, 247, 271; against feelings of smallness 36; against mourning 4, 13, 15, 18, 20, 26–28, 38, 40, 49–50, 52, 54, 59, 113, 145–147, 165, 167–168, 243, 267; against persecutory anxiety 26, 145, 163, 256
delusion/delusional 17, 127, 133, 135, 138, 144, 176, 234, 240–242

dependence and identity 3, 19, 26, 37, 78, 96, 114, 172
depressive position 17–20; and mourning 146; and paranoid schizoid position 16–17, 35–38, 61, 64, 142, 146, 247, 249, 271, 283
derivative fear 245–246, 256
detachment 84, 210, 270, 282
Deutsch, H. 47
Devil 128, 140, 143–144
Di Ceglie, G.R. 31, 271, 275
disidentify 97
disillusion 18, 39, 46, 104, 151, 159, 242; gradual disillusionment 33, 39, 149, 151
disorientation 31, 99, 101–106, 108–109, 112, 114, 118
Divine Comedy (Dante) 31, 99, 102–107, 110, 117–118, 121n3
doubt 15, 70, 89, 91, 96, 104, 118, 125, 180, 221–222, 224, 243, 252, 256, 271, 278, 287
dream 218–219

ego: bodily 44; destructive superego 52, 245, 247–248; emancipation of 52, 247, 252, 266; enrichment of 6, 146; fragmentation of 19, 67, 255; functioning 8, 20, 54, 96, 247, 253, 267; futurity 271; ideal 6–7, 18, 93; and identity 8–10; impoverishment of 20, 47, 55, 66–67; integration of 43, 145–146, 148–149, 166; integrity of 10, 35–36, 258; primitive 44, 61, 246; psychology 5, 8, 10; and superego 7, 11, 20, 41, 47–48, 50–52, 54, 60, 110,

INDEX

144, 164, 197, 230, 245–248, 250, 252, 254, 256, 258, 260, 266, 268, 271
emotional states – alive 42, 270–271, 274, 287–288
enaction 130
envy 66–67, 106, 112, 117, 127, 141, 158, 207, 234, 261, 267, 282, 284, 289; fear of 260
Erikson, E. 8–10, 13
evacuation 45, 83, 197, 219
'The Experience of the Skin in Early Object Relations' (Bick) 29–30
experiential memory 274

Feldman, M. 194
Ferenczi, S. 49–50
fluidity 1, 73; vs. rigidity 54
foreign body 174–175, 186, 188–189
fragmentation 26, 40, 43–44, 54, 93, 145, 215, 255; anxiety and 216–217; and integration 26, 40, 54
Fraiberg, S. 172
Freud, A. 60, 174
Freud, S. 6–8, 12–13, 20, 28, 30, 36, 44, 49, 51–52, 58–60, 100, 145–147, 199, 221, 229–231, 247, 250, 256, 259, 275; Leonardo da Vinci, study of 59, 65

Garland, C. 34
gaze 51, 102, 106, 113–115, 127, 156, 161, 234
ghosts in the nursery 172, 202, 211
Greenacre, P. 29, 47–48, 156
grievance 60, 249, 259

Grinberg, L. 5–6, 147, 274
Group Psychology and the Analysis of the Ego (Freud) 12
guilt and depressive position 64, 70, 102, 106, 114, 138, 163–164, 180, 201, 231, 235–236, 247–249, 257, 260–261, 264–265, 279, 281, 284

Hanly, C. 7
Harris, M. 212
Hartmann, H. 8, 10
Hartung, T. 80
Hinshelwood, R. 5
humiliation 7, 18, 31–32, 39, 51, 91, 165, 278
hysteria 215, 220–222, 227
hysterical personality 220–221, 229
hysterical symptoms 45

idealisation 7, 33–35, 38–39, 50, 78, 126, 145–148, 153, 161, 166, 241, 256
identificate 28, 66–67, 71, 75, 211
identification 59–60; with the aggressor 60, 174, 189, 252–253; with bad object 17–18, 25, 33–34, 38, 40, 43, 61, 66, 74, 117, 181; failure of 9–10, 27, 32, 72, 195, 199, 250, 270, 287; fluid 71–74; introjective 6, 15, 17, 34, 53, 60–65, 124, 148, 156, 171, 174, 199, 256, 274; material 90–93; melancholic 20, 41, 50, 52, 71, 74, 147, 230–231, 237, 247, 250; omnipotent 7, 16–17, 26, 33, 36–37, 48, 50, 52, 66, 79, 95, 145–147, 167, 230–231, 234, 241–242, 270, 274, 282; pathological 3, 58–59, 64–65,

INDEX

74, 147, 230; with primary objects 10, 12, 28, 31, 41–42, 44, 100, 124, 216, 228; projective 3, 16–19, 27–28, 35, 37, 39, 41–42, 48, 61–65, 74, 80, 93, 111, 124, 147–148, 171–172, 270, 274, 280, 282; unconscious 28, 59–60, 63, 66, 74–75, 220

identity: achievement of 4, 17, 25–27; borrowed 3, 48, 245, 254–255; and class 14–15, 51, 152, 277, 289; clinical example 67–71; confusion 6, 9, 17, 30, 37, 41, 46–47, 65, 104, 116, 118, 171, 179, 189, 198, 206, 212, 215–216, 219–220, 229, 284, 286; cultural aspects of 14–15; definition 5–8; diffusion 10, 255, 269; disintegration of 26, 36, 173; disturbance 1, 3–4, 27, 29–30, 32, 47–48, 81, 187, 193, 269, 283; feminine 159, 218; formation 2, 4, 26, 100, 173–174, 275; and gender 2, 14, 19, 46, 282, 284, 286, 289; and group identity 1–2, 4, 9, 12, 15, 47, 86, 109, 141, 286; integration of 79; masculine 83, 90, 211; mature 9, 38; mourning 4, 12–13, 15, 18, 20, 27–28, 38, 40, 49–50, 52, 54, 59, 75, 81, 113, 133, 145–147, 165, 167–168, 231, 243, 253, 267; and narcissism 6–7, 16, 28, 36, 59, 148, 173; personal 4–5, 19, 26–27, 48, 50, 52–54, 114, 192, 212, 228, 232, 243, 247, 269–275, 277, 282, 288, 290; and 'race'/racism 14–15, 64, 163; sense of 164–167; separate 2, 27, 36–38, 148, 165, 173, 192, 246, 260; social aspects of 2, 5, 14–15; stability of 51, 149, 219

illusion 33, 38–39, 49, 79, 134, 145, 148–149, 155, 242

imitation 2, 18, 205–206

impostor 48, 152, 156

inadequacy, sense of 10, 20, 52, 81, 202, 207, 257

incorporation, of the object 61

inferiority 20

insight 38–39, 161–164, 176, 199, 207, 228, 259–260, 277, 282

integration 3, 9–10, 17, 26, 34–36, 40–41, 43, 54, 79–81, 86, 101–102, 115, 117–119, 142–143, 145–146, 148–149, 167, 173, 250, 287

internal autocracy 246, 257, 260

internalisation, of good object 25, 27, 34–35, 40–43, 50, 54, 61, 67, 73–75, 78, 110, 113, 116–117, 140, 142, 149, 248, 250, 288

internal object: alien 41, 80–81, 91, 171, 174, 178–179, 184, 186, 189, 276, 288; concrete 64, 211; identification with 7, 10, 18, 28, 30, 43, 46, 49, 59–61, 73, 81, 83, 93, 95, 147–148, 151–153, 163, 165, 174, 201, 205, 210–211, 213, 216, 228–229, 236–237, 248, 250–251, 253, 260

internal persecutor 182

introjected object 62

introjections 25–26, 29, 35–37, 43, 45, 60–64, 75, 100, 174, 189, 250, 274; and identifications 226–227

intrusive object 41, 171, 173–174, 176–177, 179, 186, 189

296

INDEX

Jackson, J. 43–44, 53
Jaques, E. 102
jealousy 66–67, 127, 158, 261, 289
Joseph, B. 156

Kernberg, O. 10, 34
Klein, M. 3–5, 11–12, 16–18, 20, 25, 28, 30, 32, 34–35, 39–42, 51, 54, 60–63, 66, 75, 77–78, 101, 106, 111, 120, 146–147, 149, 171–172, 178, 212, 221, 241, 246, 248, 270, 272
Kohut, H. 10–11

The Language of Psychoanalysis (Laplanche and Pontalis) 58
Lawrence, S. 30
Learning from Experience (Bion) 42, 274
Leonardo da Vinci, study of (Freud) 59, 65
life cycle 31
Likierman, M. 63
liquid fear 245–246, 249, 254, 268
Loewald, H. 54, 271
loss: of love object 31, 230–231; and mourning 13, 54, 59, 81, 146; of self love 6, 28
love: and hate 33, 77, 117, 143, 207, 230; object 20, 31, 41, 105, 209–210, 230–231
Love, Guilt and Reparation (Klein) 54–55

madness 125, 133, 178
Mahler, M. 4, 10, 13, 31–32
manic: defences, against mourning 146, 167, 241; omnipotence 27, 32, 39–40, 49–50, 78–79, 127, 145–146, 282; state 86; triumph 73, 151, 237, 249, 259
masochism 258
massive projective identification 37, 39–40, 148
mastery, sense of 10, 31, 247
maternal reverie 26, 43
Mawson, C. 100
melancholic solution 147
Meltzer, D. 111
memory: and identity 107, 109, 154, 167, 272–274, 283–285; and phantasy 6, 11–12, 30, 53, 61, 231, 272
mental connectedness 192, 212, 232, 275
merged states 65–66
mimicry 47
mirror and sense of self 1, 3–4, 6–7, 11, 15–17, 19, 25–26, 30, 33–34, 37, 40–41, 43, 45, 50–52, 58, 60, 75, 77, 80–81, 83–84, 86, 125, 147–148, 155, 158, 167, 192, 213, 218, 242, 272
mistake 34, 130, 133–134, 136
model: of identity 25; of mind, Kleinian 3–5, 11, 16, 25, 61, 78
Money-Kyrle, R. 275
moral judgement 247
moral/morality 47, 60, 114, 117, 129, 140, 142–144, 247
Moses and Monotheism (Freud) 275
mother: and child 250–251, 275; 'good enough mother' 33, 53; infant and 15, 26, 99–100
mourning: and depressive position 16–20, 36–37, 51, 111, 117–118, 140, 145, 167, 231–232, 247, 271; failed 50; and melancholia

INDEX

12, 28, 51, 59, 147, 174, 199, 230–231, 256; pathological 3, 10, 18–19, 26, 34, 37, 46, 59, 64–65, 86, 92, 146–147, 153, 230; perpetual 52; work of 59, 147

narcissism and identity 6–7, 16, 28, 36, 59, 148, 173
narcissistic organisation: emergence from 37, 173; narcissism as defence 36–38, 43, 77–78, 82–84, 140, 173–174, 180, 287; narcissistic perfection 6, 168, 259; narcissistic relationship 40, 47, 50, 54, 67–68, 78, 129, 143–153, 166–168, 178, 187, 221–222, 234, 236–238, 240–242, 246–249; personality 6, 8, 10, 30, 35, 43, 59–61, 64, 97, 154–155, 248, 250, 271
Nayman, S. 154
no-entry defence 173–174, 189
nostalgia 38, 153–156
Notes on Some Schizoid Mechanisms (Klein) 77–78
Numa, S. 173, 271

object: damaged 164, 257; impenetrable 106, 173–174; inaccessible 274
object relationship: bad 17–18, 25, 33–34, 38, 40, 43, 61, 66, 74, 117, 181; early 25, 29; good 25, 27, 34–35, 40–43, 50, 54, 61, 67, 73–75, 78, 110, 113, 116–118, 139–140, 142, 149, 163, 250, 288; intrusive 41, 171, 173–174, 176–177, 179, 186, 189
oedipal situation 47, 86, 166, 237

oedipus complex: oedipal configuration 51, 96, 166; oedipal couple 46, 124, 283; oedipal defeat 49; oedipal illusion 49, 152
omega function 172
omnipotence: and control of the object 27, 32, 39–40, 49–50, 78–79, 145–146, 282; omnipotent phantasies 7, 16, 50, 147, 231, 241–242, 270, 274
orientation: and disorientation 99–100, 102–106, 109, 112, 118–119; mutual 31, 100, 115, 119, 275
O'Shaughnessy, E. 232, 266

Paradise lost 40, 102, 106, 109, 113–118, 120, 154, 165
paranoid-schizoid position 16–17, 35–38, 61, 64, 142, 146, 247, 249, 271, 283
paternal transference 10, 46, 83, 86, 95, 211, 227, 237, 249, 281
perceptual hallucinations 80
persecutory anxieties 26, 145, 163, 256
personality: rigid 52–54, 59, 269; structure 3, 47, 97, 247, 250; unintegrated 3; weak 18, 142, 166
phantasies: delusional 127, 133, 138, 176, 234, 241–242; omnipotent and concrete 7, 16, 50, 147, 230–231, 241–243, 270, 274; and reality 49, 54, 147, 173, 242; unconscious 6, 11–13, 16, 26, 30, 53, 61, 101, 120, 156, 231, 235; of unity 148
poetic identity 106, 108–109, 111, 114–115

INDEX

porous child 174
predictive dreams 182
pregnancy/pregnant 128, 218, 222, 251, 256
projection: failure of 173, 175, 185; taking back of 13, 182
projection-rejecting object 63
projective identification: acquisitive 65, 80; excessive 53, 270; massive 37, 39, 124, 148
psychic growth, and development 26, 147
psychic retreat 18, 37, 65, 150, 165, 270
psychosis 34, 67, 78, 126, 135, 141, 186
psychotic-ways of relating processes 67, 93–94, 97, 123–124, 176–177, 179, 182, 184–185, 189, 248, 271, 280, 282
Purgatory 102, 108–109, 111–114, 120

race 14
realisation 39, 105, 139, 240, 272–273, 283
reality: internal and external 2, 96, 104, 146, 155, 247; and phantasy 49, 54, 147, 173, 242; psychic 38–39, 49, 77, 125, 146, 148, 150–151, 162; sense of 18, 48–49, 145
re-introjection 26, 35, 100
relational psychoanalysis 11–13
relinquishing omnipotence 49
reparation 18, 106, 112–113, 149, 249, 264
replacement baby 173, 251
Rey, H. 255–256

rigidity 37, 51, 54, 140, 142, 242, 271, 286
Rosenfeld, H. 36–38, 65, 148, 172
Ryan, C. 120
Rycroft, C. 9

sameness and difference 271–272
Sandler, J. 150
Segal, H. 182
self 16; aspects of 13, 27, 35, 38, 40, 65, 164–165, 268, 271; esteem 10–11, 15, 32, 46, 49–50, 258; false 46; idealisation 7, 38; ideal self 7, 34, 146–147; image 6, 17, 29, 34, 38, 147, 178; observation 7, 247; parts of 16, 18, 29, 35–37, 40–41, 43, 45, 62–63, 77, 117–118, 144–145, 149, 163, 165, 248, 250, 255, 271; true and false 46
self-psychology 10–13
sense of identity: emergence of 25, 37, 99, 106, 155, 173; inauthentic 28, 46–47, 154, 156; obstacles to development of 1, 3, 36; stable 1, 4, 25, 78, 92, 123–124; subjective 7, 9, 33, 272, 274; unintegrated 3, 30, 100, 217; unstable 10, 51, 125, 250, 255; weak 251
separateness: and identity 31–32, 36, 43, 46, 49–51, 97, 114, 243; and loss 19, 38; and separation 156–159
sex/sexual/sexuality 8–9, 14, 29, 46, 49, 60, 126, 129, 168, 175, 177–180, 186–190, 203, 205–206, 221–222, 225, 228, 260, 277, 289

INDEX

shame 7, 10, 15, 18, 31, 36–37, 51–52, 114, 127, 164–165, 177, 195, 254, 257, 285, 287
Simpson, D. 173
simulacrum 140
Skogstad, W. 173
Sodre, I. 37, 39–40, 49, 65–66, 70, 148, 173, 231–232, 242
Sohn, L. 66, 153, 211
somatic representation:
  –hypochondriacal 80;
  –psychosomatic 79–80
somatic symptoms 30, 79–80, 85, 96, 153
somatisation 215, 222, 229
splitting: healthy 34, 36, 42, 75, 148, 172, 189; of object 33; pathological 34, 37; of the self 33
Steinbrecher, M. 80
Steiner, J. 1, 8–9, 18, 31, 37–38, 40, 51, 114, 165, 231, 242
Stern, D. 101
stigma 9, 15, 112
stomach 77, 85, 136, 209, 253, 261
superego: autocratic 245, 258; benign 20; early 60; harsh 41, 51, 248; moralistic 247; murderous 264–268; obedience to 47–48, 246; primitive 51, 254, 270; severity of 41, 247, 250
superiority 18, 150, 164, 250
survivor guilt 257
symbiotic union 31, 38, 54, 168
symbolic thinking and concrete thinking 49–50, 52
symbolisation 45

Tausk, V. 44
thinking 1, 4, 7, 28, 38, 42, 45, 49–50, 52–53, 82, 97, 99–100, 138, 140, 143, 148, 180–181, 193, 210, 249, 257, 264, 270–272, 274, 281, 286, 288
third position 7–8, 46, 202, 205, 211
The Thread of Life (Wollheim) 52
time: and memory 54; psychic 54
total situation 1
transference: and countertransference 13, 19, 30, 50, 80, 93–94, 126, 149, 151, 159, 161, 168, 192–194, 198, 216, 258, 277; illusion 38, 149, 200
triangular space 7, 129, 232
Tustin, F. 173

unconscious phantasy: of fusion 16; of merging 231

vagina 141
Virgil 107–114, 116–119
vulnerability 18, 26, 32, 37, 64, 70, 140, 165–166, 245–246, 256, 289

Waddell, M. 9
weaning 128, 139
Werman, D. S. 153
Williams, G. 64, 172–173
Williams, P. 172–173
Winnicott, D. 32–33, 39, 46, 102, 148–149, 167, 249
Wollheim, R. 6, 52–54, 192, 232, 271–273, 275